PROMINENT MEN & WOMEN OF PROVO

MCMLXXXIII

PROMINENT MEN AND WOMEN OF PROVO 1983

Larry L. Richman
Editor

RICHMAN PUBLISHING

Prominent Men & Women of Provo 1983
Limited Edition

ISBN 0-941846-00-8

Printed in the United States of America

PREFACE

This book features biographies of outstanding members of the Provo community, selected from the ranks of business and professional people, educators, and civic and political leaders. They are featured here because they have demonstrated outstanding leadership and professional achievement, or because they have given exceptional service. We publish this collection as a tribute to these people, with the hope that it will encourage participation by others in similar endeavors and inspire in them equal levels of achievement.

The information was gathered by means of direct communication with the biographee. Data forms were sent to all candidates. The information they supplied was included as completely as possible within the boundaries of editorial and space restrictions. Our staff has made no attempt to validate the information submitted and assumes no responsibility for such.

The criteria for selection of biographies for this book were not as rigid as Who's Who in America or other national registers. Our aim was to include a broader range of people who have contributed to the community, including people who either live or work in Provo. Listing in this volume was not contingent on the purchase of a copy of the book; we did not offer it for sale until after the biographies were selected and the book was printed.

There are, of course, others who deserve to be in this book. We either could not get sufficient biographical information about these people to do them justice, or because of modesty, they have requested that their biography not appear, and we have respected their wishes.

– The Editor

TABLE OF ABBREVIATIONS

AA	Associate of Arts Degree
Acad	Academy
Admin	Administrative, Administration
Adv	Advisor, Advisory
Agcy	Agency
Amer	America, American
AS	Associate of Science Degree
Assn	Association
Assoc	Associate(s)
Asst	Assistant
Atty	Attorney
B	Birth Date
BA	Bachelor of Arts Degree
Bldg	Building
BS	Bachelor of Science Degree
BSA	Boy Scouts of America
BYU	Brigham Young University
C	Children
Cert	Certificate, Certified
Champ	Champion, Championship
Chap	Chapter
Chm	Chairman
Co	Company
Com	Committee
Comm	Commission
Conf	Conference
Consul	Consultant
Conv	Convention
Coord	Coordinator, Coordination
Corp	Corporation
Ctr	Center
Del	Delegate
Dept	Department
Dir	Director
Dist	District
Econ	Economics
Ed	Education, Editor, Edition
EdD	Doctor of Education Degree
Engr	Engineer
Exec	Executive
Fac	Faculty

Fed	Federal, Federation
Found	Foundation
Gen	General
Govt	Government
Grad	Graduate
Hon	Honor, Honorary
Incl	Including
Indus	Industry, Industrial
Info	Information
Inst	Institute, Institution
Instr	Instructor, Instructional
Intermtn	Intermountain
Internatl	International
JD	Juris Doctorate (Law) Degree
Jr	Junior
Lang	Language
Ldr	Leader
Ldrshp	Leadership
LDS	Latter-Day Saint
Lit	Literature
M	Married
MA	Master of Arts Degree
Mag	Magazine
Mem	Member, Membership
Mfg	Manufacturing
Mgr	Manager
Mgt	Management
Mil	Military
MLS	Master of Library Science Degree
MS	Master of Science Degree
MTC	Missionary Training Center
Mtn	Mountain
Natl	National
Off	Office, Officer
Org	Organization
P	Parents
PG	Pleasant Grove, Utah
PhD	Doctor of Philosophy Degree
Pol	Political
Pres	President
Prin	Principal
Prof	Professor
Prog	Program

Proj	Project
Publ	Published Writings
Reg	Region, Regional
Rel	Religion, Religious
Rep	Representative
Res	Research
Ret	Retired
Sci	Science
Sec	Secretary
Serv	Service(s)
SL	Salt Lake
SLC	Salt Lake City, Utah
Soc	Society, Social
Sr	Senior
Stk	Stake
Stud	Student
Supt	Superintendent
Supvr	Supervisor
Syst	System
Tchr	Teacher
Tech	Technical, Technology
Treas	Treasurer
U,Univ	University
US	United States
UTC	Utah Technical College
V-chm	Vice Chairman
VP	Vice President
Yr	Year

SAMPLE BIOGRAPHICAL ENTRY

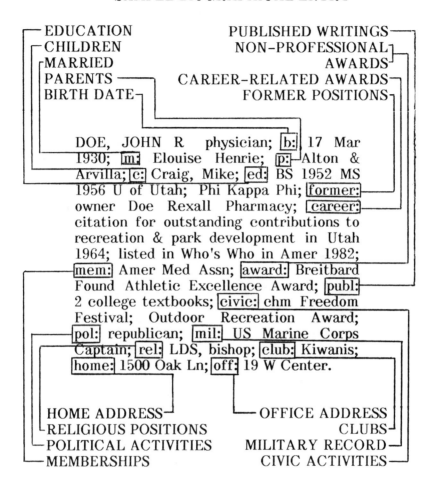

EDUCATION
CHILDREN
MARRIED
PARENTS
BIRTH DATE

PUBLISHED WRITINGS
NON-PROFESSIONAL
AWARDS
CAREER-RELATED AWARDS
FORMER POSITIONS

DOE, JOHN R physician; b: 17 Mar 1930; m: Elouise Henrie; p: Alton & Arvilla; c: Craig, Mike; ed: BS 1952 MS 1956 U of Utah; Phi Kappa Phi; former: owner Doe Rexall Pharmacy; career: citation for outstanding contributions to recreation & park development in Utah 1964; listed in Who's Who in Amer 1982; mem: Amer Med Assn; award: Breitbard Found Athletic Excellence Award; publ: 2 college textbooks; civic: chm Freedom Festival; Outdoor Recreation Award; pol: republican; mil: US Marine Corps Captain; rel: LDS, bishop; club: Kiwanis; home: 1500 Oak Ln; off: 19 W Center.

HOME ADDRESS
RELIGIOUS POSITIONS
POLITICAL ACTIVITIES
MEMBERSHIPS

OFFICE ADDRESS
CLUBS
MILITARY RECORD
CIVIC ACTIVITIES

ADAMS, JOHN HORTT   accountant; admin at BYU; b: 16
Mar 1921; m: Betty Ellis; p: Merle V & Emma H; c: John
Robert, Larry Duane, Jeffrey Ellis, Cynthia, Pamela; ed:
BS accounting 1947; grad work; Scholarship to U of Utah;
former: tool designer, Lockheed; accountant, Geneva
Steel; sec treas Utah Savings & Loan; mem: Soc of
Savings & Loan Controllers; Sertoma Club of Provo; Alpha
Kappa Psi; Natl Advisory Board, Amer Security Council;
publ: *Your Private Property Rights: Know and Protect
Them;* civic: Boy Scout com; pol: Republican state &
county del, local officer; mil: Cadet Midshipman US
Merchant Marines, WW II; Asiatic Pacific Area, Amer
Area, Victory Medal WW II; rel: LDS, stake presidency, h
council, bishop; home: 1390 N 1450 W; off: D-177 ASB,
BYU.

AIKEN, PHIL L   chiropractic physician; b: 22 Aug 1924;
m: Lorena M; p: Evan L & Ruth L; c: Miriam, Laura; ed:
BYU; Dr of Chiropractic 1949 Lincoln Chiropractic
College; postgrad cert Chiropractic Orthopedics 1970 &
postgrad study in roentgenology Los Angeles Chiropractic
College; career: Fellow Internatl College of Chiropractors
1973; Distinguished Serv Award Utah Chiropractic Assn
1979; mem: Amer Chiropractic Assn, various positions;
Diplomate Amer Board of Chiropractic Orthopedists 1973;
publ: "Bilateral Weight Measurement"; editor *The Utah
Chiropractor;* mil: US Naval Hospital Corps WWII 1943-5;
Korean Police Action 1951; rel: Provo Community
Congregational Church; United Church of Christ; chm of
board of Deacons; club: Story Lodge 4 F&AM; off: 190 E
100 S.

ALBRECHT, W STEVE   prof Grad School of Mgt BYU; b:
6 Feb 1947; m: LeAnn; p: W Torval & Elnore R; c: Scott
10, Conan 9, Tyler 5, Chad 3; ed: BS accounting 1971
BYU; MBA 1973 PhD accounting 1975 U of Wisconsin; Phi
Kappa Phi; CPA; Amer Accounting Assn Fellowship; Ernst
& Ernst Doctoral Fellowship; AAA Doctoral Consortium
Fellow; grad cum laude BYU; Beta Alpha Psi; academic
scholarships BYU; former: prof U of Illinois & Stanford U;
career: U of Wisconsin Grad Student Teaching Award
1974; Outstanding Tchrs List U of Illinois 1976; Inst of
Professional Accountancy Faculty Excellence Award BYU
1979 & Research Excellence Award BYU 1980; Peat

Marwick research grants; mem: Amer Acounting Assn; Utah Soc of Cert Public Accountants; Amer Inst of Cert Public Accountants; award: Outstanding Young Men of Amer 1980; Faculty Outstanding Achievement Award 1981; publ: *How to Detect & Prevent Business Fraud* Prentice-Hall; 53 articles; 12 papers; radio, TV interviews, movies; review board *The Accounting Review;* civic: scouting; Freedom Festival; coach Little League Baseball, Basketball, Football, Soccer; pol: Republican; rel: LDS; home: 1920 S Park Ln, Orem; off: 330 JKB, BYU.

ALEXANDER, THOMAS GLEN   prof of History BYU; dir Charles Redd Ctr for Western Studies; b: 8 Aug 1935; m: Marilyn Johns; p: Glen M & Violet Bird; c: Brooke Ann, Brenda Lynn, Tracy Lee, Mark Thomas, Paul Johns; ed: AS engineering 1955 Weber State; U of Utah; BS 1960 MS 1961 history Utah State U; PhD history 1965 U of Calif at Berkeley; former: visiting res prof Utah State U 1965; visiting instr Kearney State College 1966; instr BYU Semester Abroad in Salzburg 1968; adjunct assoc prof S Illinois U 1970-1; BYU Archives & Records Mgt Com 1973-8; BYU Press Publ Com 1976-9; career: listed in Who's Who in the West 1970-1, Directory of Amer Scholars, Personalities of the West & Midwest 1973, Outstanding Educators of Amer 1975, Dictionary of Internatl Biography 1975-6; Mormon History Assn Award for best article on Mormon History 1967-8, 76, 80; Morris Rosenblatt Award for outstanding article in Utah Historical Quarterly 1968-9; Karl G Maeser Research Award 1976; mem: Org of Amer Historians; Western History Assn; Utah Valley Branch, Utah State Historical Soc; Mormon History Assn; Utah Acad of Sci, Arts & Letters; Phi Alpha Theta; Pi Sigma Alpha; Phi Kappa Phi; Natl Council on Public History; John Whitmer Historical Assn; publ: *A Clash of Interests: Interior Department and Mountain West, 1863-96;* co-auth *Water for Urban Reclamation: The Provo River Project; A Dependent Commonwealth: Utah's Economy from Statehood to the Great Depression; Manchester Mormons: The Journal of William Clayton, 1840-1842;* editor *The Papers of Ulysses S. Grant, vol. 5: April 1 – August 31, 1862; Essays on the American West, 1972-1973, 1973-74, 1974-75; Utah's History; Soul Butter and Hog Wash and Other Essays on the American West; Voices from the Past: Diaries,*

Journals, and Autobiographies; The Mormon People: Their Character and Traditions; articles & reviews; assoc editor *The Journal of Mormon History* 1973-4; rel: LDS, seminary tchr, clerk, elders pres, h priest ldr, exec sec, h council; home: 3325 Mohican Ln; off: 4069 HBLL, BYU.

ALLEN, SANDRA LYNNE BIRCH   asst prof, coord of ballet, co-dir theatre ballet & classical ballet conservatory BYU; b: 8 Sep 1942; m: Herbert James Allen; p: Albert Rippon & Erma LaVon Kim Birch; c: Spencer James 13, Marc Stewart 11, Jon Jeffrey 7, Camilla 4, Richard Mack 3; ed: BFA 1964 MFA 1967 U of Utah; honors at entrance scholarship 1960; Dean's Meritorious Scholarship 1963; former: dir Ballet Arts 1970-82; soloist Utah Civic Ballet; mem: pres Utah Ballet Tchrs Assn 1980-1; awards: Outstanding Young Woman of the Yr 1975; choreography: *Petrushka; Coppelia, Capriccio Espagnol; Two-Timin' in Double Time; The Circle of a Woman's Reach; Opus Romantique; Forever and Ever; Love at Home; Final Farewell; Les Danses Classique; Comix; Mozartiana; Concerto No. 2; Ballectron; Tarantella; The Red Shoes; Mandolina; Polovetzian Dances; Faust; Symphonic Silhouettes;* rel: LDS, primary & sunday school tchr; home: 220 E 3200 N; off: 289 RB, BYU.

ALLRED, G HUGH   prof of Marriage & Family Therapy BYU; private practice MFT; b: 22 May 1932; m: Carolyn; p: Golden & Josephine Leavitt; c: Steve H, Lynnette, Sharlene, Gregory H, Jennifer; ed: Yale (Chinese) 1951-2; BA 1957 MA 1960 BYU; U of Alberta; EdD U of Oregon; former: counselor & asst prof Ed Psych BYU; mem: fellow AAMFT; approved supvr UAMFT; NASAP; Phi Delta Kappa; Utah Parent Teachers Assn; award: listed in several natl & internatl biographies; publ: 7 books; articles; civic: Mormon Tabernacle Choir 9 yrs; Mar & Fam Therapy Licensing Board 8 yrs, chm 3 yrs; lectures; mil: US Air Force 1951-5; rel: LDS, church writing coms, ed week lecturer, elders presidency, bishopric, h council; home: 1104 N Terrace Dr; off: 262 CCB, BYU.

ALLRED, WALLACE E   BYU prof; chm Secondary Ed Dept; b: 26 Apr 1932; m: Bonnie Norman; p: Reid H & Anna E; c: Kenneth W, Janet Steeley, Nancy Hale,

Marilyn Jenkins; ed: BS 1956 MEd 1957 BYU; MS 1965 Oregon State; PhD 1971 U of Utah; Phi Kappa Phi; NSF Fellow; Outstanding Educators of Amer; former: tchr BY High School; admin BYU Lab Schools; career: Distinguished Educator Award; mem: NCTM; AACTE, UATE; award: Scout Ldrship; publ: articles in Instructor, Utah School Review, ERIC, Rural Education; civic: Dist Scout Commissioner; pol: neighborhood chm, state del; mil: 2nd Lt US Infantry, Japan & Far East 1952-4; Distinguished Serv Award; rel: LDS, bishop, stake presidency; club: Rotary; home: 552 S 490 W, Orem; off: 110-G MCKB, BYU.

ALLSEN, PHILIP E   prof Physical Ed BYU; b: 10 Jun 1932; m: Patricia; p: John & Alverta; c: Kathy, John; ed: BS MS EdD; Phi Kappa Phi; Phi Delta Kappa; Sigma Delta Psi; former: athletic dir Gardena Calif; coach & tchr Ricks College; career: Coach of the Yr, Natl PCFS Award; mem: Amer College of Sports Medicine; Amer Assn of Health, Phys Ed & Recreation; Nutrition Today Soc; Natl Ed Assn; award: listed in Who's Who in Ed, Who's Who in the West, Dictionary of Internatl Biography, Outstanding Educators of US, Men of Achievement, Internatl Who's Who in Community Serv, Community Ldrs & Noteworthy Americans, Who's Who in the US, Interntl Authors Who's Who; publ: *Fitness For Life; Racquetball; Beginning Jogging; Current Questions of Physical Fitness;* 25 articles; civic: Little League; mil: Naval Officer 1954-9; rel: LDS, bishopric, h council; home: 284 E 3450 N; off: 269 SFH, BYU.

ANDERSEN, ARIEL A   scientist, author, inventor, businessman; b: 6 Jul 1905; m: Ines Morgan; p: Joseph W & Carrie Thoresen; c: Marlo R, Cordell, Gayle Lubin, Howard L, Jolene Burckle; ed: BS chemistry MS biochemistry Utah State U; PhD physiol bacteriology Iowa State U; Res Assistantship & Res Assoc Iowa State U; former: res asst & instr Utah State U; res sci USDA and US Defense Dept; career: suggestion awards; 8 patents: Ideal Fruit Canner, Ideal Pressure Cooker, air sampling instruments (4 patents), dietary supplement for potassium difficiency, others; mem: ACS; SAB; IFT; AAAS; ASM; Sigma Xi; award: listed in Amer Men of Sci, Leaders in Ed, Who's Who 1948 sup, Who's Who on the Pacific Coast,

Who Knows, Leaders in Amer Sci; publ: 40 sci papers; 3 religious papers: *The Gathering of the Jen Jribes of Israel, The Jall and the Origin of Man, Evolution and Creation;* rel: LDS, dist pres, stake mission pres; home: 2208 Temple View Cir.

ANDERSEN, CORDELL MORGAN   Guatemalan field dir Found for Indian Development and Ayuda Inc; plantation owner & operator; b: 19 Apr 1936; m: Maria Cristina Bernard; p: Ariel A & Ines M; c: Julie Duerden, David L, Cristina Snyder, Richard C, Joseph A, Marcia, Danny, Cindy Marie, Celestina; ed: BA 1963 BYU; former: VP Andersen Samplers & Consulting Serv; admin asst BYU Alumni Assn; BYU Alumni Distinguished Serv Award 1977; mil: US Army Reserve medical specialist & instr; rel: LDS, branch pres, dist pres, elders pres, ward clerk; home: 1135 Cherry Ln; 3a Av A Pamplona, Guatemala City; off: 2208 Temple View Cr.

ANDERSEN, FERRON L   prof & chm of Zoology BYU; b: 10 Jul 1931; m: Stenna Turley; p: Wm L & Jean P; c: Lynnette, Stan, David, Darvel, Linda, Denise; ed: BS zoology Utah State U; MS vet med sci U of Ill; PhD zoology Utah State U; former: faculty Coll Vet Med Univ of Ill; career: 12-yr Natl Inst of Health; mem: Amer Soc of Parasitologists; Soc of Protozoologists; Rocky Mtn Conf of Parasitologists; publ: 50 sci articles; civic: former chm Pornography & Decency Comm, Orem; mil: Capt Med Serv Corps; rel: LDS, bp, youth ldr 25 yrs; home: 209 S Inglewood, Orem; 575 WIDB, BYU.

ANDERSEN, WILLIAM RALPH   prof of Botany; b: 11 Dec 1930; m: Connie Lyon; p: O R & Harriett Ricks; c: Sallie, David Ralph, Steven John, Timothy Lyon, Joshua Lyon; ed: BS 1956 MS 1958 Utah State U; PhD 1963 U of Calif; Sr Sci Post-Doctorate Fellow, Natl Inst of Health, Brandeis Univ 1972; former: asst prof U of Minnesota, St Paul 1963-6; career: research grants from Natl Sci Found, Natl Inst of Health, US Dept of Agriculture Cooperative Grants Office; mem: Genetics Soc of Amer; Amer Soc of Plant Physiology; Natl Geographic Soc of Amer; Sigma Psi; Amer Assn for the Advancement of Sci; publ: 30 journal articles; 1 book chapter; 30 sci papers; pol: active support 2 Orem City council mem; rel: LDS; home: 1046 E

400 N, Orem; off: 297 WIDB, BYU.

ANDERSON, A GARY   assoc prof Church History & Doctrine BYU; b: 8 Apr 1933; m: Annette Dean; p: Allen H & Dorothy Bedell; c: Ronald, Hal, Jan, Angela, Kim, Lori, Clark, Tiffany, Tyler; ed: Assoc Degree Snow College; BS 1958 U of Utah; MS 1960 BYU; EdD 1968 BYU; former: institute dir St George 1962-71; career: dir Semester Abroad Prog in Israel 1977; mem: Mormon History Assn; Utah State Historical Soc; publ: *Know Them Which Labor Among You;* civic: YBA & Little League coach; pol: republican state & county del; mil: US Marine Corps PLC Prog 1953; rel: LDS, bishop, h council, MTC branch pres; home: 237 E 230 S, Orem; off: 72 JSB, BYU.

ANDERSON, ALLAN J   part owner Provo Paint Center; b: 3 Jun 1932; m: Audrey M; p: Lynn & Grace; c: Kim, Kori, Chris; ed: military high school; former: mgr WP Fuller Paint Co; award: Jr Chamber of Commerce; mil: US Marines; advisor Korean Marines; rel: Prod; club: Eagles; Jr Chamber of Commerce; home: 247 N 150 E, Orem; off: 201 W Center.

ANDERSON, KEITH P   prof of chemistry BYU; b: 6 Oct 1919; m: Mary Davis; p: Everett E & Julia Phillips; c: Phillip, Douglas, Brian; ed: AB BYU 1946; PhD Cornell Univ NY 1950; Chemistry Award BYU 1946; former: Chief Radiological Warfare Div, Dugway Proving Grounds 1951-2; asoc res prof of physics U of Utah 1952-3; Univ of Calif staff, Los Alamos, N Mexico 1950-1; career: Fulbright lectureships, Spain 1960-1, Columbia 1966; mem: Amer Chem Soc; Amer Assn Adv of Sci; Sigma Xi; Utah Acad of Arts & Letters; publ: numerous sci papers; mil: Officer in Intelligence, Cert of Merit, Supreme Hq Allied Exp Forces; rel: LDS; home: 3758 Foothill Dr; off: 124 ESC, BYU.

ANDERSON, KIRK R   physician, internal medicine; b: 26 Sep 1949; m: Laura Lee; p: Robert H & Carol; c: Brenda 9, Miriam 7, Robert 5, Ryan 3, Beth 1; ed: MD 1977 U of Utah; Phi Kappa Phi BYU 1973; grad cum laude BYU 1973; career: board certified Amer Board of Internal Medicine 1981; mem: Amer Medical Assn; Amer Soc of Internal Medicine; Utah State Medical Assn; rel: LDS, elders pres, exec sec; home: 1120 E 350 N, Orem; off: 1055 N 500 W.

ANDERSON, NEIL J   testing coor & instr English Language Ctr BYU; b: 10 Jun 1955; m: Kathleen Reaser; p: Robert Neil & Reva J; c: Cameron Neil 4, Todd James 3, Amelia Kathleen 1; ed: BA Spanish MA Teaching English as a 2nd Language BYU; former: pres TESL Soc BYU; mem: Tchrs of English to Speakers of Other Languages; Intermtn TESOL; Deseret Language & Linguistics Soc; publ: *Discourse Analysis in the ESL Classroom; Culture Shock; Test Construction for Classroom Use;* rel: LDS, bishopric; home: 998 Cedar Ave; off: 149 FB, BYU.

ANDERSON, RUDY F   educator, dir Mountainland Head Start; partner McKee Child Enrichmen Ctr; b: 16 Nov 1949; m: Karen; p: Merrill R & Enid M; c: Kindra 8, F Damian 6, Jaron 5, Devon 3, Tressa 1; ed: MS Early Childhood Ed; mem: Natl Assn for the Ed of Young Children; chm Utah County Week of the Young Child 1980-2; civic: Home School Educators Assn; scouting; rel: LDS, h council, stake YM pres; home: PO Box 1427, Orem; off: 286 N 100 W.

ANDRUS, HYRUM LESLIE   prof Church Hist & Doct BYU; b: 12 Mar 1924; m: Helen Mae Hillman; p: Newton Leslie & Zina Alberta Allen; c: John Leslie, Richard Milo, David Hyrum; ed: BS 1951 Ricks College; MS 1952 BYU; PhD 1955 Syracuse U; former: dir Rel Studies Ricks College; career: Karl G Maeser Research Award; Master Tchr Award; listed in Dictionary of Internatl Biography, Internatl Scholars Directory, Internatl Who's Who in Community Serv, Contemporary Authors, Directory of Amer Scholars, Personalities of the West & Midwest, Who's Who in the West; publ: *Helps for Missionaries; Joseph Smith and World Government; Joseph Smith the Man and the Seer; Liberalism, Conservatism and Mormonism; Doctrinal Commentary on the Pearl of Great Price; God, Man and the Universe; Principles of Perfection;* rel: LDS; home: 530 E 1980 N; off: JSB, BYU.

ANSEL, RAYMOND E   pastor Assemblies of God; b: 5 Feb 1943; m: Sharon E; p: Ferman & Nina; c: Sherry 17,

Raymond Bo 16, David 12, Amy 5; ed: 16 yrs Westminster High School, Denver; College, Waxahatchie, Texas; Comprehensive Diploma, Berean School of the Bible; former: Youth Rep & Men's Rep State of Utah; career: Ordained Minister, Sectional Presbyter over state of Utah; mem: Utah Valley Homebuilders Assn; award: Grand Prize Best Craftsmanship & Best Construction, Bud Leach Racquetball Courts, Utah Masonary Unions; publ: children's stories; civic: hospital work; Big Brothers & Big Sisters board mem; board of dir Private Industrial Council; Mountain Land Assn of Govt; pol: campaigns for Mayor James Ferguson; rel: Assembly of God; club: Lions; home: 2995 Bannock Dr; off: 3410 N Canyon Road.

ARMSTRONG, VIRGINIA SCHERBEL   BYU staff physician, BYU Women's Athletics Team physician; b: 16 Apr 1919; m: Vaughn William; p: Paul Scherbel & Annette Neslen Scherbel; c: Vicki Lyons, Vaughn Scherbel, William Paul, James Richard, Virginia, Valori Annette, ed: RN 1940 Dr. WH Groves LDS Hospital School of Nursing; BA 1946 MD 1948 U of Utah; former: private med practice 1952-68; school physician 1959-62; public health & pediatrics physician Colorado Public Health 1962-76; mem: Amer Red Cross Nurses Assn; Amer Nurses Assn; Amer Med Assn; Colorado Med Assn; Colorado Women's Med Assn; Amer Med Women's Assn; civic: PTA, cubscout denmother; mil: US Army Nurse Corps 2nd Lt WWII; rel: LDS, youth ldr & tchr, home: 1120 E 2680 N; off: BYU Health Ctr.

ARNOLD, FRANK H   Head Basketball Coach BYU; b: 1 Oct 1934; m: Bee W; p: Gervase E & Maxine N; c: Kelly, Kristyn, Kippline, Gibson, Kaline; ed: BS Idaho State College; MS BYU; former: asst coach UCLA, U of Oregon, jr college, high school; career: 2 Coach of the Year Awards WAC Conf; mem: board of dir & chm officials com Natl Assn of Basketball Coaches; Mens Games Player Selection Com, Amature Basketball Assn USA; publ: *Man-Man Defense; Rise & Shout* autobiography; mil: US Air Force Reserves; rel: LDS, 70 group ldr; home: 3131 Navajo Ln; off: 2108 MC, BYU.

ARNOLD, MARILYN   prof of English, dir Ctr for the Study of Christian Values in Literature BYU; b: 26 Nov

1935; p: H Lynn & Rhoda C; ed: BA, MA, PhD; Hinckley Fellow BYU; EB Fred Fellow U of Wis; grad with highest honors; Phi Kappa Phi; former: Asst to Pres BYU; Asst Dean of Women U of Wis; Asst Dir Student Financial Aids U of Wis; career: prof of the Month BYU; mem: MLA; Utah Acad; Philological Assn of Pacific Coast; publ: articles in journals, magazines, books; rel: LDS, Sunday School Gen Board; Gen Church Curriculum Com; Relief Society task forces; home: 2726 Edgewood; off: A-279 JKBA, BYU.

ARNOLD, RHONDA exec dir Utah County Crisis Line & Info Referral Serv; b: 9 Aug 1949; p: Frank & Vera Caywood; c: Brete 11; former: pres of board Utah Crisis Line; career: Award for Outstanding Serv as pres of board; civic: Joint Action in Community Serv; rel: LDS, Jr. Sunday School Coord, Relief Soc tchr; off: P.O. Box 1375.

ASHFORD, JOSETTE BRITTE prof BYU; b: 26 Mar 1920; p: Andre Britte & Bertha Morin; ed: PhD French medieval literature, accounting; social work diploma; Fullbright grant 1968-9; former: accountant, social worker in Europe; genealogist; career: prof of the Month 1978; professional development leave 1979; mem: Medieval Assn of Amer; Rencesval Internatl Epic Assn; Rocky Mtn Medieval & Renaissance Assn; L'Esprit Createur; Computerized Analysis of Medieval Literature; Laboratoire d'analyse statistique des langues anciennes; publ: articles in Olifant, Univ of Liege, Belgium, Symposium 1981; text in French phonetics; civic: lecturer in many local clubs; rel: LDS; stake Sunday School board, welfare accountant, Relief Society Gen Board; home: 234 E 2190 N; off: 339 MSRB, BYU.

ASHMAN, JAMES DUANE Dr dental surgery; b: 23 Apr 1933; m: LaMon; p: Everett & Florence; c: Teresa, John Todd, Tracy, Tyler, Jami; ed: BYU 3 yrs; DDS Northwestern Dental School grad with honors; Omirron Kappa Upsilon; mem: pres Utah Dental Assn 1980-1; former VP treas Utah Dental Assn; former pres Provo Dist Dental Soc; ADA; Acad of Dentist BYU; Acad of Implantology; GU Black Soc; Utah Straight Wire Orthodontic Soc; award: all-state football player; HS student body pres; civic: chm Provo City Board of Adjustments; mil: US Army 2 yrs; Coast Guard 2 yrs; rel: LDS, bishop, h council; off: 1275 N Univ Ave No. 11.

ASHTON, DAVID MCKAY   Provo City Data Processing Mgr; b: 9 Jun 1944; m: Shawna Higgs; p: Conway A & Emma Rae McKay; c: David C 11, Betsy Bryn 1; ed: BS math MS computer sci U of Utah; MBA Col State U; cum laude; Owl & Key; former: applications group mgr Solar Energy Research Inst; branch & reg mgr Scientific Time Sharing Corp; mem: Amer Computing Machinery Assn; Amer Mgt Assn; award: 1st place music competition; soloist Utah Symphony; recorded 2 records with Utah Symphony; Eagle Scout; publ: "Use of Small Computers & Graphics in Education" NERA 1973; civic: Rotary Club Internatl; pol: Republican; mil: hon discharge 1971; rel: LDS, Sunday School pres; 70s group ldr; home: 974 W 600 S; off: 351 W Center.

ASHTON, LARRY   pres Fiber Technology Corp; b: 23 Dec 1931; m: Joan Parcell; p: Jed L & Leone Hales; c: Todd, Rebecca, Melinda, Clint, Brent, Camilla, David, Lori, John Lindsay; ed: BSME U of Utah; former: VP Fiber Sci, Gardena, Calif; pres ENTEC, SLC; civic: UTC Gen Advisory Com; mil: Utah Natl Guard; rel: LDS, youth progs; home: 680 E 1600 S, Mapleton; off: 765 S 100 E.

ASHWORTH, DELL SHEPHERD   proprietor, Dell S Ashworth & Assoc, Architect; b: 20 July 1923; m: Bette Brailsford, Faughn Montague Bennett; c: Brent Ferrin, Mark Shepherd, Anne Elizabeth, Christopher John (Kit); ed: BYU 1940-2, 46; U of Calif at Berkley 1946-9; BA architecture; former: architect in Provo since 1949; designed Provo City Ctr; partner, Ashworth Architects 1953-71; proprietor, TAG Architects & Engineers 1971-5; proprietor, B Ashworth's, Costa Mesa, Calif; career: listed in Who's Who in the World, Who's Who in the West, Dictionary of Internatl Biography, Natl Registrar of Prominent Amer, Community Ldrs of Amer, Internatl Who's Who in Community Serv, Men of Achievement, The Amer Registry, and 12 others; mem: dir Provo Industrial Development Corp; dir Utah Valley Cultural Ctr Com; chm Provo City Planning Commission; Amer Inst of Architects; civic: pres Provo Chamber of Commerce

1969; dir Provo CORE Development Corp; stake chm BYU Destiny Fund; chaplain & pres Sons of the Amer Revolution; chm O&E Provo Dist Com Boy Scouts; mil: US Navy WW II CM 2/C Pacific Theatre; Amer Theatre Ribbon; Victory Medal; Asiatic Pacific Theatre Ribbon w 3 stars; Philippine Liberation Medal w star; rel: LDS, bishop, h council, sunday school pres; club: pres Provo Kiwanis Club; off: 36 E 400 N.

AUSTIN, RICHARD M   CPA; Asst Dir of Accounting & Financial Reporting BYU; b: 21 Jul 1934; m: Sherrie Dixon; p: Michael J & Lillian M; c: Shauna 20, Sandra 19, Michael 16, Scott 15, Julie 11, Keith 10; ed: BA accounting BYU; 1 yr grad school; former: LDS Church Auditor; mem: CPA; rel: LDS, bishop; home: 339 N 900 E, Springville; off: D-148 ASB, BYU.

BACKMAN, ELMER A   owner Backman Foundry & Machine Inc; b: 16 Nov 1918; m: L D'On; p: Herman & Marie; c: Suzann Renae, Ted E; ed: high school, electrical engineer, molder, pattern maker; athletic scholarships; Excellence for Electrical Work; former: RR, foreman of Provo Foundry & Machine; career: write-ups in metals magazines; mem: Amer Foundrymen's Soc; Meehanite Metal Corp; mil: US Navy WWII; rel: Lutheran, Missouri Synod; Elder, congregational chm 12 yrs; home: 1169 N Grand Ave; off: 565 S 900 W.

BACKMAN, JAMES H   prof of Law; b: 31 Dec 1943; m: Carolyn Furner; p: LeGrand P & Edith Price; c: James 11, David 10, Jonathan 8, Stephen 6, Heidi 4, Joseph 1; ed: BA 1969 Harvard; JD 1972 U of Utah; Order of the Coif; BA magna cum laude; former: clerk with Judge Ozell Trask 9th Circuit Court of Appeals; associate Backman, Clark & Marsh in SLC; visiting prof U of Illinois; mem: Utah State Bar; publ: articles on consumer law, landlord/tenant, water law, public lands; civic: Family Life Commissioner with wife Edgemont PTA; pol: research dir 1980 Wright for Governor campaign; rel: LDS, bishoprics, scoutmaster; club: Harvard Alumni Assn of Utah; home: 3676 N 600 E; off: 430 JRCB, BYU.

BAKER, LEGRAND LISTON   assoc librarian, asst prof of history BYU; b: 2 Nov 1937; m: Marilyn Larsen; p: Glen &

Crystal; c: Dawn 19, Brian L 16, Tonya 13, Jason T 3; ed: BS 1963 BYU; MS 1966 PhD Amer Rev War & Writing of Constitution 1972 U of Wisconson Madison; former: assoc researcher with prof Merrill Jenson U of Wisc Madison; asst prof history U Arkansas Monticello; instr Lamar Co Community College; mem: Assn of Amer Historians; Mormon History Assn; Utah Historical Soc; Utah Library Assn; publ: co-auth "Wise Men Raised Up"; *Partial Comparison of Egyption Jheology and the Gospel of Jesus Christ;* pol: Republican state del; rel: LDS, stake missionary, bishopric, stake clerk, scoutmaster; home: 142 E 2000 S, Orem; off: 5030 HBLL, BYU.

BARBER, GREG   sergeant BYU Security/Police; b: 9 Mar 1950; m: Carol; p: Lowell & Phillis; c: Tami 11, Geoffrey 8, Rachel 6, Kara 5, Krista 2; ed: AAS Central Wyo College; Dean's Honors; former: police officer; cleaning specialist in textiles; career: mem of Outstanding Team FBI Anti-sniper School 1977; President's Recognition for Outstanding Serv to BYU 1980; mem: Utah Assn of SWAT Teams, sec 3 yrs; award: Eagle Scout; civic: scouting; pol: dist chm 4 yrs, Republican; county del; rel: LDS, sunday school pres, elders presidency & instr; off: B-66 ASB, BYU.

BARNEY, WILLIAM DURELL   asst chief Fire Dept; b: 17 Mar 1933; m: Joyce Y Randall; p: Jesse & Virginia; c: Sonya, Randall, Fara Dawn, D Wayne, Cherise; ed: E Arizona Jr College; BYU; UTC; former: Provo City Policeman; paramedic; fire inspecter; fire marshall; career: EMT Utah State & Natl Reg of Emergency Medical Tech, UTC, Basic Auto Extraction, Paramedic Weber State College, Hazardous Materials Emergency Response, Dynamics of Supervision, UTC, Fire Officer Mgt, UTC, Mgt & Tactics, UTC, Arson Fire Investigation, Natl Fire Acad, Emmitsburg, Maryland; mem: Utah Firefighters; Natl Firefighters; Utah Paramedics Assn; award: All State Football Player, Arizona High Schools 1950; Athletic Scholarship E Ariz Jr College 1951-2; civic: paramedic lectures to Utah Valley Hospital, BYU, schools, churches; BSA cubbing and scouting; mil: US Army Korean conflict 1953-5; rel: LDS, exec sec, elders presidency; club: VP Ferimous Union; Utah Professional Firefighters Exec Board; home: 1815 N 1350 W; off: 80 S 300 W.

BARRETT, M SCOTT   asst dir BYU Development Office; b: 29 Jun 1947; m: Mary Ann Brown; c: five; ed: BS bus admin 1972 BYU; Student Govt VP Student Relations; Utah Registered Abstracter; Utah Title Insurance Agent; Notary Public; former: VP Central Utah Title Co; off mgr Boley Realty Inc; pres Barrett Title & Abstract Co; mem: Utah County Homebuilder's Assn; Mortgage Banker's Assn; Natl Assn of Homebuilders; Utah Land Title Assn; Amer Land Title Assn; civic: N Utah County Kiwanis Club; sec Sertoma Club of Provo; club: pres Circle K Club; home: 1314 Jordan Ave; off: BYU Development Office.

BARRETT, STEPHEN L   dir Alumni Relations BYU; b: 12 Jun 1934; m: Crystal Broderick; p: Walter William & Myrtle Jeppson; c: Douglas 15, Jennifer Lee 12, Emilee 1; ed: BS 1963 pol sci BYU Hawaii; MEd 1968 ed admin BYU; former: asst dir Annual Giving, LDS Church Development Office & BYU; coor alumni activities BYU Alumni Assn; high school tchr in Utah & Hawaii; school counselor in Calif; mem: Council for the Adv & Support of Ed; Amer Soc of Assn Executives; Amer Alumni Council; publ: *Alumni Travel Manual;* 8 articles; mil: US Army, Chaplain's asst 1959-61; rel: LDS, stake YM pres, counselor, bishopric; home: 376 S 400 E, Orem; off: Alumni House, BYU.

BARRON, HOWARD H   prof of Rel Instr BYU; b: 7 Aug 1920; m: LaVerda R; p: Homer H & Lucile S; c: Verdalee, Bryce Howard, Bryan Homer; Marlene, Mark Ralphs; ed: BS 1943 MS 1950 Utah State U; doctorate 1953 U of Utah; Alpha Zeta; Alpha Tau Alpha; Phi Kappa Delta; former: asst county agent Weber Co; principal Altamont High School & Elem; early morning seminary tchr; asst prof Secondary Ed BYU; visiting prof Secondary Ed New Mexico A&M; dir San Jose LDS Inst; chm Dept of Bible & Modern Scripture BYU; career: speaker Sidney B Sperry Symposium 3 Mar 1977; award: pres Ag Club for School of Ag; pres Vocational Agric Club; Utah State Farmer 1938-9, State Officer 1939-40, Future Farmers of Amer; publ: *Orson Hyde: Missionary, Apostle, Colonizer; Judah, Past & Future; Of Everlasting Value; More Precious Than Gold;* 3 church history syllabi; civic: sec Plain City Dairy Days, Weber Co 1948-9; com mem Provo Miss Liberty

Belle pageant 1954; pol: Republican county & state del; mil: US Army Southwest Pacific & Philippine Islands 1943-6; Rifleman; Good Conduct; rel: LDS, h council, bishop, stake presidency; club: LDS Cultural & Social Clubs; home: 475 E 1070 S, Orem; off: 140 JSB, BYU.

BARTHOLOMEW, JEWEL ALEXANDER assoc prof Nursing BYU; b: 4 May 1930; m: E Byrd Bartholomew; p: Payton Holt & Bessie Hatton Alexander; c: David, Paul, Michael, Stephen, Christopher; ed: BS 1969 BYU; MS 1976 U of Utah; RN; Cert Nurse-Midwife; research in Temperature Adjustment in the Newborn; former: team ldr Utah Valley Hospital; mem: Amer College of Nurse-Midwives; Amer Nurse's Assn; Natl League for Nursing; Assn for the Care of Children's Health; Natl Perinatal Assn; Utah Nurse's Assn, former board mem dist 3 and nominating com; Utah Perinatal Assn; civic: March of Dimes; LDS Social Serv consultant; rel: LDS, Relief Soc ldr, chm Scout Com; youth ldr; home: 197 E 980 N, Orem; off 534 SWKT, BYU.

BARTON, CLIFF S prof of Civil Engineering BYU; b: 18 Jul 1919; m: Emma Whitehead; p: Walter K & Jennie S; c: Joan Raymond, C Bruce, Anne Marie Giffen, Clyde W, John K; ed: BS Utah State U; MCE PhD Rensselaer Polytechnic U; former: aerospace design engr Lockheed Aircraft Co; mechanical engr Watervliet Arsenal; asst prof Rensselaer Polytechnic Inst; asst dean BYU 1969-82; career: Outstanding Engr US Army for redesign of army cannons & manufacturing system 1959; mem: ASEE, Tau Beta Pi; ASCE; SESA pres 1969-70; Amer Acad of Mechanics; Sigma Xi; CEA; publ: 50 articles; civic: board of dir Utah Golf Assn; Timp Golf Assn; mil: US Army Air Forces 1944-6; rel: LDS, bishop, h council, dist presidency, branch pres; home: 1101 Elm Ave; off: 270 CB, BYU.

BATEMAN, LYNN L physician, internal medicine; b: 29 Dec 1936; m: Joan; p: Lynn L & Helen S; c: Brad, Jeffery, Arianne, Melissa; ed: BYU 3 yrs; U of Utah 4 yrs MD; former: developer of Respiratory Care Dept Utah Valley Hospital; mem: Amer Med Assn; Amer College of Physicians; private teaching med & nursing students; mil: US Air Force; rel: LDS, bishop; home: 866 E 1600 S,

Mapleton; off: 777 N 500 W.

BAUM, ROYANN HAYWARD   artist, owner Something
Special Gallery; b: 15 May 1943; m: Roy Ladell Baum; p:
Roy Kelsch & Dorothy Soulier Hayward; c: Laura Lee,
Craig, Suzanne, Rodney Dell, Darren Roy, Jason H;
former: pres Womens Council of Provo; pres Art Section
Provo; VP Utah Chapter of Tole Painters; career: many
1st 2nd 3rd place awards; mem: Intermtn Soc of Artist;
Chamber of Commerce; Utah Valley Artist Guilde; rel:
LDS, cultural arts & homemaking ldr, tchr; home: 1650 N
1250 W; off: 46 W Center.

BAUMANN, RICHARD WILLIAM   dir Monte L Bean Life
Sci Museum & assoc prof; b: 24 July 1940; m: Myrna Rae
Morrill; p: William & Elsie Elizabeth Anderson; c: Karin
16, Heidi 15, Jeffrey William 12, Rebecca 10, Susan 9,
Peter 6; ed: BA 1965 MS 1967 U of Utah; PhD 1970 U of
Utah & U of Montana; former: research guest, Max Planck
Soc, Germany 1970-1; asst prof Southwest Missouri U
1972; assoc curator, Smithsonian Inst 1973-5; career: Phi
Sigma; Sigma Xi; mem: Amer Assn of Museums;
Entomological Soc of Amer; N Amer Beuthological Soc;
Utah Acad of Sci, Arts & Letters; Southwest Assn of
Naturalists; Southwesters Entomological Soc; publ: *The
Stone Flies of the Rocky Mtns;* 25 small papers; mil: 1st
Lt MSC US Army; rel: LDS, bishop, h council, stake exec
sec, explorer ldr; club: Natl Audubon Soc; Sierra Club;
home: 1617 W 1050 N; off: 290 MLBM, BYU.

BEARDALL, C DOUGLAS   professional credit &
investment consultant, ACA Corp; b: 12 Jun 1951; m:
Jewel Nelson; p: Clyde L & Irene B; c: Jeffrey Douglas 4,
Holly Ann 3, Jennifer Diane 2; ed: BYU; Scholarship
Achievement Award; former: mgr Credit Bureau of Provo;
chm Provo Chamber of Commerce; career: Sertoman of
the Year; Outstanding Young Man, Provo JayCees; cert
instr Amer Collectors Assn; pres Provo Finance Co Inc;
mem: Amer Collection Assn; Amer Recovery Assn; Natl
Rifle Assn; Amer Firearm Assn; Amer Pawnbroker &
Bailbondsman Assn; award: Pistol Marksman Awards &
Rifle Sharpshooter; publ: *Miracle of Love, Latter-day
Bondage, For Missionaries Only, Death and the LDS
Family, Life Organizer, Qualities of Love, Cookbook for*

All Seasons; civic: pres Orem Sertoma Club; regional dir Speech & Hearing Found; pol: local dir Conservative Caucus; rel: LDS, h council; home: 3016 N Commanche Ln; off: 105 E 300 S.

BECKETT, DONALD ROBERT   broadcast engr KBYU TV/FM; b: 1 Feb 1925; m: Helen Stoddard; p: Louis Stanford & Grace Emily Feveryear; c: Cynthia, Bruce Robert; ed: AA Glendale College; UCLA; Sigma Xi Sigma; Laureate 1946; Outstanding Achievement in physics & chemistry at Glendale; former: NBC, Burbank, Calif; ABC, Los Angeles, Calif; publ: Great Ideas Contest; pol: Republican; rel: LDS, bishopric; home: 838 N 60 E, Orem; off: C-302 HFAC, BYU.

BELL, ELOUISE M   assoc prof English BYU; b: 10 Sep 1935; ed: BA U of Arizona; MA BYU; grad work U of Mass; Phi Beta Kappa; Phi Kappa Phi; former: tchr U of Arizona & U of Mass; career: Outstanding Young Woman of Utah 1970; Cert Excellence in Teaching Natl Assn of Depts of English 1971-2; listed in Dictionary of Internatl Biography; mem: governing board Assn for Mormon Letters; publ: monthly column in *Network* named best column in state by Utah Holiday magazine 1979; other articles; lyrics for "Behold Thy Handmaiden", et al; rel: LDS, tchr, church writing com 6 yrs, Young Women gen board 5 yrs; home: 827 N 435 E, Orem; off: A-214 JKB, BYU.

BELL, MICHAEL   owner The Woodsman; b: 22 Sep 1946; m: Loene; p: Frank & Beverly Williams; c: Aaron 1; ed: BS chemistry BS zoology San Diego State; former: gymnastics instr 14 yrs; chemist; award: coaching & teaching; civic: Chamber of Commerce; rel: LDS, bishopric, scoutmaster; home: 502 E Paradise Dr, Orem; off: 275 E 300 S.

BENNETT-MATTEO, SUSAN M   BYU faculty; b: 6 Feb 1954; m: Sante Matteo; p: Ruth V & Glenn E Bennett, Sr; ed: BA Russian & French 1976 Goucher College; MA French Miami U; MA Slavic lit & linguistics Ohio State U; passed PhD generals; Phi Beta Kappa; Phi Kappa Phi; former: tchng asst Miami U & Ohio State U; award: Kiwanis Club Citizenship Award 1972; home: 1445 S 100

W, Orem; off: 244 FB, BYU.

BENNION, DOUGLAS N   prof of Chemical Engineering
BYU; b: 10 Mar 1935; m: Delores Yvonne Wridge; p: Noel
L & Mildred H; c: Debra, Spencer, Donald, Delores,
Edwin, Charles, Daniel; ed: BS Oregon State U; PhD U of
Calif at Berkeley; former: prof of Engineering U of Calif
LA; mem: Electrochemical Soc (pres 1977-8); Amer Inst
of Chemical Engineers; Amer Chemical Soc; publ: 50
papers in sci journals; civic: scoutmaster troop 747; mil:
US Army Corps of Engineers 1958; rel: LDS; home: 1742 N
Driftwood Dr; off: 350 CB, BYU.

BENNION, JOHN WARREN   superintendent Provo School
Dist; b: 25 Nov 1936; m: Sylvia; c: Philip 16, Stanford 13,
David 10, Bryan 6, Grant 2; ed: BS 1961 MA 1962 U of
Utah; PhD 1966 Ohio State U; U of Utah Studentbody
Pres; Owl & Key, Beehive Honorary Soc; EE Lewis Award,
Ohio State U; Sherwood Shankland Honorary Scholarship
1967, Amer Assn of School Administrators; former: tchr
Granite High School; asst instr & admin asst to dir of
School of Ed, Ohio State U; admin intern, Parma Ohio
School Dist; Asst Sup of Schools for Curriculum &
Research, Elgin Illinois Public Schools; asst prof Indiana
U; Sup of Schools, Rochester NY; visiting asst prof,
Nazareth College; asst prof State U of NY; Sup of
Schools, Bloomington Minn Public Schools; mem: School
Mgt Study Group; Phi Delta Kappa; Amer Assn of School
Administrators; Assn of Early Childhood Ed; Assn for
Supervision & Curriculum Development; publ: 3 journal
articles; 2 articles in *Improvement Era;* mil: Natl Guard
1955-62; rel: LDS, bishop; club: Provo Rotary Club; home:
530 E 4450 N; off: 280 W 940 N.

BERG, CARL D   pres Berg Mortuaries; b: 2 Oct 1945; m:
Lana C; p: Max W & Miriam C; c: Gretchen 13, Mercedes
11, Brijette 5; ed: BA 1972 BYU; mem: Natl Selected
Morticians; Order of the Golden Rule; Utah Funeral
Directors; mil: US Army Reserve; rel: LDS; club: Provo
Rotary Internatl; home: 210 S 500 W; off: 185 E Center.

BERG, LANA CRANDALL   VP Berg Mortuaries; b: 17
Nov 1944; m: Carl D Berg; p: Hart B & Bette Crandall; c:
Gretchen 13, Mercedes 11, Brijette 5; ed: BYU 1963-5; U

of Utah 1965-6; rel: LDS; home: 210 S 500 W; off: 185 E Center.

BERGE, DALE L "BUD"   prof of Anthropology; b: 5 Sep 1934; m: Geraldine "Gerri" Mitton; c: Kurt W 15, Tara M 13, Matt J 7; ed: BA 1961 MA 1964 BYU; MA 1967 PhD 1968 U of Arizona; Sigma Xi; former: res asst, teaching asst, instr, asst prof, assoc prof, BYU; research, New World Archaeological Found; teaching asst & assoc U of Arizona; research asst & assoc, Arizona State Museum; career: prof of the Month BYU 1974; listed in Community Leaders of Amer 1972, Dictionary of Internatl Biography 1972, Amer Men & Women of Sci 1974, 77; Men of Achievement 1980, Who's Who in the West 1980; Com of Public Archaeology, Soc for Amer Archaeology; exec com Ctr for Health & Environmental Studies BYU; Charles Redd Fellowship 1979-80; mem: fellow Amer Anthropological Assn; Soc for Amer Archaeology; Soc for Historical Archaeology; Historical & Cultural Sites Review Com, State of Utah; publ: 29 articles & monographs; mil: US Navy Reserve 1952-8; US Army 1958-60 Military Intelligence; Good Conduct Medal; rel: LDS, branch pres; home: 3426 Piute Dr; off: 930 SWKT, BYU.

BERRETT, LAMAR C   prof BYU; b: 28 Mar 1926; m: Darlene Hamilton; p: John Harold & Stella Wright; c: Marla, Kim, Michael, Susan, LeAnn, Nathan, Evan, Ellen, Jared; ed: BS U of Utah; MS EdD BYU; former: mem Graduate Council 1969-71; Church History Area Dir, Rel Studies Ctr 1975-; chm Church History & Doctrine Dept BYU 1964-75; mem: Soc for Early Historical Archaeology; Amer Profs for Peace; Utah State Historical Soc; Mormon History Assn; Sons of Utah Pioneers; publ: *Discovering the World of the Bible; The Wilford C Wood Collection* vol 1; mil: WWII 2nd Infantry Div 110 combat days European Theatre; 3 Battle Stars; Tech-Corporal; rel: LDS, stake clerk, bishop, h council, mission presidency; home: 1032 E 400 S, Orem; off: 154 JSB, BYU.

BERRYESSA, MAX   prof of Ed; b: 22 May 1923; m: Janet G; p: Walter S & Lillian D; c: Richard, Scott, Dean, Guy; ed: AS BS MS EdD; Honor Student; Outstanding Ed Major 1947 Weber State College; former: chm BYU Elementary

Ed Dept; Tchr Ed Advisor UNESCO; career: Karl G Maeser Distinguished Teaching Award; mem: pres Assn for Childhood Ed internatl; pres Utah ACE; pres Utah UEA Elem Sect; pres Utah ATE, AIGE, PDK; publ: 17 journal articles; civic: Little League coach; board Marrcrest Homeowner Assn; Grindstone Planned Community; Quail Valley Homeowner Assn; mil: US Navy; rel: LDS, All Church Corr Com, h council, bishop; home: 2830 Marrcrest W; off: 210-H MCKB, BYU.

BEUHRING, RYAN R   BYU Training & Development; b: 4 Oct 1947; m: Jane C; p: Robert & Elfriede; c: Sheli 17, Kelley 15, Ryan 11, Jacob 3, Daniel 1; ed: AA mathematics BS psychology MA ed psychology; mem: ASTD, ASPA, CUPA; civic: Big Brothers Big Sisters of Central Utah; mil: Army sgt; Bronze Star, Vietnam in-country decorations; Good Conduct; rel: LDS, stake mission pres, elders quorum pres; home: 274 S Ellis Dr, Orem; off: Training & Dev, LIDH, BYU.

BILLINGS, LEWIS K   sr exec VP & gen mgr Billings Computer Corp and Caldisk Div; m: Patti Jo Kelly; mem: chm Utah Valley Manufacturers Council; civic: board of dir Provo Chamber of Commerce; off: 2000 E Billings Ave.

BILLINGS, RUSSELL M   dentist; b: 8 Jan 1926; m: Janet Stringham; p: A Vivian & Gladys McBeth; c: Becky Higginson, Mindy Maddox, Joanna McGregor, Russell L; ed: BS BYU; DDS U of KC Dental School; mem: Provo Dist Dental Soc; Amer Dental Assn; mil: 1st Lt Infantry Platoon Ldr WW II; rel: LDS stake Sr Aaronic Com, scouting treas; club: Rotary Internatl; Riverside Country Club; home: 422 E 4300 N; off: 85 W 500 N.

BINGHAM, RONALD D   prof Ed Psychology; b: 27 Jan 1936; m: Marjean; p: Delos E & Marcia S; c: Ronette 20, Melanie 17, Marci 16; ed: PhD counseling Penn State U; NDEA Academic Fellowship; former: tchr, counselor, admissions dir, consultant; career: pres Utah Assn of Counselor Ed & Supervision; pres Utah Personnel & Guidance Assn; mem: Amer Personnel & Guidance Assn; Assn for Tchr Ed; Mental Health Assn; Assn of Mormon Counselors & Psychotherapists; publ: journal articles; civic: VP Provo Board of Ed; pol: republican; mil: US Air

Force; 6 mo active duty; 6 yrs reserve; rel: LDS, bishop, h council, stake aux pres; club: former Kiwanis; home: 1177 E 640 S; off 320-H MCKB, BYU.

BIRD, ROY KENNEDY   asst prof of English BYU; b: 18 Sep 1947; m: Carol Penny Cherrington; p: Roy Hall & Glenna Kennedy; c: David 10, Lora 8, Bryan 6, Geoffrey 4; ed: BA 1972 English MA 1974 English lit BYU; PhD 1982 William Marsh Rice U; Phi Kappa Phi; Rice Fellowship; former: editor & writer BYU Press 1974-6, BYU Centennial History; mem: Modern Language Assn; publ: *Ideas of Order: A College Reader;* civic: Utah Youth Soccer Assn coach; pol: del state Democratic conv; rel: LDS; home: 1504 S 100 W, Orem; off: 203-C SFLC, BYU.

BISHOP, JERRY L   off mgr ELWC Business Office BYU; b: 21 Jun 1947; m: Trudy; p: Lynn R & Lyla M; c: Alison 7, Jared 5, Kristyl 4, Jeffrey 2, Andrew 1; ed: BS 1972 BYU; scholarship; career: 5-yr Service Award; mem: Delta Phi Epsilon; Utah Bus Ed Assn; mil: Natl Guard 1970-6; rel: LDS, elders pres, asst stake clerk, stake sunday school pres; home: 429 N 250 E, Orem; off: 327 ELWC, BYU.

BLACK, BRENT RULON   receiving clerk BYU; b: 8 Aug 1958; m: Terrie C Black; p: Allen R & LaRene W Buck; c: Jeremy Brent 1; ed: UTC; FORMER: mgr Winchell's Doughnuts; truck driver; award: swimmer for BYU & Sp Fork City; buffalo riding at rodeos; rel: LDS; club: Friends Club; home: 55 E 600 N.

BLACK, RUSSELL C   Athletic Dir & Instr UTC; b: 4 Feb 1932; m: Eyvonne Porter; p: Mark C & Nina Warner; c: College" article; civic: Heart Fund Drive; PTA officer; Girl Scout Ldr; rel: LDS, youth ldr, genealogy mission; home: 1215 S 50 W, Orem; off: UTC, Box 1609.

BLACKWELL, ROBERT H   Dept Chm Radiology Technology UTC; b: 1 Apr 1938; m: Brenda A; p: Harry & Virginia; c: Michelle 13, Matthew 10, Daniel 3; ed: Vocational & Secondary Teaching Certs; BS zoology BYU; grad work; former: College Curriculum Chm; Chm Life Sci Com; Chm Medical Cluster; teacher; career: nominated Teacher of Yr 1980-1; Honorary Dental Asst 1978-9; mem: Utah Ed Assn; Natl Ed Assn; Utah & local

Vocational Assn; Natl Cooperative Ed; award: scouting, music, coaching; civic: Sertoma Internatl; pol: campaigns; mil: US Naval Reserve 8 yrs; rel: LDS, scout ldr, music chm; club: former mem, Timpanogos Knife & Fork Club; home: 707 E 150 N, Orem; off: UTC, PO Box 1609.

BLOMQUIST NUTTALL, LINDA RENAE   writer, BYU Curriculum Development; b: 17 Jul 1958; m: Kent Ross Nuttall; p: Wayne T Blomquist & Ruth Ellen Jeppson; ed: BA English 1980 BYU; Bybee Award; Presidential & Dean's Scholarships; Honors Prog High Honors; Cum Laude; Natl Merit Commendation; former: cartographer, draftsperson, writing tutor & tchr BYU; award: Kiwanis Citizenship Award; Outstanding Young Woman of Amer; publ: poems & essays; rel: LDS, welfare coor; home: 860 Columbia Ln No. 27; off: 173 SWKT, BYU.

BOHN, ROBERT F   assoc prof Bus Mgt BYU; b: 10 Feb 1942; m: Peggy A Pettit; p: James & Madge; c: Jeff 15, David 12, Matthew 8, Michael 5, Mark 1; ed: BA; MBA; PhD; scholarships; former: domestic & internatl banker; career: BYU prof of Month; nominated Outstanding prof of Yr; listed in Who's Who in Financial Planning; founded nation's 1st undergrad degree in Financial & Estate Planning; mem: Financial Mgt Assn; Western Finance Assn; Internatl Assn of Financial Planners; publ: *A Budget Book & Much More;* journal articles; 100 newspaper articles; civic: lecture & workshops; Family Life Conf Com; board of dir Utah County Mental Health Assn; mil: US Army Captain MSC; rel: LDS, Church Family Resource Mgt Com, consultant to Church Correlation Com on family finance, h council, stake mission pres; home: 3636 N Little Rock Dr; off: 377 JKB, BYU.

BOOTHE, RANDALL WAYNE   artistic dir Young Ambassadors; coor BYU Entertainment Div; b: 30 Jan 1951; m: Susan Johnson; p: Wayne Ronald & Velma Wells; ed: music theory Lewis & Clark College; BA fine arts 1975 BYU-hawaii; MM music ed 1979 BYU; grad Summa Cum Laude; Academic & ldrship Scholarships BYU-Hawaii; Richard K Frederick Music Scholarship, State of Oregon; Academic Scholarship BYU; valedictorian; former: dir BYU Vocal Jazz Emsemble; clinician Walt Disney Production; BYU instr; dir All Amer

Singers & Showband, Disneyland; artistic dir BYU Sounds of Freedom; dir Choral Music Dept BYU-Hawaii; musical consul Polynesian Cultural Ctr, Hawaii; music dir, arranger, composer Hawaii Public TV; award: Outstanding Young Men of Amer 1980; Eagle Scout; rel: LDS; home: 37 N 200 W, Spanish Fork; off: 20-A KMB, BYU.

BOSWELL, JOHN WALLACE recorder Provo LDS Temple; b: 29 Sep 1909; m: Edda M Jones; p: John henry & Mary Elizabeth Garrett; c: Margo Trotter, Dana Kaye Ellertson, John Wallace II; ed: BS bus admin & accounting 1931 BYU; former: off mgr Provo Foundry & Machine Co; supvr accounting Geneva Steel; staff asst Columbia Geneva Steel; supvr gen accounting US Steel, Lander, Wyo; asst to mgr work accountant Geneva Steel; career: listed in Who's Who of the West 1963-4; civic: pres Utah Lake Lions Club 1959-60; Boy Scouts of Amer 50 yrs; BSA Silver Beaver 1969; rel: LDS, h council, bishop, stake presidency, Provo Temple presidency; club: Timpanogos Knife & Fork Club (VIP); Jr Chamber; home: 1386 Cedar Cr; off: 2200 N Temple Dr.

BOWEN, DONNA LEE asst prof BYU Dept of Govt; ed: BA 1968 U of Utah; Ctr for Arabic Studies Abroad, Amer Univ in Cairo; MA 1972 PhD 1981 U of Chicago; summer progs in Tunisia & Iran; Natl Inst of Mental Health grant; Fulbright-Hays Fellowship; NDFL Title VI language fellowships; career: Ford Found Research Proj on Islamic Ed in Morocco; publ: articles; book reviews; papers; home: 49 E 600 N, Orem; off: Dept of Govt, BYU.

BOYER, ROYANNE D BYU faculty; Placement Dir, Organizational Behavior Dept; b: 10 Jan; m: Glen L; p: Roy Robert & Louise Reynolds Dunn; c: Pat, Heather, Holly; ed: BA speech & dramatic arts; MA organizational behavior BYU; former: Braniff Airways; Amer Airlines; Jones & Laughlin Steel; mem: Consortium of Wone in Higher Ed; Southwest Inst of Research on Women; HERS-west Higher Ed Resource Serv; civic: former pres PTSA Orem High School; pol: county chm Young Republicans, Oklahoma; rel: LDS, Relief Soc, Primary, MIA; home: 157 E 4380 N; off: 340 SWKT, BYU.

BOYTER, SCOTT M admin mgr BYU Dept of Music; b:

19 Jun 1947; m: Sherrie Lynn; p: Neil K & Mae M; c:
Laura Michelle 7, Tonia Leigh 2, Diana Lynn 2 mo; ed: S
Utah State College 1965-7; grad US Army Finance School
1972; BS BYU admin mgt 1973; honor stud S Utah State
College 1967; Outstanding Graduate Award, BYU Admin
Mgt 1973; former: admin aid to dean College of Fine Arts
& Communications BYU 1973-6; mem: Amer Mgt Assn;
Admin Mgt Soc; Amer Philatelic Soc; Professional
Business Assn, BYU Chapter; Utah Personnel Assn, BYU
Chapter; award: listed in 1979 Outstanding Young Men in
Amer; pol: Young Republicans; mil: Army Reserve platoon
sgt & branch chief, 395th finance sect, Ft Douglas; Spirit
of Amer Honor Award; Army Reserve Components
Achievement Award with Oak Leaf Cluster; Armed
Forces Reserve Medal; rel: LDS, bishopric, stake exec
sec; club: Key Club Internatl; Postal Commemorative Soc;
home: 331 N 875 E, Orem; off: C-550 HFAC, BYU.

BRADSHAW, JERALD   prof of Chemistry; b: 28 Nov
1932; m: Karen Lee; p: Sherwin H & Maree Wood; c:
Donna, Melinda; ed: BS U of Utah; PhD UCLA; former:
research chemist Chevron Research, Calif; career: prof of
Yr BYU 1974; Maeser Research Award BYU 1977; mem:
Amer Chemical Soc; adv board Internatl Soc of
Heterocyclic Chemistry; Utah Acad of Sci; Sigma Xi;
publ: 5 patents; over 90 sci papers; mil: US Navy 4 yrs; ret
Cdr Navy Reserve; USS Oriskang; Naval Intelligence; rel:
LDS, h council, bishop; club: former pres Timpanogos
Kiwanis; home: 1616 Oaklane; off: 227 ESC, BYU.

BRADSHAW, MERRILL   composer & prof of Music BYU;
b: 18 Jun 1929; m: Janet Spilsbury; p: Melvin K & Lorene
Hamblin; c: Karen, Tracy Lynn, Brian Richard, Keith
Merrill, Marie, Charles Callis, Daniel James; ed: BA 1954
MA 1955 BYU; M Mus 1956 DMA 1962 U of Ill; grad
awards BYU, U of Ill; Phi Kappa Phi; Pi Kappa Lambda;
former: fellow, asst in music U of Ill; music tchr Chanute
Air Force Base; career: Maeser Creative Arts Award
1967; Distinguished Faculty Lecture 1981; mem: MENS;
ASCAP; award: Who's Who in Music; Who's Who in
Community Service; Who's Who in the West; publ:
*Mosaics; Music for Worship; Miniature Preludes; Mormon
Hymn Fantasies;* articles & monographs in various
journals; numerous musical compositions; civic: chm Arts

Council of Central Utah; Provo City Cutural Arts
Commission; pol: del Republican conv; rel: LDS, bishop, h
council Gen Church Music Dept; scoutmaster; home: 248
E 3140 N; off: E-544 HFAC, BYU.

BRAITHWAITE, LEE F   prof of Zoology BYU; b: 26 Sep
1936; m: Judith Johns; p: Leonard R & Violet Cox; c:
Brent, Lynette, Julee, Ellen, Brian, Marc, Bruce, Nathan,
Cheralyn, Heather; ed: PhD; career: Karl G Maeser
Teaching Excellence Award; mem: Soc of Western
Naturalists; publ: 2 textbooks; 23 sci articles; mil: US
Army Reserves; rel: LDS, bishop, h council; home: 169 N
600 W, Orem; off: 189 WIDB, BYU.

BRANAM, OLIVER C   owner & operator Ollie's Garage;
b: 8 Sep 1923; m: Barbara Colleen Ivie; p: Walter Marion
& Carrie Stith; c: Robert H, Thomas Walter, Barbara J
Vakilian, Wendy S; ed: auto mechanic Trade Tec
Muskoggee, Okla; former: adult ed instr; career: Master
Tec, Chry Co, DR of Motors Perfect Circil, Special
Training Chry Factory; mem: Automotive Assn of US;
award: Boy Scouts of Amer Eagle & Silver Beaver; civic:
former pres Amature Radio, ham operator; pol: state del
Democrat; rel: LDS, sunday school tchr, scout finance
chm; club: Lions Club, Civil Defense, Emergency Radio
Alert; home: 564 S State St; off: 791 E 600 S.

BRENNER, ROBERT HAROLD   technician Industrial Ed,
tchr auto mechanics, special courses, ed week, BYU; b: 4
Mar 1938; m: Sydeny Ann Geary; p: Harold F & Lucile
Rapier; c: Joy Ann Paiz, Kathy Lyn Hirst, Robert
Stephen, Timothy John, Tamara Lucile, Thomas Kevin; ed:
BYU; career: 15-yr Service Award Gen Motors; Gen
Motors Achievement Awards; BYU Service Award; mem:
Utah Council for Computer Ed; Computer Users Group;
civic: Boy Scouts of America scoutmaster; rel: LDS, exec
sec, bishopric, sunday school supt; home: 161 S 280 E,
Orem; off: 230 SNLB, BYU.

BREWSTER, BRANDON SCOTT   asst prof of Chemical
Engineering BYU; b: 25 Apr 1951; m: Elaine Carr; p: Blair
Hayes Brewster & Bonnie Bytheway Miller; c: Sara 6, Ben
4, Jacob 2; ed: BS 1975 ME 1977 PhD 1979 chemical
engineering, U of Utah; DC Jackling scholarship;

Presidential Honors; BS Magna Cum Laude, DMMMCF
Fellow; mem: AICHE; ASEE, Phi Kappa Phi; Sigma Xi;
publ: *Heat Transfer and Pressure Drop in Coal-Air
Suspensions Flowing Downward Through a Vertical Tube*
PhD Thesis; mil: AF Reserve; Utah Air Natl Guard; rel:
LDS; home: 2730 Arapahoe Ln; off: 350 CB, BYU.

BRIGGS, LELAND S   physican; pres staff Utah Valley
Hospital; b: 23 Apr 1933; m: Mary; p: L Stanford & Pay; c:
Lezlie, Michelle, Rebecca, Jason, Shaun; ed: MD; AOA
Medical Scholastic Honor Soc; career: former pres Utah
Heart Assn; mem: Utah County Med Soc; Utah State Med
Soc; Amer Med Assn; Utah Heart Assn; rel: LDS, bishop, h
council; off: 1055 N 500 W.

BRIMHALL, WILLIS H   prof of Geology BYU; b: 17 May
1925; m: Lynette McRae; p: Rulon W & Ida Hone; c:
Gregory, Jeffrey, Mark, Michelle, Denise, Scott, Susan,
Jennifer, Debra; ed: BS 1949 BYU; MS 1951 U Arizona;
PhD 1966 Rice U; mem: Amer Chemical Soc; Amer Assn
for the Adv of Sci; Geological Soc of Amer; Soc of
Exploration Geochemists; publ: papers in sci journals;
civic: consultant, Environmental Geology; mil: USNR
Aviation Electronic Technicians Mate 2c 1943-6; rel:
LDS; home 789 S 590 E, Orem; Dept of Geology, BYU.

BRIMLEY, VERN JR   asst to sup Community Affairs
Provo City Schools; b: 31 May 1931; m: Dawn Baker; p:
Vern & Thelma; c: Lisa Marie, Sheryl, Shana; ed: BS MA
EdD; Fulbright Fellowship; Danforth-NASE Fellowship;
former: dir Federal Progs, principal, Wasatch School, tchr
BYU Lab School, Franklin, Provost, acct exec, KEYY,
KLOR-TV; career: IDEA Fellow; Kettering Foundation
Fellowship; Exchange Tchr to Great Britain; Acad of
Amer Educators; included in Outstanding Educators in
Amer; Utah Network Instr TV Exec Com; mem: Natl Ed
Assn; Utah Ed Assn; Ed Assn English Speaking Union; Natl
Union of Tchrs (honorary); publ: co-author *Financing
Education in a Climate of Change;* articles on ed; civic:
Provo Chamber of Commerce; Community Action Board;
Board Mem Credit Union; Cultural Arts Ctr Board of
Trustees; rel: LDS, branch pres, h council; home: 3121
Comanche Ln; off: 280 W 940 N.

BRINGHURST, PAUL Parking Serv Supvr, BYU Traffic Off; b: 18 Oct 1949; m: Sue Tripp; p: Ray N & Virginia Bringhurst; c: Noelle 9, Jared 7, Carrie 5, Erin 2; ed: BS business & mil sci 1974 BYU; grad Utah Police Acad; cert Sep 1981; former: career: Employee of the Yr 1982 BYU Security/Police; civic: Army Reserve Co Commander; mil: US Army Officer 4 yrs; Commendation Medal; rel: LDS, 70s pres, ward mission ldr, branch presidency; home: 356 S 50 W, Orem; off: 1430 N 700 E.

BRITSCH, R LANIER prof of History & Asian Studies BYU; b: 16 Nov 1938; m: JoAnn M; p: Ralph A & Florence T; c: Carl 18, Catherine 15, Curtis 13, Sheri 12, Randall 8, James 5; ed: BA 1963 asian studies, anthropology BYU; MA 1964 history BYU; PhD 1967 asian studies, religious Claremont Grad School; NDFL Fellowship for study of Japanese lang & culture 1965-6; Fellow of Blaisdell Inst for Adv Study of World Cultures and Religions; career: Fulbright-Hayes Seminar in Indian Political Inst & History, India 1968; LDS Church Historian's Fellowship 1974; mem: Assn for Asian Studies; Internatl Assn for Mission Studies; Amer Soc for Missiology; Mormon History Assn; award: District Achievement Award BSA; publ: 26 articles in journals & periodicals; mil: USAR 1957-65; rel: LDS, branch pres; h council; stake presidency; home: 518 E 500 S, Orem; off: 411 KMB, BYU.

BROADBENT, JAMES M orthodontist; b: 19 Apr; m: Janet Hamilton; p: Marden & Norma; c: Justin 4, Tyler 2; ed: BS BYU; DDS, MS, Ortho Cert Northwestern U; CV Mosby Book Award; career: diplomate Amer Board of Orthodontics; mem: Amer Assn of Orthodontists; Rocky Mtn Soc of Orthodontists; former pres Utah Orthodontic Soc; former pres Provo Dist Dental Soc; Utah & Amer Dental Assn; Clinical Research Associates; Tweed Orthodontic Found; Greater SL Ortho Study Group; award: Kentucky Colonel Award, State of Kentucky; civic: sec-treas Utah Youth Soccer Assn; Century Club Boy Scouts of Amer; rel: LDS, bishopric, scoutmaster; club: Executive Club; home: 581 E 3750 N; off: 777 N 500 W No. 205, and 3707 N Canyon Rd No. 7D.

BROADBENT, LARRY JAY dentist, consultant; b: 20 Apr 1945; m: Nathalie C; p: Jay S & Beverly Harrison; c:

Cameron Jay, Chad Joseph, Casey James; ed: Doctor of Medical Dentistry U of Oregon; BYU Honors Prog; mem: Amer Dental Assn; mil: Capt US Army Dental Corp; rel: LDS; home: 1255 S 1500 E, Mapleton; off: 1275 N University Ave No. 21.

BROOKS, LELAND G   salesman, Robert T Smith Real Estate; b: 11 May 1913; m: Anna Lou Peterson; p: George & Flora Morris; c: Teena (deceased), Jeffrey, Sue Ann, Linda, Chris; ed: Masters Degree in education; former: coach Virgin Valley High, Bunkerville, Nev, Lincoln High, Orem, automobile salesman; mgr, Equitable Realty & Heritage Realty; career: Oldsmobile salesman awards; Top Retail Salesman for Denver dist; mem: BYU Track Team; pol: ran for City Commissioner; rel: LDS, h council, bishopric; club: Lions; home: 1439 Cherry Cr; off: 1900 N Canyon Rd.

BROTHERSON, JACK D   prof of Botany & Range Sci BYU; b: 18 Sep 1938; m: Karen Jeanne Earl; p: William N & Karen Beth; c: Mark 15, Sean 14, Eric 11, Jeanne 8, Rachel 6, Eric 5; ed:) BS MS BYU; PhD Iowa State U; NDEA Fellow; NSF Fellow; career: Creative Research Award 1980; mem: Ecol Soc of Amer; British Ecological Soc; Int Soc for Range Mgt; publ: 50 articles; rel: LDS, elders pres, bishopric, h council; home: 488 N 600 E, Orem; off: 493 WIDB, BYU.

BROWN, DON JAY   dir Training & Development BYU Personnel Serv; b: 1 Sep 1943; m: Barbara Jean; p: William Max & Bessie Bunnell; c: David William 14, Carol Jean 11, Robert Lowell 9, Matthew Jay 3; ed: BS public relations MA communications BYU; Kappa Tau Alpha; former: asst dir BYU Gen Serv; career: Amer Soc for Training & Development Serv Award, Educational Institutions SIG, Personnel Assn of Central Utah Leadership Serv Award; mem: Amer Soc for Training & Development (former pres Utah chapter & chm, Natl Ed Institutions Group); Amer Soc for Personnel Admin; former pres Personnel Assn of Central Utah; Acad of Mgt, Amer Film Inst; civic: exec dir Utah Valley Community Leadership Acad; rel: LDS, h council; club: Cougar Club; home: 751 S Geneva Road, Orem; off: LIDH, BYU.

BROWN, RONALD GENE   mgr U-Serve Gas of Provo; b: 12 Mar 1957; m: Georgianna Fambrough; p: Ronald Gary & Eloise Shirley Vaughan; c: Nathaniel Johnathan 1; ed: BA BYU; Distinguished Grad BYU AFROTC; former: head mechanic Pigeon Mtn Husky; career: Outstanding Sales Improvement 1980-1; mem: Small Businessmen of Amer; awards: Mayor Verl G Dixon Leadership Award; 1975 Road Rally Champion; publ: *The Tempest is Raging; Family Home Evening; The Stettley Actioneer; Moses Thatcher and the Mormon Hierarchy: A Question of Dissidence;* civic: Utah Special Olympics; Muscular Dystrophy Assn; mil: Cadet Commander BYU AFROTC; 2nd Lt US Air Force Titan Missle Launch Officer; Vandenburg II 1980 Camp Academics Award & Honor Flight; Commandant of Cadets Outstanding Sr Award 1981; rel: LDS; club: Orem Sunrise Lions; Jr Chamber of Commerce; Natl Rife Assn; Write Your Congressman; home: 401 S State.

BUDD, MARIEL PASKETT   exec sec; b: 19 May 1939; m: Richard Douglas Budd; p: Melvin Oscar & Relia Hale Paskett; c: Richard D Jr 19, Lauri 18, Spencer Warren 16; ed: Stevens Henager Business College; BYU; Cert Professional Sec; mem: treas CPSA West; rel: LDS, Relief Soc tchr, YWMIA pres; home: 434 N 200 E, Lindon; 323 KMB, BYU.

BULLOCK, KENNETH C   prof of Geology BYU; b: 8 Sep 1918; m: Annie G; p: Irving & Cora C; c: Kenneth G, Virginia, Mary Anne, Sherilyn; ed: BS 1940 MA 1942 BYU; PhD 1949 U of Wisconsin; Van Hise Research Asstship, U of Wisc; former: chm Dept of Geology BYU 1956-62; career: council mem Utah Geological & Mineral Survey; mem Internatl Geological Field Inst to Brazil; mem: fellow Geological Soc of Amer; Soc of Mining Engineers of AIME; Sigma Xi; Sigma Gamma Epsilon; Utah Geological Assn; publ: *Iron Deposits of Utah; Fluorite Occurrences in Utah; Minerals & Mineral Localities of Utah;* bulletins; sci papers; civic: Boy Scout Examiner; Mineral Resource Com for Utah County; pol: dist chm; mil: Lt JG US Naval Reserve, WW II 1944-6; Amer Theatre; Good Behavior; rel: LDS, bishop, h council, stake presidency; home: 1035 N 900 E; off: 129 ESC, BYU.

BURNSIDE, WESLEY M   prof of Art History, dir of Art

Acquisitions BYU; p: Mason N & Fannie Bills; ed: BS 1941 MS 1949 BYU; PhD 1970 Ohio State; publ: *Maynard Dixon Artist of the West; Early Utah Artists;* mil: 13th AAF, S Pacific 1943-6; rel: LDS; home: 605 Sagewood; off: Art Gallery, BYU.

BUSHNELL, J MERRILL   VP & gen mgr Waterworks Equipment Co; m: Lucille; c: Bruce, Ned, Pammy; ed: BA 1947 BYU; MBA 1949 Stanford U; former: industrial engineer, purchasing agent, asst gen mgr, Pacific States Cast Iron Pipe Co; mem: board of dir Utah Industrial Relations Council; former pres Utah Manufacturers' Assn; advisory board First Security Bank, Provo 1972-82; board of advisors Mtn Bell Utah; board of dir Mtn Bell Denver; award: BYU Distinguished Alumni Award 1980; civic: exec board Utah Natl Parks Council BSA; BYU Business School Natl Advisory Council; rel: LDS, stake pres; club: former pres Provo Kiwanis Club; home: 2005 N 1450 E; off: PO Box 1219.

BUTLER, H JULENE   gen ref librarian & instr BYU; b: 12 Feb 1948; p: Paul W & Helen T Young Butler; ed: BA 1970 MLS 1971 BYU; former: cataloger HBLL 1971-5; mem: Utah Library Assn; Amer Library Assn; TESOL; Phi Kappa Phi; publ: "A Physical Disability Need Not Keep You From Preparing Your Family History"; civic: Disabled Student Faculty Advisory Council BYU; rel: LDS, tchr, sec, name extraction missionary; home: 1636 N 240 W, Orem; off: 3226 HBLL, BYU.

CALL, CRAIG M   attorney; preservationist; board of dir Caribou Four Corners Inc; corp sec & mgr Calls Inc; licensed gen contractor; b: 1948; m: Janine Winder; ed: Blue Mtn Community College; U of Washington; BS business 1972 JD 1976 BYU; former: dir Central Utah Office Congressman James V Hansen 1981; founder Alpine Oil Co; proprieter The Eggertsen House Restaurant; proprieter Downtown Provo Mercantile Co; founder Historic Utah Inc; lecturer & panelist on preservation topics Natl Assn of Housing & Redevelopment Officials, Utah State Historical Soc & BYU; career: licensed Realtor Assoc; redeveloper 18 properties in and near Provo listed in Natl Register of Historic Places; Award for Significant & Imaginative Serv to the Community while in Law School 1976 by BYU Law School Faculty; Award for Outstanding Work in Historic Preservation by Utah State Historical Soc 1976 and Utah Heritage Found 1977; listed as one of 24 New Pioneers in Utah Valley and one of 79 People to Watch in '79 by Mountainwest Magazine 1977-9; finalist with Mayor James Ferguson for the Distinguished Serv Award, Provo Jaycees 1979; mem: Utah Bar; Osborne Call Family Partnership; Osborne Call Found; corp sec & exec dir Chesterfield Found; pres Utah State Heritage Found 1979-81; publ: *Provo Historic Bldgs Jour;* articles on religion and historic preservation; civic: vice-chm Provo City Council 1982; neighborhood chm; Provo City Downtown Mall Com; Provo City Downtown Parking Com; corp sec Timpanogos Transit Authority; VP & dir Provo Chamber of Commerce; volunteer liaison between BYU and Provo City; BSA; pol: Republican, Reagan Campaign 1976; rel: LDS, bishop; club: Provo Kiwanis Club home: 1496 N 1550 E.

CAMPBELL, DOUGLAS M   prof of Computer Sci BYU; b: 4 May 1943; m: Jill; p: Quinn & Joan; c: Heather 14, Micah 13, Matthew 11, Susannah 8; ed: Harvard 1961-3, 65-7; U of N Carolina, Chapel Hill 1967-71; Phi Beta Kappa; Morehead Grad Fellow; former: visiting prof U of Maryland 1974, U of Michigan 1978-9; career: Karl G Maeser Research Award 1981; mem: AAUP; AMS; MAA; ACM; publ: *Whole Craft of Number;* home: 758 E 100 N, Orem; off: 364 TMCB, BYU.

CANAAN, DAVID E   owner David E Canaan Design; b: 23 Feb 1949; m: Judy; p: Robert E & Edithmae Dalton; c: Jon 10, Jill 8, Paul 6, Scott 4; ed: BYU; former: faculty BYU & U of Utah; prod mgr BYU Graphic Communications; art dir Allen & Canaan Advertising; career: New York Art Dir Club Award; Natl Communication Div of United Way Awards; numerous gold & silver awards in natl, reg & local competitions; mem: pres elect Art Directors, SLC; former board mem Communications Assn of Utah Valley; former pres Executive Club of Utah Valley; publ: columnist, ADSLC Trade Publ; civic: former PR Dir United Way of Utah County; mil: Utah Air Natl Guard 6 yrs; natl recognition for publ design; rel: LDS, counselor Utah State Hospital branch, elders pres; home: 4136 Crestview; off: 950 N University.

CANNON, DONALD Q   prof of Church History & Doctrine BYU; b: 24 Dec 1936; m: Jo Ann; p: Quayle & LaNor; c: Brian 20, Kelly 17, Sean 17, Patrick 10, Brendon 9, Erin 7; ed: BA MA history U of Utah; PhD history Clark U; NDEA Fellowship; Phi Kappa Phi; former: assoc prof of history U of Maine at Portland – Gorham; career: univ research grants; mem: Mormon History Assn; Utah State Historical Soc; publ: *A New Light Breaks Forth; The Exodus and Beyond;* articles on LDS history; book reviews; civic: BSA Merit Badge Counselor; mil: Capt US Army Intelligence; Army Commendation Medal; rel: LDS, bishop, stake presidency, h council; home: 817 N 435 E, Orem; off: 139 JSB, BYU.

CARLSON, GARY   VP of Research CTI; b: 6 Mar 1928; m: Barbara L; c: Reginald, Nancy, Tom, Elizabeth, Jane; ed: BA MA PhD UCLA in industrial psychology; former: dir BYU Computer Serv 1963–79; mem: ACM; AAAS; publ: 35 journal articles; civic: State Computer Steering Board 1975–7; state & local coms; pol: Republican state del, precinct chm; mil: US Army Spec 3rd Class Artillery Survey 1953–5; Top Marksman; rel: LDS, h council; home: 3289 Mohawk Cr; off: 1455 S State, Orem.

CHAMBERLAIN, JONATHAN MACK   psychologist, researcher, writer; b: 26 Aug 1928; m: Beverly; p: Guy & Vera Heaton; c: Lori Judd, Charles J, Lisa Palmer, Mark T, David G; ed: BA English & French 1958 BYU; MEd counseling & guidance 1964 PhD counselor ed & psychology 1967 U Wyoming; BYU Honor Student; NDEA Inst Scholar Academic Yr 1963–4; Phi Delta Kappa; licensed psychologist and marriage & family therapist; former: secondary school tchr; instr Adult Basic Ed; dir psychological serv Project Head Start, SE Utah; dir Reg Child Study Serv, ESEA, SE Utah; school psychologist; dir Student Employment & Financial Aids, U of Wyoming; counselor U of Wyoming Counseling Ctr; consultant, State Board of Ed, Utah State Prison, several school dists, med orgs; career: honorable mention Outstanding Home Study Course of the Yr 1975; Outstanding Tchr of Yr, BYU Div of Continuing Ed 1979; mem: Utah Personnel & Guidance Assn; Amer School Counselor Assn; Amer College Personnel Assn; Utah School Counselor Assn; Natl Ed Assn; Utah Psychologist in Private Practice; Utah Assn

School Psychologists; Utah Assn for Counselor Ed & Supervision; Utah Psychologist Assn; Internatl LDS Counselors Assn; Utah County Assn for Mental Health; pres Thomas Chamberlain Family Org; publ: *Eliminate Your SDB's** -- **Self-Defeating Behaviors* & 3 supplements; *Teenage Sex: Why not?;* articles; courses; training programs; handbooks; news releases; civic: pres Orem Kiwanis Internatl 1981-2; mil: US Air Force Career Guidance Spec; M Sgt; 1951-3; rel: LDS, 70s pres, stake mission ldr, exec sec, h council, bishop; home: 280 W 1700 S, Orem; off: 144 SWKT, BYU.

CHANDLER, DAVID L assoc prof History BYU; b: 9 Oct 1938; m: Jennett; p: Paul & Zola; c: Jill 18, Brad 16, Lance 15, Heidi 15, Penny 15, Grant 11, Ginger 10, Carrie 9, Scott 7; ed: BS 1963 cum laud; MS 1965 cum laud; PhD 1972 cum laud; NDEA Fellow 1963-6; former: res assoc Internatl Ctr for Med Res & Training, Cali, Columbia 1967-8; instr Southern Univ 1968-9; asst prof BYU 1970; mem: Amer Historical Assn; Conf on Latin Amer History; publ: *Health & Slavery in Colonial Colombia;* 3 articles on slavery; rel: LDS, ward clerk, elders pres, branch pres, dist pres; home: 11167 N 5100 W, Highland; off: Dept of History, BYU.

CHANDLER, HOMER C exec dir Mountainland Assn of Govts; b: 12 Feb 1925; m: Mary Helen; p: William James & Mary Nancy; c: Bruce, Wayne, Susan, Douglas, Ronald, Marlene; ed: master's degree in Public Admin; former: City Mgr So Salt Lake, Monticello, Utah, and Millbrae, Calif; exec dir Columbia Reg Assn of Govts, Portland; mem: Internatl City Mgr Assn; Amer Soc of Public Admin; Natl Assn of Reg Councils; mil: US Army WW II, South Pacific Theatre of Action; rel: LDS, bishop, h council; home: 4003 N 650 E; off: 160 E Center.

CHATTERLEY, LOUIS JOSEPH prof of math ed BYU; b: 13 Aug 1933; m: Sandra Little; p: Morton J & Carrie B; c: Matthew, Michael, Jeffrey, Bryan, Timothy, Jennifer, Edward; ed: BS 1955 BYU; MS 1962 U of Utah; PhD math ed 1972 U of Texas Austin; grad with honors BYU 1955; former: tchr Kanab High School & Evergreen Jr High; career: Academic Yr Inst NSF 1966; mem: Natl Council Tchrs of Math; Utah Council Tchrs of Math; award:

athletic awards; civic recognition Kanab, Utah; publ: 7
articles; civic: Little League; Boy Scouts of Amer; pol:
state & local del; rel: LDS, scoutmaster, bishopric, h
council, sunday school tchr; home: 796 E 400 S, Orem; off:
350 TMCB, BYU.

CHERRINGTON, DAVID JACK   prof of Org Behavior
BYU; b: 28 Oct 1942; m: Marilyn Daines; p: Jack A &
Virginia Freebairn; c: David Richard 15, Nathan John 13,
Jennifer 12, Jill 8; ed: BS 1966 BYU; MBA DBA 1970
Indiana Univ; Phi Kappa Phi 1966 BYU; Sigma Iota Epsilon
1968 Indiana U; former: board of dir University YMCA,
Champaign, Ill; career: $1000 Award for Outstanding
Research 1971 U of Ill; mem: Acad of Mgt; Amer Soc of
Personnel Admin; Amer Mgt Assn; award: Outstanding
Athlete Award in high school; publ: *The Work Ethic:
Working Values & Values that Work; Personnel
Management;* co-auth: *The Business Management
Laboratory; How to Detect and Prevent Business Fraud;*
34 research articles; rel: LDS, MTC branch pres; home:
1123 E 120 S, Orem; 1064 SWKT, BYU.

CHOI, SOO-YOUNG   asst prof of Korean; b: 2 Jan 1946;
m: Ock-Ja Choi; p: Hong-Min Choi & Bong-Yea Kim; c:
Pearl 6, Joseph 5, Jacob 3, Michael 1; ed: PhD in Instr Sci
& Tech; Magna Cum Laude; mem: Amer Ed Res Assn;
publ: "The Relationship of Test Performance to ISDP
Rating in Organic Chemistry Texts" *Journal of Instr
Development;* mil: Korean Army 3 yrs; rel: LDS, branch
pres, bishopric; club: Korean Clubs; home 1A-4 Wymount,
BYU; off: 250 FB, BYU.

CHRISTENSEN, DEAN CHRISTIAN   ret BYU Prof; public
school tchr; b: 25 Feb 1913; m: Afton Nielson; p: Oscar &
Mary Lund; c: Jed Dean, Sherrie, Kim, Laurie, Wendy; ed:
Snow Jr Coll 1933; Utah State U 1938; MA 1948;
doctorate 1957; Phi Kappa Phi; former: supt Duchesne Co
School Dist; prin Wellsville Jr High; Utah State U Lab
School Dir; career: chm Honors Prog Evaluation Com
BYU; guest prof Amer Univ Beirut, Lebanon 1963-4;
mem: chm Higher Ed Com UEA; NEA; AASS Prin; AAS
Admin; pres Sec Admin Assn; publ: on ed supervision &
admin; civic: chm Provo City Beautification; pol: State
Rep 2 terms, Utah State Senate, dist chm 4 yrs; mil: US

Marines Air Corps WWII 3 yrs Pacific Theatre; rel: LDS, bishop, stake president; home: 189 N 300 E.

CHRISTENSEN, JERRY B   owner Jerry's Used Cars, Inc; b: 17 Jul 1931; m: Wilda; p: Soren & Bertha; c: Blaine, Ralph, Jeff, Tom Diana; former: gen sales mgr P E Ashton Co; career: Professional Salesmaster Award; rel: LDS; home: 199 E 4380 N; off: 950 S University Ave.

CHRISTENSEN, JOHN OWEN   Gen Ref Librarian BYU Library; b: 8 Aug 1949; m: Nancy Morrish; p: Thomas H & Helen M; c: Katie 3, Amy 1; ed: BS 1973 U of Washington; MLS 1975 BYU; Rensselaer Award for Sci & Math; Valedictorian of MLS class 1975; former: librarian UTC at SLC; mem: Utah Library Assn; Beta Phi Mu; award: Eagle Scout; publ: "Comparison of Arrival Algorithms for Automated Serials Claiming Operations", ERIC; rel: LDS, bishopric, exec sec, scoutmaster; home: 2305 W 710 n; off: 3222 HBLL, BYU.

CHRISTENSEN, LLOYD DeREESE   owner Lloyd's Business Machines; b: 15 Nov 1926; m: Marilyn Jensen; p: Calvin Nathin & Juanita Sandersen; c: Reese, Rebecca, Tim, Todd, Peter, Tracy, Kelly; ed: BYU business 2 yrs; former: Morgan Typewriter; mem: 25-yr mem Orem Kiwanis Club, former pres; civic: Provo Chamber of Commerce 28 yrs; pol: Orem Citizen party 2 elections; mil: Navy 1944-6, San Francisco; Korean conflict, 9 mo Japan typewriter shop on USS Hamel; rel: LDS, bishop, h council, explorer ldr, Aaronic Priest ldr 28 yrs; home: 774 E 1000 S, Orem; off: 324 W Center.

CHRISTENSEN, ROSS TAYLOR   prof emeritus of archaeology & anthropology BYU; b: 28 Aug 1918; m: Ruth Richardson; p: H Oswald & Nettie Taylor; c: Wende Mercado, Linda Ditzler, Paul T, Sylvia Allred, Charles E, Becky Jones, Carol Lee, Cindy, Lisa; ed: 8 colleges & univ in USA, Brazil & Peru; PhD 1956 anthropology U of Arizona, Tucson; former: BYU archaeology faculty 1952-79; chm Dept of Archaeology 1960-7; dir 5th BYU arch expedition to Middle Amer 1958; career: Pan Amer Fellow in Peruvian archaeology 1950; field lecturer Tel Aviv U excavations at Tel Beer-Sheba, Israel 1976; Natl Screening Com, Western Div, Inst of Internatl Ed 1974;

mem: sec, treas, editor Soc for Early Historic
Archaeology, Provo; Amer Schools of Oriental Research;
Soc for Amer Archaeology; Amer Anthropological Assn;
publ: *Progress in Archaeology;* articles & papers; pol:
Republican county & state del; mil: US Army Air Force
1943-5; rel: LDS, bishopric, group ldr US Armed Forces;
home: 1574 S 240 E, Orem; off: Salmon House, BYU.

CHRISTOPHER, JOHN RAYMOND lecturer on herbal
usage, Doctor of Naturopathy, pres Christopher
Publications Inc; b: 25 Nov 1909; m: Della; p: Lee &
Milissa; c: John, Ruth, David, Janet, Steven; ed: associate
in business, master of herbology, doctor of naturopathy;
former: practiced until 1971; lectured internationally for
past 10 yrs; career: Ann Arbor Distinguished Serv Award;
America's foremost authority on herbs (from natl survey
of health professionals); mem: Natl Health Federation;
Natl Naturapathic Assn; award: Doctor Christopher herb
formulas widely distributed in US and Canada; publ:
*Childhood Diseases, The School of Natural Healing,
Capsicum, Just What is the Word of Wisdom;* mil: WW II
Ft Lewis, Wash, Medical Dispensary Head; rel: LDS,
Tabernacle Choir 15 yrs; club: Boy Scouts troop ldr &
Eagle Scout; home: Spanish Fork Canyon, PO Box 474,
Spanish Fork; off: 708 W Columbia Ln.

CHRISTY, HOWARD ALLAN editor BYU Press, asst
editor *Journal of Mormon History;* b: 9 May 1933; m:
Lynne; p: Bruce V; c: Caroline 17, Bruce Verner III 12,
Megen 10, Carleton Michael 5; ed: BA forestry 1955 U of
Washington; MA history 1978 BYU; career: Dale L Morgan
Award for best scholarly article in *Utah Historical
Quarterly* in 1978; mem: Utah State Historical Soc;
Mormon History Assn; pres Utah Valley chapter Utah
State Historical Soc; publ: co-editor *Atlas of Utah;*
articles; mil: US Marines Lt Col ret 1975; Silver Star;
Navy Commendation Medal for combat serv in Vietnam;
rel: LDS, bishopric, exec sec, clerk, tchr, scout ldr; home:
3653 Little Rock Dr; off: 217 UPB, BYU.

CLARK, BRUCE BUDGE prof of English BYU; b: 9 Apr
1918; m: Ouida Raphiel; p: Marvin E & Alice Budge; c:
Lorraine, Bradley, Robert, Jeffrey, Shawn, Sandra; ed: BA
1943 U of Utah; MA 1948 BYU; PhD 1951 U of Utah; Phi

Kappa Phi; former: chm BYU English Dept 1960-5; dean BYU College of Humanities 1965-81; career: Cert of Merit for Distinguished Serv to Education 1967 by Internatl Biographical Assn; Karl G Maeser Award for Teaching Excellence BYU 1972; listed in Who's Who in Amer, Directory of Amer Scholars, Outstanding Educators of Amer, Who's Who in the West, Dictionary of Internatl Biography, Who's Who in College & Univ Admin; Leaders in Education, Internatl Scholars Directory; mem: Modern Language Assn; Natl Council of Tchrs of English; Utah Acad of Arts & Sci; Utah State Advisory Council on Teaching of English; Amer Assn for Adv of the Humanities; publ: editor *Directory of LDS Educators in Higher Education & School Administration;* co-auth *Out of the Best Books,* 6 vols; *Romanticism through Modern Eyes; Oscar Wilde: A Study in Genius and Tragedy; Richard Evans' Quote Book; Idealists in Revolt: An Introduction to English Romanticism; The Need Beyond Reason and Other Essays: College of Humanities Centennial Lectures 1975-6; Great Short Stories for Discussion and Delight;* articles; civic: advisory board Orem Community Hospital; mil: US Army 1943-6; rel: LDS, bishop, h council, patriarch; club: Browning Soc; home: 365 E 1655 S, Orem; off: 269 JKBA, BYU.

CLARK, H CLIFFORD   prof Elementary Ed BYU; b: 16 Mar 1929; m: Clara Lee; p: Henry C & Mary Ashby; c: David, Kent, Leesa, Steven; ed: EdD 1963; former: coord of Elem Ed BYU; career: Distinguished Faculty Award Weber State College; mem: Natl Council Teachers of Math; School Sci & Math Assn; publ: articles & books; civic: athletic coach; rel: LDS, reg athletic dir, priesthood ldr; club: Kiwanis; home: Rt 2 Box 315, Spanish Fork; off: 267-F MCKB, BYU.

CLARK, JOYCE   partner, escrow officer Valley Title Co; b: 6 Aug 1938; m: W Kay Clark; p: Harold K & Ruth Williamson; c: Kalyne, H Don, Gregory, JoDee, Tina; ed: high school grad; professional licenses: title insurance agent & escrow agent; former: real estate related since 1956; career: Utah State Title Insurance Council; Utah State Title Insurance Advisory Com; Ed Com Utah Land Title Assn; Utah State Realtor Forms Com; mem: pres Utah County Board of Realtor's Credit Union; Home

Builder's Assn; affiliate mem Utah County Board of Realtors; Women's Council of Realtors; Executive Women Internatl; Utah Land Title Assn; rel: LDS, pres Young Women, stake primary presidency, Relief Soc presidency, tchr; home: 277 E 340 S, Orem; off: 75 S 200 E.

CLARK, MELVIN C   Provo Dist Supvr, Div of Rehabilitation Serv, Utah State Off of Ed; b: 19 May 1928; m: Juanita Stone; p: Lucius & Miriam A Carling; c: Douglas J, Kathleen C Cullimore, David R, Karen C Watkins; ed: BA 1952 BYU; MSW 1956 U of Utah; career: Natl Rehab Counseling Assn Utah Counselor of the Yr 1967; mem: life mem Natl Rehabilitation Assn, Natl Assn of Social Workers; rel: LDS, bishop, h council; home: 528 S 450 E, Orem, off: 285 N 100 E.

CLARK, RICHARD S   medical physician; b: 4 Dec 1923; m: Carolyn Moore; p: Dr Stanley M & Mary Newell; c: Patricia Millar, Richard S II, Mary Kathryn; ed: MD Jefferson Med College 1951; OB-GYN Board Certified 1961; mem: Amer Surg Soc; rel: LDS; home: 1805 Oakridge Ln; off: 225 N University Ave.

CLARK, ROBERT CRAIG   medical physician; b: 19 Jul 1925; m: Eloise Christensen; p: Dr Stanley M & Mary Newell; c: Christine Bork, Craig Jr, James Garner, Kipp Houston; ed: MD Jefferson Med College 1948; mem: Amer Med Assn; Utah County Med Soc; Utah State Med Soc; rel: LDS; home: 742 S Cherry Dr, Orem; off: 225 N University Ave.

CLARKE, ALVA JOHN   prof of Ed Admin; b: 3 Jul 1908; m: Rissa Merkley; p: Peter Gemmel & Vilate Green; c: Margaret Riley, Sybil Ferguson, Jill Harris, Jack A, Kathryn Williams; ed: BS chemistry 1938 MS ed admin 1942 BYU; EdD 1950 Colorado U; former: Supt of Schools, Alberta; tchr & principal BYU Lab School; chm Sec Ed Dept; asst dean & acting dean College of Ed BYU; chief of prog mgt USOE; advisor to ministry of ed, Tehran, Iran 1953-5; advisor chancellor of U of Tehran 1962-4; Provo City Training Officer; mem: PDK; NEA, UEA; award: Proficiency Award USOE; publ: *Foreign Aid: An Investment in People;* civic: scout ldr; Provo City Commissioner; rel: LDS, tchr, bishop; club: Kiwanis; home 2202 Canyon Rd; off: 351 W Center.

CLAYBAUGH, DONN R   industrial engineer; UTC faculty; b: 22 July 1925; m: Jeanne Cawley; p: Harry Carl & Asenath E Thomas; c: Ann Johnson, Denny, Ken, Jonn, Connie Oyler, Winn, Bennett, Brennan; ed: BS industrial mgt 1950 U of Southern Calif; Cert in Industrial Engr, Methods Engr Council 1952; grad work on MBA Calif State College, Long Beach; former: mgr facilities planning Northrop Corp Aircraft Div; mgr industrial engr Aerojet Gen Corp; career: registered professional engr in Calif; chm natl study committees for Aerospace Industries Assn, Wash DC; mem: sr mem Amer Inst of Industrial Engineers; Disabled Amer Veterans; publ: articles in trade magazines; civic: Save the Amer River Com, Sacramento, Calif 1963; 1st Annual Provo River Cleanup 1981; chm Utah County Beautification Com 1982; pol: Republican dist chm 1979-80; mil: US Navy WW II; Navy Commendation Award; Pacific Theatre Battle Ribbons with 13 battle stars; rel: LDS, temple worker, h council, bishopric, stake missionary; home: 1095 N Jordan; off: UTC 1395 N 150 E.

CLAYTON, KEITH JOSEPH   pediatrician; b: 20 Jul 1941; m: Connie Hall; p: Vaughn M & Eunice Edvalson; c: Keith Jr 13, David 12, Michael 11, Lisa 9, Julie 8, Matthew 6, Amy 2; ed: BS BYU; MD U of Utah; Florence Strong Patient Care Award 1970; mem: Amer Acad of Pediatrics; publ: many on patient ed; mil: US Army Reserve 1968-74; rel: LDS, bishop, stake pres; home: 3006 Indian Hills Dr; off: 1675 N 200 W.

CLOWARD, MYRLE LIVINGSTON   asst dir BYU Food Serv; m: Wells Pershing Cloward; p: Heber & Mary J Oldroyd Livingston; c: Dr Sherman L, Connie Cloward Parsons, Kelly Cloward Pettit; ed: Provo High, BYU; career: 1980 1st place natl award for menu planning; citation for meritorious serv 1981 Natl Assn of College & Univ Food Serv; BYU Cert of Recognition for Services to Athletic Depts; mem: Utah State Restaurant Assn; Natl Restaurant Assn; area dir Natl Assn of College & Univ Food Serv; pol: Republican; active for Sen Garn, Hatch; election com for Ray Beckham; rel: LDS, temple worker, stake Relief Society counselor, bishop's wife; club: pres Literatae Provo Literary Club; home: 2733 N University Ave; off: 199 ELWC, BYU.

CLOWARD, WELLS PERSHING   dir BYU Food Serv; b: 14 Jun 1918; m: Myrle Livingston; p: Thomas & Laura Staheli; c: Dr Sherman L, Connie Cloward Parsons, Kelly Cloward Pettit; ed: BYU; former: owned 2 restaurants 1946-53; established BYU Food Serv 1953; layout, design, staffing & establishing food serv for Provo & Ogden Temples, Church Office Bldg, & LDS School in Mexico; career: 2 Natl Awards of Excellence by School & College Food Serv Internatl; 2 Internatl Awards for Institutions; Gold Spoon Award by Utah State Restaurant Assn; mem: reg pres, natl VP, Natl Assn of College & Univ Food Serv; Natl Restaurant Assn; Utah State Restaurant Assn; pol: Republican; active for Senators Garn & Hatch; Ray Beckham election com; mil: US Navy WW II Pacific Theatre; 5 battle stars; rel: LDS, bishop, h council, geneology com chm; club: board of dir Kiwanis Club; home: 2733 N University Ave; off: 199 ELWC, BYU.

COMPTON, LANE A   dir Cooperative Ed; prof of Physical Sci BYU; b: 11 Apr 1920; m: June Wheeler; p: George A & Margaret Estella Mattson; c: Janet, Sandra, Kent, Bruce, Christine; ed: AS Weber College; BS MS EdD U of Utah; fellow Utah Acad of Sci, Arts & Letters; pres Utah Acad of Sci, Arts & Letters; chm Rocky Mtn Sci Council; pres Assn of Cooperative Educators & Employers of Utah; former: public school tchr; mem: Natl Sci Tchr's Assn; Utah Sci Tchr's Assn; Cooperative Ed Assn; Phi Delta Kappa; publ: *Cooperative Education Workbook;* civic: Chamber of Commerce; pol: precinct level; mil: T/4 Army Medical Corps; rel: LDS, bishop; home: 2986 Apache Ln; off: C-249-51 ASB, BYU.

COMPTON, MERLIN D   prof Spanish & Portuguese BYU; b: 22 Jul 1924; m: Avon Allen; p: George A & Margaret Mattson; c: Terry Ann, Todd Merlin, Tamara Jane, Timothy George, Tina Louise; ed: BA 1952 MA 1954 BYU; PhD 1959 UCLA; Phi Kappa Phi; Sigma Delta Pi; former: asst prof Adams State College; assoc prof Weber State College; mem: Amer Assn of Tchrs of Spanish & Portuguese; publ: *Ricardo Palma Jwayne;* articles on Ricardo Palma; mil: US Army Air Force 1943-6; Staff Sgt; rel: LDS, bishop; home: 1465 E 330 S; off: 143 FOB, BYU.

CONKLIN, CURT EUGENE librarian BYU Law Library; b: 8 Apr 1947; m: Marjorie; c: 6; ed: BA 1972 MLS 1977 BYU; mem: AALS, UCLC, ULA; publ: *Library of Congress Subject Headings - KJ Cross-Reference;* civic: Sertoma Club; rel: LDS; home: 1080 E 560 N; off: 358-B JRCB, BYU.

COOK, PAUL FRANKLIN instructional developer, assoc prof of Ed Psychology, licensed psychologist; b: 12 Mar 1936; m: Jan; p: Merrill E & Margaret Richards; c: Randall 16, John 15, Gregory 13, Joseph 10; ed: BS 1960 Utah State U; MS 1966 PhD ed psych 1968 BYU; Phi Kappa Phi; former: Sr Research Scientist, Amer Inst for Research; asst dir Reg Testing & Resource Ctr; career: listed in Amer Men & Women of Sci: Social & Behavioral Sci 1978; mem: sec/treas Assn Mormon Counselors & Psychotherapists; Assn for Supervision & Curriculum Development; Amer Personnel & Guidance Assn; mil: US Army officer 1960-2; Army Intelligence; rel: LDS, bishopric, curriculum writer; home: 3713 N 600 E; off: 121 KMB, BYU.

CORDERY, JACK DAVID Compliance Officer in Charge, Provo Field Staton, US Dept of Labor ESA; b: 19 Oct 1932; m: Marilyn Willmore; p: Alfred John & Eva E; c: Julia Ann, Lisa Jane, John, Thomas, Joseph; ed: BS MS Public Admin U of Utah; graduated with honors; former: Wage-Hour Investigator, Oakland, Calif and SLC; career: Superior Performance Awards 1969, 71, 79; 25-yr duty pin; US Dept of Labor Distinguished Career Serv Award by Asst Sec of Labor 1982; mem: various heritage & historical groups; publ: *Veterans Preference in the Civil Service* not publ; civic: historical & restoration projects, scouting; pol: Presidential Task Force; mil: Hq Co US Army, Wash, DC; rel: LDS, h council, bishopric; club: Bonneville Knife & Fork; home: 1526 Harrison Ave, SLC; off: Rm 105 FOB, 88 W 100 N.

COTTRELL, MILFORD C BYU prof; b: 30 Jan 1926; m: Shirley Griffith; p: S Ross & Mary Lourene Sims; c: Stephen Milford, Cheryl Meecham, David Mark, Laura, Marianne; ed: BA mathematics 1948 U of Wyoming; MS ed admin 1956 EdD 1961 BYU; Post Doctoral Fellow, U of Oregon 1966-7; former: dir LDS Inst of Religion, U of

Wyoming; Supt Church Schools, W Samoa; public school
tchr; seminary principal; coor Research & Field Serv
BYU; coor Intern Doctoral Prog BYU 1971-3; consultant
to ed agencies; mem: Phi Delta Kappa, Amer Ed Res
Assn; publ: article "What do you Expect?" in Instructor;
Bilingual & Career Opportunities Projects for Navajo; rel:
LDS, bishop, h council; home: 741 E 3750 N; off: 302-C
MCKB, BYU.

COVEY, STEPHEN R   assoc prof Organizational Behavior
& Business Mgt BYU; m: Sandra Merrill; c: Cynthia,
Maria, Stephen, Sean, David, Catherine, Colleen, Jenny,
Joshua; ed: BS 1952 U of Utah; MBA 1957 Harvard U;
DRE 1976 BYU; former: admin asst to Pres of BYU
1965-9; dir Univ Relations 1967-9; officer & dir several
corporations; visiting prof U of Utah, Belfast Tech
College, Church College of Hawaii; faculty, Natl Real
Estate Marketing Assn, Young Presidents Org, Travel
Abroad & Wilderness Survival Progs BYU; training &
consulting in business, ed & govt; career: Karl G Maeser &
Adult Ed Awards for Teaching Excellence; mem: Natl
Univ Ed Assn Div of Conf & Institutes Faculty Serv Award
1982; publ: *Spiritual Roots of Human Relations; How to
Suceed with People;* articles in business & religious publs;
weekly newspaper column on human relations 1970-1;
manuals on teaching, leadership & training; rel: LDS,
bishop, mission pres, h council, Church Priesthood
Missionary Com, MIA Gen Board, Priesthood Tchr Devel
Com, Church Ldrship Com, mission rep, regional rep, ad
hoc gen church coms; off: 1024 SWKT, BYU.

COWAN, RICHARD O   prof of Church History &
Doctrine BYU; b: 24 Jan 1934; m: Dawn; p: Lee R & Edith
O; c: Sandra, Linda, Reed, Lee, Patricia, Donna; ed: PhD
1961 Stanford U; Phi Beta Kappa 1957; career: BYU prof
of Yr 1965; Maeser Teaching Excellence 1979; mem: Utah
Historical Soc; Mormon History Assn; publ: *The Kingdom
Is Rolling Forth; The Doctrine & Covenants: Our Modern
Scripture;* rel: LDS, MTC historian, adult curriculum
writer, stake presidency; home: 1205 E 930 N; off: 235
JSB, BYU.

COX, SOREN F   prof of English and Linguistics, BYU; b:
4 Aug 1925; m: Fern Mary Saunders; p: Thomas Franklin &

Anna Anderson; c: Mary, Carilee, Ann, Dale Soren, Paul Franklin; ed: BA 1952, MA 1956, English, BYU; PhD 1964 Communications, U of Minnesota; former: Coord Composition, Assoc Chm English, Chm Linguistics Dept BYU; Dir Lang Ctr, Nanyan Univ, Singapore; career: Asia Found Grant 1970-2; Fullbright-Hayes Award 1971-2; mem: Natl Council of Tchrs of English; College Conf on Composition & Communication; Deseret Lang & Linguistic Soc; publ: *About Language;* pol: dist & ward chm Democratic Party; mil: US Navy 1944-6; rel: LDS, bishop, Singapore Mission Pres, stake pres; home: 1729 W 1400 N; off: A-289 JKBA, BYU.

CRACROFT, RICHARD HOLTON   prof of English, dean College of Humanities BYU; b: 28 Jun 1936; m: Janice Alger; p: Ralph & Grace White; c: Richard Alger 18, Jeffrey R 16, Jennifer 14; ed: BA 1961 MA 1963 U of Utah; PhD 1969 U of Wisconsin; Ford Summer Fellowship, Phi Kappa Phi, U of Utah Jr & Sr Honorary Awards, Skull & Bones & Owl & Key; former: dir Business Enterprises for the Blind, State of Utah; student instr U of Utah & U of Wisc; mem: Natl Council, Tchrs of English; Amer Lit Section, Modern Language Assn; award: Eagle Scout; 2nd team All State Football & pres sr class at East High School; pres soph class U of Utah; publ: co-auth *A Believing People: The Literature of the Latter-day Saints; 22 Young Mormon Writers; Washington Irving: The Western Works;* 60 articles in Mormon Lit, Western Lit, Amer Lit & LDS periodicals; research editor *Amer Western Literature;* assoc editor *Dialogue, Utah Chronicle;* mil: Utah Natl Guard 8 yrs; Sgt 144th Hospital Evac & 142 Mil Intelligence Co; rel: LDS, bishop, h council, stake pres; home: 770 E Center; off: A-129 JKBA, BYU.

CRAGHEAD, JACK A   owner Craghead Plumbing & Heating Co; b: 10 Aug 1917; m: Ruth B; p: J Will & Irene; c: Gary W, Robert G, Sandra, James W, Richard L, Jackie L, Cori Ann; former: vice commander Amer Legion; civic: Provo City Park & Recreation Board 16 yrs, former chm; former pres Provo Chamber of Commerce; former pres Central League; mil: US Navy WWII; club: former pres Provo Rotary; former pres Provo Downtown Coaches Club; Footprinters; Cougar Club; Elks Lodge; Old Time Athletic Assn; home: 1991 N 150 E; off: 61 N 400 W.

CRANDALL, LOUIS E   pres Western Advertising Agency; b: 27 Jul 1929; m: Mabel; p: Louis P; c: Janie, Mary Louise, Annette, Ruth Ellen, Louis Jr; ed: Arizona State Univ, advertising & public relations; former: commercial artist Arizona Public Serv Co; owner Crandall Assoc Advertising Agcy, Phoenix; developed Legend City, Tempe, Ariz; organized Four Seasons Ski & Recreation Ctr (now Heritage Mtn); civic: board chm Boys Club of Utah County; former mem Utah County Planning Commission; UVIDA board; chm Provo City Ctr Development Com; rel: LDS, h council, Utah Valley Public Communications Coor; home: 325 S 1450 E; off: 275 E Center.

CRANDALL, VERN JAY   prof of Computer Sci & Stat BYU; consultant, instr in software design IBM; b: 18 Mar 1939; m: Linda Rae Storms; p: Bliss Hansen & Mildred Johnson; c: Lance Vernon 4, Shane Lewis 3, Scott David 2; ed: BA math stat, with honors BYU; MS experimental stat Kansas State U; PhD biomath U of Washington; Natl Inst of Health grant 1963-5, 66-68, 72; former: Systems Programmer 1954-9, Statistician 1961-3, Stat Consultant & VP of Research & Devel 1963-75, DHI Computing Serv; dir & officer several co's; career: grants from Natl Sci Found, Boeing Aerospace, IBM; mem: Amer Stat Assn; Biometric Soc WNAR; Inst of Math Stats; IEEE Computer Soc; Pattern Recognition Soc; Assn for Computing Machinery; civic: Lions Club 1969-75; pol: Republican; rel: LDS, sunday school pres, bishopric, stake exec sec, h council; home: 1224 E 700 S; off: 236 TMCB, BYU.

CRIPPS, DAVID   BYU Food Serv; b: 20 Oct 1951; p: Teddy Ray & Carol Erlene; ed: AA 1972 Bakersfield BA 1977 BYU; mem: Natural History Assn, Smithsonian Inst; award: Best Improved Bowler CICCY League; publ: 3 poems; pol: Republican; rel: LDS, choir pres, historical clerk; home: 320 E 100 N; off: Deseret Towers Cafeteria, BYU.

CROOKSTON, BYRON F   corp attorney Rocky Mtn Helicopters; b: 1 Apr 1949; m: JenaVee Smith; p: Ray B & Marvel; c: Michael 9, Stephen 7, Richard 5, Melanie 2; ed: BA cum laude 1973, MA summa cum laude 1975 org communications, JD 1979 BYU; former: instr karate &

Amer Sign Language BYU; mem: Utah State Bar; Trial Lawyers of Amer; Utah Registry of Interpreters for the Deaf; Utah Assn for the Deaf; Natl Assn of Underwater Instructors; civic: asst dir Workshops for Deaf Youth BYU 1973-9; Boy Scouts of Amer; rel: LDS, branch presidency, elders presidency, h council; club: BYU Karate Club; Shotokan Karate of Amer; home: 708 W 1220 S; off: 800 S 3110 W.

CROSSLEY, KENNETH VERN   concert mgr BYU Dept of Music; b: 15 Dec 1953; m: Lorraine Johnson; p: John & Betty; c: Carren 4, Scott 3, Kendall 1; ed: Ricks College 1971-2; Associate Degree 1976 Bachelors 1978 BYU; mem: Assn of College, Univ & Community Arts Administrators; Western Alliance of Arts Administrators; civic: Springville Community Progress, Arts City Days Com; pol: Utah Citizen's for the Arts; rel: LDS; club: Utah Valley Stamp Club; home: 295 E 1270 N, Springville; off: C-358b HFAC, BYU.

DAHLIN, THERRIN CARL   chm Circulation Dept BYU Library; b: 10 Mar 1947; m: Kathleen Gottfredson; p: Jack Carl & Thellis Margaret Eddington; c: Eric Carl 9, Melanie 5; ed: BA; MLS; grad work for ed admin doctorate; Utah Library Assn Scholarship Beta Phi Mu; Phi Alpha Theta; Phi Kappa Phi; former: assoc dept chm; reserve librarian; cataloger; mem: Utah Library Assn; publ: co-auth *Catholic Left in Latin America;* articles; civic: Cubmaster; youth ldr; soccer coach; Little League coach; pol: dist chm, dist v-chm, county del; mil: Natl Guard 10 yrs; Meritorious Serv Medal; rel: LDS, exec sec, 70s pres, elders pres, clerk; home: 1028 W 1100 N; off: 3081 HBLL, BYU.

DAINES, DELVA   prof of Ed BYU; p: Hazen B Daines MD & Sarah B; c: Sally; ed: BS MS EdD; Merrill-Palmer Inst of Human Development & Family Life, Detroit, Mich; recipient of McKay Inst & College of Ed research grants; Phi Kappa Phi; former: tchr; dist & state of Idaho Supvr of Elementary Ed; career: Utah Council of Internatl Reading Assn Award 1981 for outstanding leadership & contributions toward reading; 1975 Achievement Award as Utah Woman Educator from Utah Delta Kappa Soc Internatl; mem: Internatl Reading Assn; Amer Ed Res

Assn; Assn for Tchr Educators; Delta Kappa Gamma Soc Internatl; Natl Council of Tchrs of English; Natl Conf for Res in English; Phi Delta Kappa Honorary Ed Soc; Assn for Supervision & Curriculum Development; publ: *Reading in the Content Areas: Strategies for Teachers;* journal articles; books & course syllabi; civic: Del to Women's State Legislative Council; fund raising for Easter Seals for Crippled Children; rel: LDS, YW Gen Board, Correlation Writing Com; club: Alice Louise Reynolds Club; off: 210Y MCKB, BYU.

DANIELS, PHILIP BLISS   prof of Psychology; consultant; trainer; b: 9 Nov 1928; m: Patsy Unger; p: William Bliss & Mary LaVern Hawley; c: Matt, Darsi, Jamie Dawn, Philip Drew, Patrick; ed: BS psychology 1954, MS psychology 1957 BYU; PhD social psychology 1962 Harvard U; mem: sr partner Behavioral Sci Resources Inc; publ: *Strategies to Facilitate Problem Solving;* co-author instr manual *As Others See You: Management Profiling for Team Effectiveness;* articles; questionnaires; mil: Lt US Air Force 1954-6; rel: LDS, bishopric, stake Sunday School pres; home: 1814 N 1500 E; off 1098 SWKT, BYU.

DASTRUP, BYRON CREER   maint mechanic MTC, BYU Aux Maint, owner Dastrup Apts; b: 16 Oct 1927; m: Erika Binder; p: Ephriam Byron & Sarah Jane Creer; c: Ronaele, Paulette, Jeanette, Julianne, Eric Byron, Carl Creer, Bersy, Chris, Perer, Pennie; ed: UTC; former: Provo City Power Plant maint sup 4 yrs, mgr 13 yrs; mem: Amer Welding Soc; Adv Council Welding School UTC 10 yrs; award: BSA Silver Beaver Award; civic: 4th of July panorama shows 4 yrs & fireworks com 10 yrs; SPEBSASA Barbershop Quartet 5 yrs; board mem Little Dry Creek Water Users Assn; Scouting 36 yrs; mil: US Merchant Marines 1945-7; rel: LDS, bishopric, clerk; home: Star Rt Box 43A, Lehi; off: 109 AXMB, BYU.

DAVIES, J KENNETH   prof of Economics BYU; b: 30 Apr 1925; m: Pauline; p: Joseph T & Lora A; c: Tania D James, Scott T; ed: BNS Marquette Univ; MS economics BYU; PhD economics U of S Calif; Ford Found Economic Seminar, Stanford Univ 1960; Inst on Freedom & Competitive Enterprise, Claremont College 1956; mem: Utah Council on Economic Ed; Utah Acad of Sci, Arts &

Letters; Amer Economic Assn; Western Economic Assn; Wasatch Front Economic Forum; Assoc vice-chm Mountainlands Manpower Advisory Com; Labor Arbitration panels Utah State Employee, Dist 15 Coal Industry, Mtn State Steel Industry; publ: co-author *Economics and the American Systems; Deseret's Sons of Joil;* co-author *Micro Manpower Planning in the Public Sector* , Environmental Protection Agcy; 2 articles; pol: Republican; former chm West Provo Precinct; Platform Com; Utah & State Nominating Com; mil: Lt USNR; active duty 1942-6; rel: LDS, bishop, stake presidency; home: 877 N 700 W; off: 1230-A SFLC, BYU.

DAVIS, FRED   head wrestling coach BYU; b: 16 Feb 1934; p: Mrs Lucille Jones; c: Tannaca Duke, DaNette Kimball, Fred III; ed: BS Okla State U; former: wrestling coach McLain High School, Tulsa, OK; career: pres NCAA Wrestling Coaches 1973; NCAA Coach of the Yr 1973; East West All-Star Coach 1974; Dale Rex Award; NCAA Champ 1955, 2nd 1956, 4th 1954; on Natl Champ Team 1954-6; 3-time All-American; BYU 4th NCAA 1973, 6th NCAA 1977; coached 18 All-Americans, 46 WAC Champs, 14 WAC team titles; rel: Baptist; home: 1516 Merlin; off: 228 SFH, BYU.

DAY, BARTLEY E   asst prof Career Ed BYU, Asst to Dean of Student Life; b: 21 Sep 1923; m: Jane Irene Olsen; p: Eli A Jr & Lucile Madsen; c: Victoria Hamilton, Janice Wright, Wayne, Oliver Dean; ed: undergrad U of Utah, Alfred College NY, Lafayette College PA, Amherst MA; BS 1949 US Military Acad; MA 1967 Boston Univ; doctoral studies BYU; Phi Kappa Phi; former: prof of Mil Sci BYU; Army command & staff 35 yrs; career: Mil Legion of Honor; Meritorious Serv Medal; Joint Serv Commendation Medal; 3 Army Commendation Medals; 2 Natl Defense Serv Medals; Korean Serv Medal; Good Conduct Medal; WW II Victory Medal; Amer Theatre Medal; Army of Occupation Medal; mem: Amer Assn for Higher Ed; board mem Kiwanis Club of Provo; Order of St Barbara; Assn of US Army; Utah Personal & Guidance Assn; Assn Mormon Counselors & Psycholotherapists; Sons of Utah Pioneers; Commander in Mormon Battalion; publ: Dept of Army manuals; *Development of a Graphical Solution to the Honest John Firing Problems,* Artillery Trends 1960; civic:

Provo Freedom Festival 1975; pol: voting dist chm; del to state conv; election com; mil: 1941–77 Private to Colonel, field artillery, command & staff internatl levels & joint command hqs; rel: LDS, stake & dist presidency; bishop, h council; home: 131 S Inglewood Dr, Orem; off: 380 SWKT, BYU.

DE HOYOS, GENEVIEVE univ prof; b: 3 Dec 1924; m: Arturo; p: Jules Leon Argault & Jeanne Seguin Argault; c: Sylvia Coates, Lili Anderson, Jan Tolman; ed: BA 1954 BYU; Master Social Work 1959 Mich S U; PhD soc 1967 Ind U; Phi Kappa Phi; Alpha Kappa Delta; former: psychiatric S W Indianapolis; univ prof Butler U, Indianapolis; career: Sigma Xi; Cert Social Worker CSW; publ: *Monograph on Pima Indians; Feminism or Familism; Stewardship;* civic: board mem Utah County Volunteers in Action, Utah County LEPA, Mtnland Community Action Agency; rel: LDS, primary & MIA stake board, librarian; home: 2825 N Indian Hills Cr; off: 840 SWKT, BYU.

DE SANTIS, JOE actor, sculptor, tchr; b: 15 Jun 1909; p: Pasquale & Maria Paoli; c: David Peter, Christopher Courtney; ed: City College of NY; Leonardo da Vinci Art School NY; Beaux Arts Inst of Design; apprenticed to Onorio Ruotolo 1927–9; former: Walter Hampden Repertory Company; roles in 27 Broadway plays; over 10,000 radio broadcasts; television shows *Playhouse 90, Studio One, Philco Theatre of the Air;* TV movie *Contract on Cherry St* with Frank Sinatra; appeared in 31 motion pictures such as *Cold Wind in August, Al Capone, I Want Jo Live, The Brotherhood;* tchr of sculpture Henry St Settlement NY; Ed Alliance NY; tchr of dialects for the Amer Theatre Wing; conducted actors workshop for ANTA 1964–8; career: "The Italian Director" for *In Any Language;* mem: AEA; SAG; AFTRA; ANTA; civic: contributed equipment to Eldred Sr Ctr; rel: Catholic; club: The Masquers, Hollywood; The Players, NY; home: Box 1513.

DECKER, DANIEL LORENZO prof of Physics BYU; b: 22 Sep 1929; m: Bonnie Beardall; p: Lorenzo B & Anna Squires; c: Kenneth, Renae Everitt, Ralph, Max, Eldon, Keith, Lois; ed: BS 1953 MS 1955 BYU; PhD 1958 U of Ill; Phi Kappa Phi; former: research physicist Los Alamos Sci

Lab; Argonne Natl Lab & CEN de Saclay; career: Distinguished Faculty Lecturer BYU 1979; Fellow of Amer Physical Soc & Utah Acad of Sci, Arts & Letters; mem: Amer Assn of Physics Tchrs; Amer Physical Soc; Sigma Si; Pigma Pi Sigma; Utah Acad of Sci, Arts & Letters; publ: 89 journal articles; pol: dist voting chm; rel: LDS, bishop, exec sec, scoutmaster; home: 1321 E 820 N; off: 177 ESC, BYU.

DIXON, HARRY A   owner mgr Dixon Collection Agency; b: 4 Oct 1910; d: 29 Jun 1981; m: Cecile Clark; p: Albert Frederick & Sena Rasmussen; c: Margie Dixon Smith; ed: BYU grad in business admin/mgt 1936 BYU; former: Dixon Taylor Russell Co Stores 35 yrs; mem: Amer Collectors Assn; Mtn States Collectors; award: donor of Dixon Tennis Trophy awarded ea yr to outstanding lady tennis player at BYU; civic: Provo Chamber of Commerce; mil: US Army Air Force 1st Sgt 431st Fighter Squad 475th Group; Bronze Star; rel: LDS; clerk; club: Lions; home: 72 N 100 E.

DIXON, MARDEN   attorney & physician Washington DC & Provo; b: 24 Oct 1941; m: Carolyn C; p: William & Ruth M Dixon Christiansen; c: Annette 13, Camille 9, Bryan 8, Karen 6, Ilene 2; ed: JD 1965; MD 1971; Honors Univ of Utah College of Law; medical license Utah, Maryland, DC; former: asst chief Legal Medicine Sect, Armed Forces Inst of Pathology, Washington DC; adjunct prof BYU College of Law; former adjunct prof Georgetown Univ Law Ctr; Antioch School of Law; assoc prof lecturer George Washington Univ; mem: former pres Utah Trial Lawyers Assn; Utah State Bar; Maryland Bar; DC Court of Appeals, US Dist Court of Utah; publ: *Drug Product Liability; Legal Medicine;* professional articles; civic: instituted Spanish Immersion Prog at Cherry Hill Emen School, Orem; mil: US Navy LCDR 1972-4; rel: LDS, stake mission pres, exec sec, elders presidency; home: 331 E 1800 S, Orem; off: 1900 N Canyon Rd, Suite 304.

DIXON, VERL GRANT   retired Provo City Mayor; real estate salesman, gen contractor; b: 26 Nov 1908; m: Virginia Poulsen; p: Ernest & Mary Ann Painter; c: Linda Dixon Rose, Mary Ellen Dixon, Merrill Verl; ed: BA BYU 1932; grad study U Columbia; Grad Scout Executives

Training School; former: County Clerk 4 yrs; County Commissioner 8 yrs; Mayor of Provo 12 yrs; career: Tom McCoy Award 1966 Outstanding Municipal Official; mem: local board mem Amer Assn of Retired Persons; pres Eldred Found; pres Natl Soc of the Sons of Utah Pioneers 1971; award: Outstanding Man SVP 1976; Silver Beaver, Utah Natl Parks Council BSA; civic: chm Red Cross; exec Boy Scout Council; commander Provo Post 13 Amer Legion; pol: pres Counties Assn 1955; pres League of Cities & Towns 1965; mil: air transport pilot WW II; Bronze Minute Man Award Utah Natl Guard 1966; rel: LDS, bishop, h council, temple worker; club: Provo Golden "K" Kiwanis, Footprinters; home: 342 N 500 W.

DUFF, ROGER BARRETT   mgr & branch pres Consumer Banking HFC Thrift; b: 1 Jan 1955; m: Donna Lianne; p: John D Jr, Col Ret USAF & Georgia T; c: Cassandra 4, Jeremy 2; ed: Central Wash U 2 yrs; Wash Mil Academy 1 yr; Military Commission 1976; career: 1978, 80 Achievement Awards, 1981 Presidents Club Award, household Internatl; mem: Better Business Bureau; Natl Guard Officers Assn; award: Outstanding Young Men of Amer 1978; pol: Republican, county coms in Wash State; mil: enlisted 1972, military acad, commissioned officer, entered Natl Guard 1976, commander 19th Special Forces in Provo; Army Commendation; Army Good Conduct; Washington, Calif, Oklahoma Commendation; 9th Sig Bn Vietnam Campaign Ribbon; Parachutists Badge; Aviator; rel: LDS, elders quorum pres, athletic dir; club: Elks Club; Utah Natl Guard Assn; 19th Special Forces Officer Club; Calif Natl Guard Assn; home: 527 E 1600 N, Orem; off: 132 W Center.

DUNFORD, BEVERLY   business mgr Utah Valley Symphony; b: 30 Sep 1927; m: Alma Rex Dunford; p: Edward James & Jessie Souter Duckett; c: Craig R, Barry R, Valerie Christensen, Lori Taylor, Annette Nelson, Deborah Hansen, Kathleen; ed: BYU 3 yrs; scholarship; civic: mgr Symphony 21 yrs; Provo Cultural Board; rel: LDS, Relief Soc pres, stake primary, tchr; club: Comitas Literary Club; home: 461 E 2875 N.

DURAHAM, THOMAS L   Asst prof of Music, BYU; b: 26 Aug 1950; m: Rebecca C; p: Lowell M & Betty D; c:

Carter 6, Laura 4, Lisa 1; ed: BM, MM U of Utah; PhD U of Iowa; magna cum laude, Phi Kappa Phi, dept merit scholarship U of Utah; former: tch asst, U of Utah; grad instr, U of Iowa; career: 1st prize, Sadie Rafferty Natl Composition Competition; 2nd prize Jackman Music Corp Competition for Composers; Mormon Handcart Park Commission; mem: Phi Kappa Phi, Utah Acad of Arts, Letters & Sciences; award: Outstanding Young Man of America 1980; publ: *Jesus The Savior Is Born* Deseret Music 1979 SATB; *God Be With You* 1980; civic: mem Mormon Tabernacle Choir; rel: LDS, music dir, exec sec, quorum instr; home: 151 S 240 E, Orem; off: E-563 HFAC BYU.

DURRANT, EARLENE   assoc prof Physical Ed BYU; b: 1 Feb 1940; p: Owen A & Lela Blonquist; ed: EdD; Phi Kappa Phi; former: tchr secondary school; head Women's PE Dept BYU-Hawaii; career: Outstanding Senior BYU; mem: Natl Athletic Trainer's Assn; Amer College Sports Medicine; Natl Assn Health PE, Recreation & Dance; award: Serv Award Hawaii Assn PE, Health & Recreation; Outstanding Faculty Mem BYU Dept of PE; publ: softball textbook; prof mag articles; civic: Big Brother's Big Sister's board; rel: LDS, sunday school, Relief Soc, MIA; home: 728 N 400 E, Orem; off: 1104 SFH, BYU.

DUSARA, SHAVJI "JIM" PURSHOTTAM   Head Soccer Coach, physical ed instr BYU; b: 5 Aug 1936; m: Vasanti; p: Purshottam Ukabhai Dusara; c: Shreedhar 14, Mehul 7, Saloni 5; ed: BA physical ed & sports England; Masters & Doctrate BYU; former: athletics dir Natl Univ of Tanzania (Dar es salaam); Natl & Olympic Coach Track & Field in Tanzania, East Africa; career: Coach of the Year WAC 1978-81; Rocky Mtn Inter-Collegiate Soccer League 1976; 100 games win cert Natl Soccer Coaches Assn of Amer; mem: Natl Soccer Coaches Assn of Amer; award: Queens Scout Badge 1956; Tanzania Natl Record Holder in Pole Vault 1956, 58; Tanzania Welter Weight Boxing Champ; publ: *Development of Modern Jactics in Soccer;* civic: advisor for youth & coaches development in Utah; rel: LDS; home: 152 W 1880 N, Orem; off: 258 SFH, BYU.

DYER, WILLIAM GIBB   dean BYU School of Management; b: 4 Oct 1925; m: Bonnie Hansen; c: Gibb,

Michael, Lisa, Jeffrey, David; ed: U of Oregon; Washington State U; BA 1950 MA 1951 BYU; PhD 1955 U of Wisconsin; Maeser Teaching Award 1975; School of Mgt Distinguished Faculty Award 1973-4; former: instr Iowa State U; prof U of Utah; chm BYU Dept of Org Behavior; prog dir NTL Intermtn Div; chm BYU Leadership & Org Development Com; board of dir Behavioral Sci Resources & Fontana Corp; training consultant Natl Training Lab; overseas prof U of S Calif; career: Univ Fellow U of Wisconsin 1951; listed in Amer Men of Sci & Who's Who in the West; mem: board of dir Natl Training Laboratories Inst for Applied Behavioral Sci 1967-70; fellow NTL Inst; Senior Assoc Leadership Resources; Amer Assn for Humanistic Psychology; Internatl Assn of Applied Soc Scientists; publ: 11 books & monographs, incl *Team Building; Insight to Impact; Choices: A Father's Counsel;* 54 articles; 8 training manuals & tapes; mil: US Army Air Force navigator WWII; rel: LDS, bishop, sunday school gen board; home: 3077 Mojave Ln; off: 154 JKB, BYU.

EARL, DON L   prof of music BYU; dir BYU Symphony Orchestra; dir Mendelssohn Chorus; b: 19 Aug 1917 m: Ruth Lillian Moss; p: Ira J & Lovisa Leavitt; c: Stephen Moss, Anthony J, David L, Jerald A; ed: BA 1940 MA 1946 BYU; PhD 1952 Indiana U; former: artistic & musical dir Utah Valley Opera Assn 1959; Recreational Supvr of Music, Las Vegas 1940; violinist Grand Rapids Symphony 1940; choral dir, Bern, Switzerland 1937-9; career: Ford Found Opera Scholarship at New York City Ctr Opera Co 1959; listed in The Opera Directory, London, Dictionary of Internatl Biography 1967, Who's Who in the West 1967-8, Royal Blue Book 1968, Internatl Who's Who in Music and Musician's Directory 1977; mem: Pi Kappa Lambda; Phi Mu Alpha Sinfoni; Amer Musicological Soc; Natl Assn of Tchrs of Singing; Amer Assn of Univ Profs; Natl Opera Assn; Central Opera Serv; Provo Federated Musicians local 272; Amer Fed of Musicians pres local 272; publ: *The Cambiata* MA thesis; *The Solo Song Cycle in Germany 1800-50* PhD dissertation; *An Introduction to the Aural Skills of Musicians;* articles; civic: co-found Provo Municipal Band; conductor Utah Valley Symphony; lecturer at civic & social clubs; mil: US Navy aviator 1942-5; rel: LDS, reg music dir, h council, bishop; home: 2701 N 700 E; off: E-556 HFAC, BYU.

EASTON, SUSAN   prof Church Hist & Doctrine BYU; b: 9 Nov 1944; p: Karl Moroni Ward & Ethelyn Towler Lindsay Ward; c: Brian 13, Todd 11, John 8; ed: BA pol sci, history; MA education; EdD ed psychology & counseling; Phi Kappa Phi; Supplemental Award for acad excellence; Sundberg Award for research & writing; former: inst; asst prof; career: Outstanding Young Woman of Amer by Natl Soc; research grant BYU College of Family; mem: Mormon Historical Assn; award: On My Honor, Boy Scouts of Amer; publ: Illustrious Forebears & Guidance Services"; "Members of the Mormon Batallion"; "Pioneers of 1847"; civic: BSA merit badge counselor; rel: LDS, all-church writing com, curriculum com consultant; home: 555 Sumac Dr; off: 135 JSB, BYU.

EDDINGTON, ROBERT R   exec dir Central Utah Chapter Amer Red Cross; b: 11 Jul 1934; m: Margret Jane Shepherd; p: Reed & Elnora; c: Michael, Mark, Leslie, Rachel; ed: BS accounting cum laude BYU; Phi Kappa Phi; career: Refugee Serv Award, Refugee Assn of Utah County; civic: Provo Chamber of Commerce; pol: state & county del Republican; mil: US Air Force 20 yrs; Combat Pilot, Strategic Air Command, SE Asia; Distinguished Flying Cross; Air Medal; Commendation Medal; rel: LDS, branch pres, bishop, h council; club: Timpanogos Kiwanis; home: 1187 Ash Ave; off: 865 N 200 W.

EDENFIELD, GRADY LAMAR   school principal; b: 21 Jul 1930; m: Jane Ann Ivie; p: Paul & Pinie Green; c: Grady Lamar Jr, Suzan; ed: BS 1959 MS 1962 EdD 1972 BYU, in education; former: tchr Timpanogos Elem, Portola Elem; principal Provost Elem, Edgemont Elem, Wasatch Elem; mem: Phi Delta Kappa; UAESP; NAESP, PEA, UEA, NEA; civic: chm Planning Commission, Mapleton 1979-82; pol: Mapleton City Councilman 1979-82; mil: US Navy; rel: LDS, bishop, h council, stake sunday school presidency; home: 1033 E 900 N, Mapleton; off: 1080 N 1000 E.

EDMUNDS, MARY ELLEN   asst dir Special Training, MTC; b: 3 Mar 1940; p: Dr Paul K & Ella Mary Middleton Edmunds; ed: BS nursing 1962 BYU; former: coor Health Missionaries LDS Church; supvr Utah Valley Hospital; instr nursing BYU 5 yrs; tchr, supvr, sec & asst to pres SL Missionary Home 1965-72; career: Nurse of the Yr 1961;

civic: instr BYU Ed Week; Youth & Adult Conf speaker; rel: LDS, missionary to Taiwan, Hong Kong, 1st lady miss to Philippines 1962-4; stake mission BYU 1967-9; health mission to Philippines 1972-3; 1st lady welfare serv missionary to Indonesia 1976-8; home: PO Box 45, Springville; off: A-125 MTC, BYU.

EDWARDS, CLIFFORD HAZEN   prof of Secondary Ed BYU; b: 21 Feb 1937; m: Deanna; p: George Franklin & Thelma Larsen; c: Shon Robert 15, Steven Clifford 13, Jeffrey Glen 11, Eric Matthew 5; ed: BS MEd Utah State U; EdD U of Utah; Phi Kappa Phi; former: prof of secondary ed Illinois State U; tchr Logan High, RiverView Jr High; career: 3 research awards; mem: ASCD, AETS, NARC, NSSE, AACTE; publ: 6 books, 21 articles, 3 computer progs; mil: 1st Lt Artillery US Army; rel: LDS, h council, bishopric, stake missionary; elders quorum pres; home: 777 E Walnut; off: 149-a MCKB, BYU.

EDWARDS, CLIFFORD HAZEN   prof of Secondary Ed BYU; b: 21 Feb 1937; m: Deanna; p: George Franklin & Thelma Larsen; c: Shon Robert 15, Steven Clifford 13, Jeffrey Glen 11, Eric Matthew 5; ed: BS MEd Utah State U; EdD U of Utah; Phi Kappa Phi; former: prof of secondary ed Illinois State U; tchr Logan High, RiverView Jr High; career: 3 research awards; mem: ASCD, AETS, NARC, NSSE, AACTE; publ: 6 books, 21 articles, 3 computer progs; mil: 1st Lt Artillery US Army; rel: LDS, h council, bishopric, stake missionary; elders quorum pres; home: 777 E Walnut; off: 149-a MCKB, BYU.

EDWARDS, CLYDE C   instr UTC; b: 28 Nov 1928; m: Beverly R; p: Homer J & Naomia F; c: Eric H, JaNel, Karyn, Dary, Denise; ed: BS BYU; MA Washington State; PhD BYU; Phi Kappa Phi; NDEA Fellowship; Distinguished Military Grad; former: asst prof BYU; Ranger US Forest Serv; career: Natl Defense Pre-Doctoral Fellowship; mem: Sigma Xi; Ecological Soc; Utah Ed Assn; Natl Ed Soc; award: pres UTC Faculty Assn; publ: *Winter Behavior and Population Dynamics of American Eagles in Western Utah;* civic: Sierra Club; Wasatch Mtn Club; Audubon Soc; mil: Officer US Air Force; rel: LDS, scouting, branch presidency; home: 2025 S Main, Orem; off: M216 UTC.

ELDREDGE, J LLOYD   assoc prof of Ed BYU; b: 3 May 1935; m: Cherie; p: Wayne & Lois Thomas; c: Lloyd, Stephen, Gaylene, Kristin, Brad, Michelle, Nicole; ed: BS MS Doctorate; Phi Kappa Phi; High Honor Roll BYU; Doctorate with Distinction; former: School Principal & Superintendent; Utah Title I Dir; Utah Dir of Elementary Ed; Utah Elementary-Secondary Technical Assist Coor, Utah Basic Skills Coor; Utah Dir of Discipline in Behavior & Studies; career: honored at 4 Utah Author's Banquets & awarded governor's certs; over 60 consultant assignments; over 150 workships; over 100 speeches; pres U of Utah Phi Delta Kappa; mem: Natl Ed Assn; natl Elem Principal's Assn; Utah Soc of School Supts; Utah Assn Elementary School Principals; award: US Metrics Speakers Bureau; publ: 50 books & articles; civic: treas, 5th VP, 4th VP of Utah Congress of Parents & Tchrs; rel: LDS, elders quorum pres, bishop, h council; home: 982 E 315 S, Orem; off: 210-Q MCKB, BYU.

ELLIS, GLEN J   attorney; Provo City Attorney; b: 14 Aug 1930; m: Elaine Harding; p: Merlin & Echo; c: Mark, Diane, Moana, Beth, Reid, Lee; ed: BS 1962 JD 1964 U of Utah; Phi Delta Phi legal frat; former: mem law firm Maxfield, Gammon & Ellis 1967-75; mem: Amer Assn Trial Lawyers; ABA; Utah State Bar; Central Utah Bar; pol: Republican county & state del; rel: LDS, bishop, h council; home: 1280 W 1600 N; off: Box 1097.

ELLSWORTH, RICHARD GRANT   prof of English BYU; b: 11 Jul 1927; m: Betty Lola Midgley; p: German Smith & Adelaide Grant; c: Richard German, Madelyn, Barbara, Joseph Cordon, Carolyn, Elizabeth, James Edgar, Christina; ed: AB 1951 English BYU, MA 1952 English, U of Maryland, PhD 1959 amer civilization; former: teaching asst U of Maryland 1952-4; Pr Geo Co Public Schools elem tchr 1956; US Capitol Police 1953-7; US Fed Govt 1957-8; career: prof of the Month ASBYU 1967; mem: Utah Library Assn; Amer Library Assn; Modern Language Assn; Mormon History Assn; Amer Studies Assn; Utah Historical Soc; Amer Lit Section MLA; publ: *Am Romanticism: The Interrelationship of All Things; Getting to Know the Real You;* journal articles; civic: Provo City Public Library Board of Trustees 1965-9, chm 1967-8; board of dir Univ Campus Fed Credit Union; literary advisory board Utah State Inst of Fine Arts; pol: county & state del, Republican; mil: US Navy 1945-6; rel: LDS, tchr, counselor, bishop, branch pres, h council, clerk; home: 1267 Apple Ave; off: English Dept, BYU.

ENGEMANN, BETTY   exec dir Better Business Bureau of Utah Valley Inc; b: 1 Feb; m: Robert; p: Earl & Beth Echols Crail; c: Andrew 16, Lizanne 14, Melissa 11, Danny 9; ed: BS homemaking ed BYU; former: home serv rep S Calif Gas Co; civic: former chm Calif Citizens for Decency, San Fernancy Valley Chapter; rel: LDS, Relief Soc, sunday school, primary tchr; home: 3541 Sioux Cir; off: 40 N 100 E.

ESPLIN, ROSS   assoc prof of English BYU; b: 4 Sep 1922; m: Olive; p: Israel H & Chastie; c: Judith, Jill, Robin, Mary, Linda, Claudia, Kimo; ed: AA 1943 Dixie College; AB 1947 MA 1949 BYU; PhD 1970 U of Utah; grad with honors BYU 1947; former: high school English tchr; Language Arts Chm Dixie College 1950-3; English Dept Chm Church College of Hawaii 1960-4; mem: Rocky Mtn Medieval & Renaissance Assn; publ: 1 article; *Independent Study Courses in the Short Story; Masterpieces of English Literature;* mil: US Coast Guard 1943-5; rel: LDS, bishop, clerk; club: Provo Timpanogos Kiwanis Club; home: 3115 N Cherokee Ln; off: A-233 JKB, BYU.

EUBANKS, HARVEY   mgr Men's Locker Rooms BYU; b: 29 Jul 1928; m: Lila C; p: Harvard F Sr & Etherie B; c: Samuel G 16, Lorraine 14; ed: Florida S College, U of Florida, Los Angeles City College, San Francisco State College, BYU; BS & grad work U of Utah; former: steward Pan Amer; mil: Florida Natl Guard; US Army, Japan & Korea; Meritorious Unit Ovation; rel: LDS, pres Sunday School, MIA, exec sec; home: 2891 N 220 E; off: 129 RB, BYU.

EVANS, LAMAR F   asst to dir BYU Food Serv; b: 29 Mar 1929; m: Elise S; p: Earl D & Melva L; c: Melanie, Jeffrey, Shelley, Bradley; ed: 1 yr college; career: Citation for Meritorious Serv, 3 yrs reg pres Natl Board of Dir NACUFS; mem: Natl Assn of College & Univ Food Serv; mem board of dir & 2nd VP Utah Restaurant Assn; advisory com Camperworld; Retail Bakers Assn; Natl

Automatic Merchandisers Assn; Natl Assn of Concessionaires; civic: chm food activities Provo Freedom Festival 9 yrs; rel: LDS, 70s pres; bishop; home: 1017 E 2680 N; off: 199 ELWC, BYU.

EVENSON, WILLIAM E   dir Gen Ed, prof of Physics BYU; b: 12 Oct 1941; m: Nancy Ann Woffinden; p: Raymond Fox & Berta Woolley; c: Brian K 16, Elizabeth 14, JoAnn 11, Andrew 9, Bengte 6; ed: BS physics 1965 BYU; PhD theoretical solid state physics 1968 Iowa State U; Natl Sci Found Post Doct Fellow 1968-9; Danforth Grad Fellow 1965-8; NSF Coop Grad Fellow 1965-6; Honorary Woodrow Wilson Fellow 1965-6; former: Visiting Colleague in Botany, U of Hawaii at Manoa 1977-8; Research Assoc U of Penn 1968-70; career: prof of Month BYU 1979; mem: Amer Physical Soc; Amer Assn of Physics Tchrs; Sigma Xi; Phi Kappa Phi; Sigma Pi Sigma; Amer Botanical Soc; Hawaii Botanical Soc; Hawaii Audubon Soc; Natl Audubon Soc; award: Outstanding Young Men of Amer 1972; publ: 20 sci journal articles; civic: Scoutmaster; Cubmaster; pol: chm Utah County Democrat 1981, v-chm 1979-81, mem State Central Com 1979-81; rel: LDS, bishop, h council, elders pres, exec sec; home: 629 E 2875 N; off: 1206 SFLC, BYU.

EYER, MARY FRANCES STURLAUGSON   part-time BYU faculty; m: John Robertson Eyer; p: Frank & Corine White; ed: BA English; masters work in ed psychology; Sigma Tau Delta; Jubilee Scholarship; Who's Who in Amer Colleges & Univ; former: yearbook editor; counselor at BYU; publ: *A Soul So Rebellious; He Restoreth My Soul;* 2 poems; civic: lecturer; rel: LDS, stake sec, Relief Soc, Primary tchr; home: 335 W 170 N, Orem; off: 141-B BRMB, BYU.

FAIRBANKS, "EJ" LAMAR   dentist; b: 24 sep 1917; m: Rose Price; p: LeRoy Smith Fairbanks & Orissa Jane Smith; c: Stephen LaMar; Earl LeRoy; Darrell Eugene; David Alan; James Douglas; Linda Rose; Michael Ralph; Kerrie Ann; ed: BS agronomy BYU; DDS 1959 Kansas City U of Mo; former: Caxton Printers Caldwell, ID; Airesearch Mfg Co & N Amer Aircraft, Inglewood, CA; Mtn Fuel Supply, Provo; Bureau of Reclamation, Provo; Geneva Steel, Provo; award: invented heat engine &

patented 1972; invented comb shoe horn; non-directional windmill; publ: *Fairbanks Family in America;* civic: Utah County Cancer Soc chm 1962; mil: US Air Force pilot 1943-56; Air Medal; Distinguished Flying Cross 3 Oak leaf clusters; 2 battle stars; Reserve 1956-68; rel: LDS, supt YMMIA, scoutmaster, sunday school tchr; club: Kiwanis; home: 511 S 850 E, Orem; off: 885 N 500 W.

FAIRCLOUGH, DENNIS   asst prof, computer consult BYU; b: 24 Jul 1935; m: Marilyn; p: Albert & Mabel; c: Pamela, Christi, Lisa, Kari, Holly; ed: BSEE U of Utah; MSEE U of Santa Clara; PhD candidate BYU; Phi Kappa Phi; Tau Beta Pi; Eta Kappa Nu; former: development engr IBM; VP R&D WICAT and Novell; career: Outstanding Contribution Award IBM; mem: IEEE; ACM; ASEE; publ: articles; rel: LDS, Sunday School pres, exec sec, clerk; home: 865 N 750 E, Orem; off: 468 CB, BYU.

FARNSWORTH, F DENNIS JR   instr Gen Ed UTC, Chief Res Analyst 698th MID (S) US Army Reserve; b: 17 Jul 1941; m: Viola West; p: F Dennis & Beulah Jessup; c: Lance 11, James 9, Nathaniel 7, Victoria 5; ed: BA Asian Studies BYU 1966; MA Internatl Admin BYU 1969; honor roll; former: sup lumber div Weyerhaeuser co, Everett, Wash; career: nominated Outstanding Tchr, Gen Ed Dept UTC 1976; mem: Utah Public Employees Assn; publ: co-author *Trends in Sino-Japanese Trade* US Defense Intelligence Agcy; civic: school dist bond campaign, Wash 1970; pol: Republican, voting dist chm, del to country conv; mil: 2 yrs active Vietnam, 16 yrs USAR; Army Commendation Medal; Natl Defense Service Medal; Good Conduct Medal; rel: LDS, sunday school pres, tchr; home: 915 N 510 E, Orem; off: UTC 1395 N 150 E.

FAULKNER, JAMES EARL   prof of Statistics; statistical consultant H E Cramer Co; b: 22 Nov 1928; m: Joyce; p: James & Edna; c: Laura Smith, Holly Pipkin, William "Rocky", Becky Horlacher, James, Robert, Jerusha; ed: BS math 1950 Utah State U; MS math 1952 Kansas State U; PhD biostatistics 1964 U of Minn; Phi Kappa Phi; Pi Mu Epsilon; Sigma Xi; NIH Fellowship & Traineeships; pres Utah Chap ASA; prog chm Western Reg ASA; former: stat consultant GCA Corp 1968-72, Hercules Inc 1966-8, Toole Army Dept 1964-5; assoc res engr Minn-Honeywell

Regulator Co 1957; instr math U of Minn 1956-62, Utah
State U 1952-4; grad asst math Kansas State U 1950-2;
career: listed in Who's Who in the West, Dict of Internatl
Biography, Amer Men of Sci; dir Sci Bowl Competition,
Natural & Math Sci Conf BYU 1975-81; Gen Ed Com,
College of Physical & Math Sci BYU 1973-80; Com on
Audio-Visual Instr Materials, Amer Stat Assn 1976-; Stat
Panel, Consortium for Math & its Applications 1978-;
mem: Math Assn of Amer; Amer Stat Assn; Biometric
Soc; Natl Council of Tchrs of Math; publ: 15 articles, 2
dissertations; contributed to 3 GCA publs; 12 reports; 8
presentations; rel: LDS, bishopric, dist 70s pres, choir dir,
youth ldr; home: 991 W 800 N, Orem; off: 214 TMCB, BYU.

FEILD, MARLA KAY   systematic specialist, coor of BYU
Aquatic Ecology Lab; b: 29 Mar 1957; p: Russell Wardahl
& Betty Katherine; ed: AA Northwestern Mich College;
BS BYU; Secondary Ed Tchrs Cert Utah; rel: LDS, stake
Relief Soc board; home: 1951 N 700 W; off: 115 Page
School, BYU.

FINNEGAN, WAYNE R   buyer BYU Bookstore; b: 30 May
1944; m: Valerie Anne; p: Catherine Taylor; c: Arlene
Renae 14, David Wayne 13, Shawn Lavell 9, Christopher
Scott 4; ed: BS physical ed; mil: medic 1457 Hq Co Amer
Fork Utah Natl Guard; rel: LDS, exec sec; home: 535 W
150 N, Orem; off: 2130A BYU Bookstore.

FIRMAGE, MARGARET FELT   housewife, youth leader;
b: 5 Jun 1921; m: David Allan Firmage; p: Roy H & Edna
Little Felt; c: Kathy E Campbell, Jeri F Walton, Nita F
Jameson, Becky F Ellis, Richard A, Ronald R; ed: U of
Utah 2 yrs; award: 45 yrs Girl Scouts appreciation awards;
12 yrs Den mother appreciation awards; 12 yrs League of
Women Voters, pres 1 term; publ: *I'd Love Jo -- Where Is
Vietnam?*; civic: Girl Scouts; Boy Scouts; chm Volunteers
Red Cross; candidate for City Council; pol: Republican
dist offices; asst registrar 6 yrs; rel: LDS, stake camp dir
5 yrs, Relief Soc tchr & pres, primary & MIA; club: pres
BYU Women; League of Women Voters; Engineers Wives;
Womens Chamber of Commerce; home: 1079 Ash Ave.

FLETCHER, CHARLES THOMAS   assoc prof & coor,
Justice Admin Prog BYU; b: 9 Jan 1917; m: Donna; p: C

Eugene & Estella; c: Judith Rae Staples; ed: BS BYU; grad FBI Acad; grad studies U of Calif Berkeley & LaVerne College; former: special agent FBI 1941-67; career: BYU Law Enforcement Assn Dedicated Serv Award 1972, 76; mem: Internatl Assn of Chiefs of Police; Acad of Criminal Justice Sci; Soc of Former Special Agents of the FBI; Amer Soc of Public Administrators; civic: Governor's Com Law Enforcement Standards & Goals; Mountainland's Com on Criminal Justice Standards & Goals; rel: LDS, bishop, h council; club: Cougar Club; Kiwanis Internatl, former pres Provo Club, former Lt Governor Div I Utah County; dist coor Kiwanis Internatl Found; home: 1700 N 1450 E; off: 760 SWKT, BYU.

FLETCHER, HARVEY JUNIOR   prof of mathematics BYU; b: 9 Apr 1923; m: Deah Tonks; p: Harvey Fletcher & Karen Lorena Chipman; c: Mary Lyn Perry, Thos Harvey, John, Deanna, Amy Jean, Judy Ann; ed: BS phys MIT; MS physics Cal Tech; PhD U of Utah mathematics 1954; Phi Kappa Phi; Sigma Xi; former: chm BYU Math Dept 4 yrs; Bell Telephone Labs; Hercules; Eyring Research Inst; career: prof of the Year BYU 1969-70; mem: Math Assn of Amer; James Chipman Family Org, pres 1979-82; publ: 60 papers & technical reports; 7 natl journal papers; civic: chm Provo Freedom Festival; pol: area chm Republican Utah County Dist 38; mil: Lt jg USNR 1944-6; Naval Aviation Observer; command officer CASU F5; rel: LDS, bishop, h council, stake sunday school pres, stake presidency; club: pres Timpanogos Kiwanis 1980-1; home: 1175 Locust Cr; off: 322 TMCB, BYU.

FLINDERS, NEIL J   fac BYU College of Ed; b: 11 Jul 1934; m: Joan D Robertson; p: Percy James Flinders & Reta Herrick; c: Leisa 21, Erin 19, Karalee 16, Tracy 15, Scott 12, David 12, Shelley 10; ed: BS sociology, journalism; MS rel ed, philosophy; EdD admin & human relations; former: seminary prin, institute instr, dir of tchr training, dir res & long range planning, Church Ed Syst; mem: Far Western Philosophy of Ed Assn; publ: several books, monographs, articles, professional papers on rel & ed; civic: mem Manila Culinary Water Bd, chm Community Planning Com, pres Pleasant Grove Ed Adv Com, mem Alpine Dist Ed Adv Com; mil: 2 yrs US Army Medical Corps; rel: LDS, elders quorum pres, high council, bishop; home: RFD 2 Box 400-F, PG; off: 210-N MCKB, BYU.

FORSYTH, DON HOAGLAND   Utah County Constable (elected 1978); b: 24 Mar 1940; m: Shauna Gygi; p: Harry H & Berince Peck; c: Natalia Jo 19, Holly 15, John 13, Michael 8, Cathy 6, William 2, Jill 1; ed: BS Weber State College; former: coor Utah County Fair 1977–81; mgr Bug Hut; mem: Utah State Constables Assn; Natl Constables Assn; Utah Peace Officers Assn; Internatl Assn of Chiefs of Police; award: Sertoman of the Year, Orem Sertoma Club; Jr King of Provo 1941; civic: Boy Scouts of Amer; rel: LDS, scoutmaster; home: 846 S 500 E, Orem; off: Utah County Bldg.

FOSTER, KENNETH MONROE   instr UTC; b: 11 Apr 1929; m: Dorothy L Hewitson; p: Ralph B & Grace; c: Kenneth Jr 15, Lorrie 13, Elizabeth 10; ed: BA U of Miss; Naval Enlisted Sci Ed Prog; career: conf speaker; pres UTC Faculty Assn; mem: UEA; AVA; pol: county del Republican; mil: US Navy Lt 23 yrs; Korean & Vietnam Campaigns; UN Korean Action; Asian Occupation; China Medal; Good Conduct; rel: LDS, sunday school tchr & sec, elders sec, cubmaster, scout com; home: 915 N 840 E, Orem; off: 1395 N 150 E.

FOX, FRANK WAYNE   assoc prof History BYU; b: 7 Oct 1940; m: Elaine Tebbs; p: A W Fox; c: David Ryan 7, Michael Jordan 4; ed: BA history 1966 MA history & amer studies 1969 U of Utah; PhD 1973 Stanford; Phi Alpha Theta; Phi Kappa Phi; Henry D. Newell Grad Fellowship; former: supvr highways & highway construction, Utah State Road Commission & Highway Supply Corp; career: listed in Who's Who in the West 1981; Phi Alpha Theta Tchr of Yr 1975; Assn for Mormon Letters prize for best general publ 1980; mem: Organization of Amer Historians; Amer Studies Assn; Soc for Early Amer History & Culture; publ: *Madison Avenue Goes to War: The Strange Military Career of American Advertising; J. Reuben Clark: The Public Years;* articles; books in progress; special consulting editor *BYU Centennial History;* civic: Liberty Fund Seminar 1980–1; rel: LDS, instructor, h council, stake clerk; home: 3259 Mohawk Ln; off: 322 KMB, BYU.

FOX, MARSHALL SLINN   supvr Water Treatment & Auxiliary Boiler Dept BYU; b: 22 Jan 1929; m: Joan Miner; p: John Alfred & Margaret Chloe Boyer; c: Richard Lynn, Marsha, Debra, David Reed; ed: 1 qtr college; former: road construction equipment operator 1951-64; BYU Admin Advisory Com 1972-4; career: 15 yrs Serv to BYU in 1979; mem: former mem Operating Engineer's Union; civic: board of dir Springville Playhouse 18 yrs; mil: US Army 1951-4; rel: LDS, bishop, h council, stake presidency; club: former mem Springville 20-30 Club; home: 307 W 400 S, Springville; off: Physical Plant Bldg B-31, BYU.

FRANCIS, RELL GARDNER   writer, photographer; owner Heritage Prints; b: 27 Jan 1928; m: Janet Oaks; p: Samuel Evan & Barbara Ferguson; c: Sean 20, Lewis M 18, Dana 14; ed: BA 1954 MA 1963 art BYU; former: monument designer 1945-54; art instr Nebo School Dist 1955-74; dir City Spirit for Springville City & Natl Endowment for the Arts 1976; career: winner natl newspaper contests 1957-9; Best in Show in Photography, Utah State Fair 1966-7; Meritorious Serv Award in Photography BYU 1974; Morris Rosenblatt Award for Best Article in Utah Historical Qtrly Mag 1976; mem: Natl Ed Assn; Valley Artist's Guild; honorary life mem Springville Museum of Art; award: State Cultural Award for Springville City, Community Progress 2 yrs; Best Bicentennial Parade Float 1976; publ: *Cyrus E Dallin: Let Justice Be Done; Utah Photographs of George Edward Anderson;* articles in Amer West, Amer Heritage, Popular Photography, Utah Historical Soc Quarterly, Natl Geographic, Southwest Art magazines; civic: former board mem Springville Museum of Art; Kiwanis Club board; chm of photography Community Development; board Valley Artists' Guild; pol: letters to newspaper forums; rel: LDS, stake dir of libraries, tchr development dir; home: 750 E Chase Ln, Springville; off: 250 W Center.

FRANCIS, RULON S   BYU prof; b: 27 Jan 1928; m: Geraldine York; p: S Evan & Barbara Ferguson; c: Debra, John, Susan, Richard; ed: BS BYU; MS U of S Calif; PhD U of Utah; Cert in Physical Therapy; former: dept head Physical Therapy & Orthopedic Brace Shop, Primary Children's Med Ctr; career: Registered Physical

Therapist; Certified Athletic Trainer; mem: fellow Amer
College of Sports Med; Amer Physical Therapy Assn;
Amer Alliance for Health & Physical Ed; Natl Athletic
Trainers Assn; Phi Kappa Phi; Sigma Xi; Amer Polled
Hereford Assn; Utah Polled Hereford Soc; publ: *A Study
Manual for Corrective Physical Education; A Study
Manual With Illustrations for Diagnosis & Management of
Athletic Injuries;* 6 articles; mil: Infantry, Japan; Capt
Army Med Corps Reserve; rel: LDS, stake pres, h council,
bishop; home: 1622 W 950 N; off: 122 RB, BYU.

FREEMAN, LAWRENCE REED   BYU prof; b: 17 Dec
1941; m: Bjorg Hildegard Stoyl; p: Walter Ottley & Ruby
Reed; c: Allen Christopher 6, Bjorn Erik 4, Craig William
2; ed: PhD food sci nutrition U of Mass; NDEA Fellowship;
US Army Command Pre-doctoral Research Fellowship;
career: visiting scientist 1978-9 Central Inst for Nutrition
& Food Res, Zeist, The Netherlands; mem: Soc for
Applied Bacteriology; Amer Soc for Microbiology; Inst of
Food Technologists; Sigma Xi; Phi Kappa Phi; publ: 13 sci
journal articles; rel: LDS, bishopric, ward clerk; home:
1028 E 720 N, Orem; off: Dept of Food Sci & Nutrition,
BYU.

FRISBY, DUANE   vocational evaluator, Div of
Rehabilitation Serv, Utah State Office of Ed; b: 28 Apr
1939; m: Kaye; p: Carl D & Selda W; c: Diane 15, Larry
12, Randall 9, Keith 7, Sandi 5, Ryan 2; ed: BA industrial
ed MEd counseling & guidance grad with honors BYU;
mem: Natl Rehabilitation Assn; pres Vocational
Evaluation Work Adjustment Assn 1981-2; chapter pres
Utah Public Employees Assn; civic: Payson Area Water
Safety Com; pol: republican; mil: US Army 1962-5;
translator & interpreter in Mandarin Chinese; Good
Conduct Medal; Soldier of the Month; Scholastic
Achievement Award, Defense Language Inst; rel: LDS, h
council, bishop; home: 1085 S Canyon Rd, Payson; off:
1347 Riverside Ave.

FROERER, SCOTT B   adult educator; supvr Dept of Ed
Weeks; coor Campus Ed Week BYU; b: 7 Dec 1948; p:
Fredrick Jr & Phyllis Brown; c: Heide 9, Abbie 7, Jacob 5,
Adam 3, John 1; ed: BS history, economics, geography
BYU; former: board of dir Adult Ed Assn of Utah; publ:

compiled *Voices From the Past: Diaries, Journals, & Autobiographies* 1980; civic: v-chm Freedom Festival of Utah; rel: LDS, bishop, exec sec, temple worker; home: 2313 W 800 N; off: 276 HCEB, BYU.

FUGAL, JOHN PAUL   assoc prof Religious Instr; b: 18 Aug 1921; m: Elma Widdison; p: Jens Peter & Lavina Christensen (1955 Amer Mother of the Yr); c: Jens, Pamela, Deborah, Robert, Amy, Jared; ed: BS 1948 MRE 1959; DRE 1967; Phi Kappa Phi 1959; former: principal Pleasant Grove Seminary; tchr Amer Fork, Lehi, Pleasant Grove Seminaries; Book of Mormon Area Chm; Sharing the Gospel Missionary Preparation area chm; award: Honorary Chapter Farmer FFA 1961; Honorary Master M Man; publ: *A Review of Priesthood Correlation;* mil: Natl Guard 145th Field Artillery 1939-41; rel: LDS, h council, stake mission pres, bishop; home: 390 N Main, Lindon; off: 67 JSB, BYU.

GALE, DARWIN FRED   prof & dept chm BYU; b: 11 Mar 1931; m: Carol Tullis; p: Fred E & Oertel I; c: Kerry D, Scott K, Karen Murray, Paula Asay, Mark R; ed: Weber College; Utah State U; EdD ed psychology 1967 BYU; former: psychologist admin staff Washoe County, Reno, Nev, Nebo School Dist; career: life mem Nev State PTA; Outstanding Serv Award BYU Continuing Ed; mem: Council for Exceptional Schildren; Amer Assn Colleges Teacher Ed; Phi Kappa Phi; Phi Delta Theta; award: listed in Leaders in Special Ed; publ: "Accuracy of Questionnaire Studies"; "Children's Perception of Men Wearing Beards"; mil: US Army 1953-5; rel: LDS, bishop, h council; home: 834 E 2730 N; off: 320 MCKB, BYU.

GALE, LARRIE ELDON   asst dir David O McKay Inst; assoc prof of Instr sci BYU; b: 16 Feb 1942; m: Nell Velasco; p: Eldon & Reha Myrl Higginson; c: Eldon 17, Ronald 15, Sean 13, Tana 9, Tamra 8, Kim 5; ed: BA History & Spanish 1967 MA Spanish 1970 San Diego State College; PhD Instr Tech 1973 U of Utah; Phi Kappa Phi; Sigma Delta Pi; Alpha Mu Gamma; former: Assoc Dir Instr Serv, asst prof of ed, assoc dir Ctr for Research in Teaching Effectiveness, U of Texas at San Antonio; external evaluator to Title IV progs in Utah 1979-81; consul Kapiolani Community College, Hawaii; consul

Church Ed Sys for projs in Guatemala, Ghana & Nigeria; consultant & prog developer to several corps, school dists, and univ on training, bilingual & bicultural progs, instr resources; consultant to Bolivian govt & US Embassy on rural ed; admin asst U of Utah Ctr to Improve Learning & Instr; admin asst to dean of Grad School of Ed, U of Utah; career: listed in Leaders in Ed (5th ed), Dictionary of Internatl Biography (10th ed), Community Leaders and Noteworthy Americans (9th ed); AIDP grant as instr development consul & workshop dir for developing US colleges; mem: SIETAR; chm Internatl Interest Group, Div of Instr Development, AETC; ASTD; Internatl Congress of Ed Media; Amer Assn of Univ Profs; publ: several journal articles and papers; structured tutoring ESL Spanish training tapes; tap%slide series of children's lit; "A New Home" video prog in 5 languages for refugee camps in Thailand; reviewer for Ed Tech Publ; civic: San Diego Civic Youth Orchestra; rel: LDS, bishopric, h council; off: 113 KMB, BYU.

GAMETTE, KENT R   physician, specialist obstetrics & gynecology; b: 8 Mar 1943; m: Sharon; p: Don V & Ruth; c: Kimbery 12, Shannon 10, Gregory 7, Alisa 3, Jeffry 2; ed: BS BYU 1967; MD Cornell Univ Med College; mem: Amer Board of Ob-Gyn; Utah County & State Med Soc; publ: *Differential Diagnosis in Gynecology* textbook; mil: retired; rel: LDS, bishop; home: 1521 N 1550 E; off: 920 N 500 W.

GAMMON, RAY EUGENE   Deputy Utah County Attorney; attorney at law; b: 16 Dec 1933; m: Karla W; p: Ray & Pauline S; c: Carol 12, Karen 10, Susan 8, David 6, Steven 4, John 3; ed: BA 1960 BYU; JD 1963 U of Utah; former: Utah County Board of Adjustment, mem 1967-77, chm 1972-7; Deputy Dist Attorney, 4th Judicial Dist 1969-72; career: pres Central Utah Bar Assn 1973; mem: Phi Delta Phi; Amer Bar Assn; Utah State Bar; Central Utah Bar Assn; civic: Provo July 4th com; pol: county & state del to republican conv; mil: US Army 1956-8; Good Conduct Medal; Outstanding Soldier Award; Military Police Training Ctr; rel: LDS, bishopric, h council; home: 3317 N 650 E; off: 60 E 100 S.

GARDNER, JOHN HALE   prof of Physics BYU; b: 24 Aug

1922; m: Olga Dotson; p: Willard & Viola Hale; c: Helen Van Orman, John W, Kristin Sundell, Rebecca Crandall, Robert, Eric, Ann Marie Millheim, Margaret; ed: BS Utah State U; MA PhD Harvard U; Valedictorian of Grad Class Utah State U; Distinguished Serv Award Utah Acad of Sci; Maeser Award; former: consul, Ramo Wooldridge Corp, Space Tech Labs; mem: fellow Amer Physical Soc; fellow Inst of Physics, London; Amer Assn of Physics Tchrs; Sigma Xi; Phi Kappa Phi; mem board of dir Redd Ctr for Western Studies; mem board of dir New World Archeological Found; publ: various on nuclear magnetic resonance and electromagnetism; pol: Republican, Utah County Central Com; rel: LDS, h council, branch pres; home: 1140 Aspen Ave; off: 175 ESC, BYU.

GARNER, LYNN EVAN   prof of Mathematics BYU; b: 19 Jul 1941; m: Kaye Waite; p: Evan B & Melba Despain; c: Kaylene 20, Bradley 17, Kristen 14, Alisse 7, Brian 5; ed: BS 1962 BYU; MA 1964 U of Utah; PhD 1968 U of Oregon; Danforth Tchr Grantee 1966-7; mem: Amer Math Soc; Math Assn of Amer; Sigma Xi; Pi Mu Epsilon; publ: *An Outline of Projective Geometry;* 3 tech papers; rel: LDS, branch pres MTC; home: 681 E 3230 N; off: 282 TMCB, BYU.

GARRISON, RAY HOWARD   prof of accounting BYU; CPA; b: 23 Feb 1933; m: Mary Jean; p: James Edgar & Grace Hart Baggerly; c: Leslie 20, Kimberly 16, James 14, Jana 12, LeAnn 6; ed: BS 1960 MS 1961 BYU; Doctor of Business Admin 1966 Indiana Univ; Outstanding Sr Student in Accounting 1960 Arthur Young Found; Outstanding Grad from College of Business 4.0 GPA 1961; Gen Electric Corp fellowship; Phi Kappa Phi; Beta Alpha Psi; Beta Gamma Sigma; former: professional audit staff Peat, Marwick, Mitchell & Co CPA 1961-3; visiting assoc prof U of Michigan 1972-3; chm College of Business Communications & Curriculum Com; College of Business Computer Uses Com; Faculty Advisory Com; MBA Exec & Steering Com; IPA Exec Com; Honors Prog Advisor; career: Arthur Andersen Teaching Excellence Awards 1972 & 1976; Outstanding Prof MBA Prog 1974,5,7; Karl G Maeser Distinguished Teaching Award 1979; listed in Who's Who in Finance & Industry; mem: Amer Accounting Assn; Natl Assn of Accountants; publ: *Managerial*

Accounting: Concepts for Planning, Control, Decision Making, textbook, instr manual & workbook used in over 400 colleges & univ; journal articles; rel: LDS; home: 458 S 450 E, Orem; off: 326 JKB, BYU.

GERMANE, GEOFFREY JAMES   asst prof Mechanical Engineering BYU; b: 3 July 1950; m: Sydney L; p: James S & Alice B; c: Megan 5, Geoffrey Nathan 3, Matthew James 5 mo; ed: BS MS PhD mechanical engineering; Pi Tau Sigma, Natl Mechanical Eng Honorary; Phi Kappa Phi; career: SAE Teetor Award Recipient 1981; BYU Sigma Xi Engineering Dissertation of the Year 1978; mem: Soc of Automotive Engineers; publ: organizations & symposia; civic: Utah Legislative Com on Alternate Fuels 1980; rel: LDS, bishopric, h council, exec sec; home: 74 E 1750 N, Orem; off: 242 CB, BYU.

GIBB, SARA LEE   dir Modern Dance BYU; m: J David Gibb; c: Douglas 16, Derek 14, Angela 12, Melinda 9, Alaina 7; ed: BA theatre arts ed MS physical ed & dance BYU; Rozelle Frey Studio, Los Angeles; Banff School of Fine Arts, Canada; former: public school tchr 3 yrs; instr Ricks College 3 yrs; career: chosen by State Dept to study dance training in Moscow & Leningrad; mem: chm Dance Div, Southwest Dist, Amer Alliance for Health, Physical Ed, Recreation & Dance; officer Natl Dance Assn; publ: *Slim, Trim, Fun for Life;* rel: LDS, dir stake & reg dance festivals, stake cultural arts chm; off: 293 RB, BYU.

GIFFORD, DON R   pediatric dentist; b: 3 Oct 1947; m: Kathy; p: James Edward & Mary Alice; c: D Ray 11, Dawn Katherine 9; ed: AS Ricks College; BS BYU; DDS Creighton Univ; gen practice residency Scott AFB; pedodontic residency Children's Hospital, Cinncinnati, Ohio; chief resident, Dental Dept Children's Hospital; mem: Amer Acad of Pedodontics; Amer Soc of Dentistry for Children; Amer Dental Assn; Utah Dental Assn; Provo Dist Dental Soc; award: Lt Gov of the Year Award, Circle K Internatl, Ricks College; civic: Kiwanis Internatl; mil: US Air Force 3 yrs; Commendation Medal; Rel: LDS, exec sec; home: 420 E 2875 N; off: 2230 N Univ Pkwy, Bldg 4-A.

GILES, LEORA ALLEN   Children's Librarian Provo City

Library; b: 22 Nov 1926; m: Floyd K; p: Grover E & Frances Harris Allen; c: Terri, Pamela, James; ed: BYU; Honor Soc Scholarship BYU; former: housewife; career: Provo City Employee of the Month 1981; mem: PTA; Utah Library Assn; rel: LDS, Primary pres, stake Relief Soc presidency; clubs ALTRUSA Club of Utah Valley; home: 1777 N 1350 W; off: 13 N 100 E.

GILLUM, GARY P   Ancient Studies Librarian BYU; b: 12 Jun 1944; m: Elizabeth; p: Paul & Ruth; c: Grant 11, Bonnie 11, Adina 9, David 9, Annalyn 3; ed: BA Concordia Sr College; MLS 1971 BYU; former: music librarian, Indianapolis Public Library; career: Professional Development Grant to compile index & bibliography of Hugh Nibley's Works 1979-81; mem: Mtn Plains Library Assn; Utah Library Assn; Soc of Biblical Lit; Amer Acad of Religion; publ: *Of All Things! A Nibley Quote Book*; civic: Payson Library Board; rel: LDS sr pres 70s; home: 240 S 700 W, Payson; off: 6210-A HBLL, BYU.

GIVAN, EDWIN   Chm of the Board, Givan Ford Sales & Leasing; b: 20 Jul 1913; m: Helen; p: Ed & Louise; c: Larry, JoAnn Field; ed: LaSall & Harvard Business College; former: Admin Mgr, Ford Motor Co; Staff Budget & Cost Sup Remington Arms; Sec, VP, Pres Utah Automobile Dealers; Chm of Motor Vehicle Dealers Adv Board; Dir of Ford Dealer Advertising Fund; mem: Utah & Natl Automobile Dealers Assn; award: Championship Golf Award, Riverside Country Club; civic: Chamber of Commerce; pol: mem Natl Fed of Independent Businesses; club: Rotary; life mem Elks Lodge; former dir & pres Riverside Country Club; Bloomington Country Club; home: 2718 Marrcrest West; off: 191 S University Ave.

GLEED, J GUY JR   dental technician; b: 9 Dec 1931; m: Neola; p: J Guy & Nellie; c: Vicki Willes, Kent J; ed: Utah State U; career: Master of Dental Technology; civic: Provo City Neighborhood Chm 7 yrs; chm & pres board of dir Provo Freedom Festival; pol: Republican dist 6 chm & state del; rel: LDS, bishop, h council, stake presidency; club: former pres Sertoma Civic Club; home: 731 E 3800 N; off: Utah Valley Dental Lab, 777 N 500 W.

GOLIGHTLY, GARY D   pres Golightly Inc, Little Rascals

Clothing Store; b: 12 May 1950; m: Kathi Moore; p: Max C & beverly Keith; c: Taleese 7, Keely Ann 5, Aubree 2; ed: BYU 2 yrs; Honor Student; Danforth Ldrship Award; former: pres, VP, board mem, University Mall Merchants Assn; mem: Provo Chamber of Commerce; treas Hillside Central West Inc; civic: Provo City Councilman 1982-4; rel: LDS, bishopric; club: Executive Club of Utah Valley; home: 1996 W 1550 N; off: 117 N University Ave.

GOODMAN, A HAROLD   prof of Music BYU; b: 14 Jul 1924; m: Naomi F; p: Ralph N & Marie O'Dell; c: Steven H, Gordon D, Karen G Reeder; ed: BA U of Arizona; MM EdD (MuEd) U of S Calif; Phi Mu Alpha; Phi Delta Kappa; Phi Kappa Phi; Phi Kappa Lamda; former: music supvr Snowflake & Tucson, Arizona; career: Outstanding Educators of Amer; The World Who's Who of Musicians; Internatl Biographers; Karl G Maeser Teaching Excellence BYU; Outstanding Musician of Utah; mem: Music Educators Natl Conf; Kappa Kappa Psi; Natl Assn Schools of Music; Amer String Tchrs Assn; award: chm BYU Music Dept & Lyceum Progs; chm Music Ed at BYU & N Arizona U; pres Utah Music Educators; Western Div MENC & MENC Research Council; publ: *We Can Become Perfect; Music Education: Perspectives & Perceptions; Music Administration in Higher Learning; Instrumental Music Guide;* civic: conductor Tucson Symphony, N Arizona Symphony, Utah Valley Symphony, Utah Valley Youth Symphony; chm Provo Cultural Affairs Board; Flagstaff City Charter; Board of Young Audiences; Board of Amer Fed of Musicians; rel: LDS, bishop, stake pres, gen Sunday School board, chm Church Music Dept, temple presidency, mission pres; club: Lions Club; home: 725 E Stadium Ave; off: Provo Temple, 2200 N Temple Dr.

GOOLD, ANNA MAE   BYU Law School Placement Officer; b: 10 Mar 1925; m: Sessel W Goold; p: J M & Anna Palmer; c: Larry, Keith, Michael, Terry; ed: Utah State U; U of Calif at LA; former: doctors' sec & bkkpr; sec to asst principals at Arroyo High School, El Monte, Calif; career: J Reuben Clark Award; The Heart of the Law School Award; mem: Natl Assn for Law Placement; rel: LDS, Relief Soc pres; MIA pres; tchr; home: 337 S 700 E, Orem; off: 436 JRCB, BYU.

GOULD, DOUGLAS ALLEN   librarian BYU; b: 12 Dec 1942; m: Kaye Cochran; p: Donald D Bliss & Laurel B Bliss; c: Debra 14, Timothy 12, Joshua 10, Rebecca 7; ed: BYU bus mgt 3 yrs; former: dept mgr ZCMI; mil: Utah Army Natl Guard 6 yrs; rel: LDS, ward clerk, exec sec; home: 1B-23 Wymount Terrace; off: 3087 HBLL, BYU.

GOURLEY, TOM   Dir BYU Stud Info Serv; b: 24 Nov 1948; m: Martha; p: Tom M. Gourley, Sr & Beverly Ogan; c: Kathryn 3, Michael, Jason 1; ed: BS bus admin San Jose State; MS agribusiness BYU; former: Dir of Purchasing, Dee's Inc.; Provo City Property Mgr; indus engr, Colgate Palmolive Co.; Cert of Merit 81 CASE natl competition; mem: UACRAO, CASE; rel: LDS, stk exec sec; home: 13 E 1100 N, PG; off: A-245 ASB, BYU.

GRAVES, BARBARA   principal Provo Canyon School; b: 7 May 1951; p: William & Betty Sanders Graves; ed: BA MEd BYU; former: tchr Provo Canyon School 7 yrs, acting ed dir; career: Outstanding Teaching Serv Award 1978; rel: LDS, Relief Soc tchr & presidency, primary tchr; home: 673 W 1800 N; off: Box 1441.

GRAY, HOWARD RICHARD   assoc prof Recreation Mgt & Youth Ldrship; b: 5 Oct 1944; m: Sharon Reed; p: Elmo Austin & Nadine Dunn; c: Sheridan 13, Austin 12, Jordan 8, Mardi 5; ed: PhD 1977 Penn State U; Omicron Delta Kappa; former: chm Recreation & Leisure Serv, Radford Virginia U; career: Outstanding Board Member, Viriginia Special Olympics 1979; Natl Accreditation Council, Visitiation Team to Long Beach State U 1982, San Diego State U 1981; mem: Natl Recreation & Parks Assn; Amer Assn of Health, Physical Ed & Dance; award: Eagle Scout; Duty to God; Outstanding Teaching; publ: editor *Leisure Insights;* 40 papers & articles; civic: v-chm Policy Recreation Com; v-chm Virginia Special Olympics; dir Utah Senior Festival; mil: Utah Natl Guard, Radio Specialist; rel: LDS, h council, branch pres, bishopric; home: 181 E 300 N, Orem; off 273-M RB, BYU.

GROSJEAN, ALBERT C   jeweler Grosjean's Diamonds; b: 28 Mar 1907; m: Verrell; c: Glenn C, Maxine McIntosh; ed: business admin accounting Utah State U; accounting Columbia U; Gemological Inst of Amer; former: Sears,

Roebuck & Co, Provo, 31 yrs mgt; UTC instr business mgt 3 yrs; mem: Provo Chamber of Commerce; award: 2 Extension Awards, Lions Internatl; civic: former pres & dist govnr, Lions Internatl; pol: block chm Sen Jake Garn republican com; rel: LDS, stake auditor; home: 1956 N 360 E; off: 210 W 200 N RaLinda Bldg Suite 202.

GROVER, JERRY DEE   prof Industrial Ed; b: 29 Nov 1931; m: Kay; p: Ursel & Alice; c: Debra, Amy, Jeff, Kelly, Gay, CaraLee, Jerry, Tracy, Keith, Ken, Shawny, Stewart, Shad, Chase; ed: BS 1956 ME 1960 Utah State U; EdD 1968 BYU; former: tchr Montpelier High School, Idaho; Victor Valley Jr High, Calif; mem: AVA, UIEA, UVA, PDK, PKP, NIATC, NAIT, AIAA, ACITE; civic: scoutmaster, cubmaster; rel: LDS, h council, bishopric; home: Rt 2 Box 235, Spanish Fork; off: 230 SNLB, BYU.

GROVER, MARK LEROY   Latin Amer Studies Bibliographer BYU Library; b: 26 Jun 1947; m: Deborah S; p: M C & Irene Luke; c: Anthony Michal 5, Sylvia Irene 1; ed: BA MLIS BYU; MA PhD Indiana U; former: editorial asst Amer Historical Review; mem: Latin Amer Studies Assn; Seminar on the Acquisition of Latin Amer Library Materials Assn; publ: *The Catholic Left in Latin America;* mil: 1st Lt army Reserve; rel: LDS, 70s group ldr; home: 55 E 300 S, PG; off: 6210-D HBLL, BYU.

HAFEN, BRENT QUE   prof of Health Sci BYU; b: 17 Jul 1940; m: Sylvia Ann Jacobson; p: Max Wilford Holm & Shirley Clawson; c: Cory, Kenneth, Jennifer, Mark, Christy, John Matthew; ed: BS MS health sci U of Utah; PhD S Illinois U 1969; UCLA post-doc; Harvard Medical School; U of Calif at San Francisco; U of Colorado; Stanford U; former: territory mgr Wyeth Labs; dir Student Health Ctr, Bemidiju State College; instr Wisconsin State U & S Illinois U; pres Porta Pulse Corp; mem: Amer Assn of Trauma Specialists; Natl Assn of Emergency Medical Technicians; Amer Public Health Assn; Nutrition Today Soc; College Health Ed Com, Amer School Health Assn; Amer Social Health Assn; Amer Alliance for Health Ed; Natl Ctr of Health Ed; Eta Sigma Gamma; board Utah County Mental Health Assn; board Utah County Council on Drug Rehabilitation; publ: 35 books; 6 monographs; articles; presentations; assoc editor *Amer Journal of*

Health Ed; civic: advisory board Natl Ctr for Health Ed; chm board of trustees The Cottage Prog Internatl Inc; advisory board Utah State Div of Alcoholism & Drugs; board of dir Gathering Place Drug Rehabilitation Ctr; State Hospital Research Council; board Utah County Drug Abuse Council; BYU Ed Week speaker; co-dir Annual Inst of Criminal & Social Justice; Research Advisory Com Utah State Hospital; co-dir Emergency Medical Technician Training Prog; consul & dir workshops on drugs, community health, social problems, child abuse & neglect, suicidology, crisis intervention, alcohol, driving problems, interpersonal relationships; rel: LDS, branch pres, bishop, h council, stake presidency; home: 1269 N Grand Ave; off: 229-E RB, BYU.

HALES, ROBERT H   MD ophthalmology FACS; assoc prof U of Utah; instr BYU; ed: BS 1954 BYU; MD 1957 U of Utah; U of Calif; former: pres of staff Utah Valley Hospital; mem: diplomat Amer Board of Ophthalmology; board of trustee Utah State Medical Assn; pres Fredrick C Cordes Eye Soc; exec com, VP, Utah Acad of Continuing Medical Ed; exec com, board of trustees, VP, Utah Professional Review Org; pres Utah State Medical Assn; del Amer Medical Assn; pres Utah Ophthalmological Soc; board of councillors Amer Acad of Ophthalmology; coor council Health Systems Agcy; publ: *Contact Lenses: A Clinical Approach to Fitting;* 19 articles; civic: Board of Governor's Utah Medical Insurance Assn; exec com, v-chm, Utah State Driver License Medical Advisory Board; pres Utah County Cancer Soc; off: 1275 N University Ave.

HALL, BLAINE H   Humanities Librarian BYU; b: 12 Dec 1932 m: Carol S; p: James O & Effie Hill; c: Suzanne 19, Cheryl 17, Derek 14; ed: MA Amer Lit; Master of Library Sci BYU; Phi Kappa Phi; former: instr of English BYU; career: H W Wilson & Amer Library Assn Library Periodical Award 1976 as editor of Utah Library Assn journal *Utah Libraries;* mem: Utah Library Assn; Mountain Plains Library Assn; Amer Library Assn; Children's Lit Assn of Utah; Orem Public Library Board of Trustees; publ: co-author *Using the Library: the Card Catalog;* editor *Utah Libraries & MPLA Newsletter;* mil: US Army 1953-4; Commendation Ribbon with Medal Pendant; rel:

LDS, clerk; home: 230 E 1910 S, Orem; off: 5226 HBLL, BYU.

HALL, JOHN FRANKLIN III   asst prof of classics BYU; b: 14 Apr 1951; m: Pamela Fillerup; c: John 5, James 3, Jefferson 1; ed: BA Summa Cum Laude & Highest Honors BYU; MA PhD Univ of Pennsylvania ancient history; BYU Hinckley Scholar, University Scholar, Phi Kappa Phi; mem: Amer Assn of Ancient Historians; Amer Philological Assn; Classical Assn of Midwest & South; Amer Classical League; publ: articles in professional & academic journals; rel: LDS; home: 1387 Locust Ln; off: A-202 JKBA, BYU.

HALLADAY, ANN   supvr Ed Placement BYU; b: 16 Jul 1938; p: Vilate J & Wilford Meeks Halladay; ed: BS MEd BYU; current doct student; academic scholarship; former: elementary & special ed tchr; mem: ASCUS; former mem local, state & natl tchr assns; publ: article in *Journal of Staffing* ASCUS; rel: LDS, youth tchr; club: Yesharah; Cougar Club; home: 3672 N Canyon Rd; off: D-240 ASB, BYU.

HAMMOND, ROY B   physician and surgeon; m: Anita S; p: May C & Clyde A; c: Roy A, Kristine Shipman, Richard, Robert; ed: BS BYU, MD George Washington U; mem: Amer Med Assn, Utah State Med Assn; former pres Utah County Med Assn; former pres Utah Valley Hospital Staff; former mem Utah County Board of Health; Med Adv Utah County Draft Board; mem Board of Dir, Central Bank & Trust Co; mil: Utah Natl Guard; US Air Force; Flight Surgeon, World War II, New Guinae Theater, South Pacific; rel: LDS; club: former pres Riverside Country Club; home: 60 E Marrcrest S; off: 10 S 300 E.

HANCOCK, EUGENE MERRILL   dietitian, BYU Food Serv asst mgr Morris Cafe; b: 14 Feb 1939; m: Barbara Jean Anderson; p: Clawson B & Margaret A Poulsen; c: Susan 15, Douglas 13, Jean 12, Rebecca 10, Amanda 5, Rachel 3; ed: BS foods & nutrition 1966 BYU; former: ass mgr U of New Mexico Food Serv; mem: Amer Dietetic Assn, registered dietitian; mil: US Army Reserve; rel: LDS, elders pres, 70s pres, ward clerk, exec sec, sunday school pres; home: 535 N 1025 W, Orem; off: Morris Cafeteria, BYU.

HANSEN, H REESE   assoc dean & prof BYU Law School;
b: 8 Apr 1942; m: Katheryn Traveller; p: Howard F &
Loila Gayle; c: Brian T 18, Mark T 17, Dale T 14, Curtis T
11; ed: BS honors 1964 Utah State U; JD 1972 U of Utah;
Phi Kappa Phi; Order of Coif; Herbert M Schiller
Memorial Scholarship; Grad Research Fellow 1971-2;
former: atty Strong, Poelman & Fox, SLC 1972-4; mgt
Mtn State Telephone Co 1964-69; mem: Utah State Bar;
chm Services Com Law School Admissions Council; dir
Law School Admissions Serv Inc; board of litigation Mtn
States Legal Found; exec dir Sect on Prelaw & Admissions
to Law School, Assn of Amer Law Schools; publ: co-auth
Idaho Probate System; Utah Probate System; revision
editor *Manual for Justices of the Peace, State of Utah;*
rel: LDS, stake presidency, bishop; club: Provo Jaycees;
Timp Lions Club; home: 447 E Stadium Ave; off: 342
JRCB, BYU.

HANSEN, LEE DUANE   prof of Chemistry BYU; b: 13
Apr 1940; m: Judith Woolstenhulme; p: Alva Duane &
Mary Froerer; c: Velinda Dawn 20, Thea Jo 18, Clifford
Wayne 17, Judith Aleta 15, Jared Reed 12, Karina Ann 10,
Jeremiah James 7, Timothy Alva 5, Benjamin Lee 3; ed:
BS chemistry 1962 BYU; PhD chemistry 1965 BYU;
former: Prof of Chemistry U of New Mexico, Albuquerque
1965-72; mem: Sigma Xi; AAAS; publ: 80 journal articles;
1 book; several chapters in professional books; civic: Boy
Scouts of Amer; rel: LDS, scouting coor; home: 1937 S
Main, Orem; off: 267 FB, BYU.

HANSEN, RONALD G   pres Eyring Research Inst Inc; b:
23 May 1924; m: Merrel Carter; p: Leo & Merle; c: Sandra
Wamsley, Ronald C, Julie Ann Kruitmoes, Karen Sue
Bancroft, Hettie Ann Scott, Melinda Sue, Melanie Ann
Evans, Pamela; ed: BS bacteriology and public health 1949
Utah State Agricultural College; MA speech & hearing
1950, PhD speech sci 1954 Ohio State U; prof Speech &
Hearing Pathology; Distinguished Serv Award 1973;
former: Provost for Res and Assoc Dean of Grad School
Southern Illinois U 1965-73; Dir of Applied Sci at
Technology Inc, Dayton, Ohio 1963-5; Chief Progs Div
Aerospace Medical Div; Chief Audiology Lab, School of
Aviation Medicine; Chief Biological Acoustics, Aerospace
Medical Lab; Chief Acoustics, Aeromedical Lab; mem:

Acoustical Soc of Amer; Amer Speech & Hearing Assn; Aerospace Medical Assn; Illinois Speech & Hearing Assn; exec com Natl Council of univ Res Administrators; Council of Deans; Sigma Xi; Governor of Illinois Reg Medical Advisory Group; Boy Scouts of Amer; publ: 53 publ; editorial staff Journal of Occupational Medicine; civic: VP & Dir Provo Chamber of Commerce; VP & Dir United Way of Utah County; VP & Dir Provo Kiwanis; Dir Provo Cultural Affairs Commission; mil: Flying WW II; 15 yrs aerospace medical research; military serv schools in radio, gunnery, instr course 1942; Air Medal, 5 Oak Leaf Clusters; 5 Campaign Award; Distinguished Serv Award; rel: LDS; dist pres, bishopric, h council; home: 1081 S Carterville Rd, Orem; off: 1455 W 820 N.

HARDY, DOUGLAS KIRKMAN   owner R Spencer Hines Restaurant & Catering; b: 16 Jul 1945; p: Horace H & Lynne Kirkman; c: Heather Lynne 8, Holly Ann 6, Troy Brandon 5, Whitney Marquette 4, Cameron Paige 3; ed: BS BYU; former: Provo & SL real estate development; San Francisco restaurant mgt; career: Utah Holiday Magazine "7 Finest Restaurants in Utah"; Utah Heritage Found Award of Merit; mem: Beehive State Chefs Assn; Amer Culinary Fed of New York; Utah Heritage Found; Utah Historic Soc; award: Provo City Annual Beautification Award; R Spencer Hines Natl Historic Landmark Trust for Historic Preservation, Washington DC; civic: Provo & SL Area Chamber of Commerce; BYU Student Govt; pol: republican; mil: Vetern 19th Special Forces US Army Airborne Medic; Green Beret; rel: LDS, tchr, YSI, welfare farm coord; club: Alumnus BYU Young Men & Samuel Hall Soc; home: 949 E 1120 S, Orem; off: 125 S 400 W.

HARMON, C J   pres Harmon's Inc Cadillac Pontiac; chm of board Far West Bank; b: 11 Dec 1922; m: Ruth Ercanbrack; p: Clarence H & Myrl L; c: Brant, Linda, Mark, Hal, Gina; ed: grad BYU in accounting & business admin (finance & banking); grad Gen Motors Inst bus mgt; former: owner Harmon motor Co, Spanish Fork; career: Pontiac & Cadillac Dealer Councils; factory sales awards; mem: former VP Utah Automobile Dealers Assn; civic: BYU Presidents Club; BYU Cougar Club; Governor's Council on Consumer Affairs; Provo City Airport Board; mil: US Air Force 1st Lt; lead pilot with 567th bomb squad 389th bomb group B-24 bombers WW II; grad Officers Training Prog; Air Medals; rel: LDS; club: former Rotarian; former pres Riverside Country Club; home: 1570 Willow Ln.

HARMON, FRANK W   prof of Elementary Ed BYU; b: 23 Nov 1925; m: Ruth R; p: Frank N & Lillie E; c: Brent R, Craig R, Lori, Richard, Carol; ed: BS 1952 MS 1956 U of Utah; EdD 1963 Columbia Univ; BS high honors; World Book Scholarship 1960; former: tchr Davis County 1952-6, Great Neck, NY 1956-60, Queens College 1961-3; career: consultant to USOE Follow Through 1968-72; mem: UEA, DEA, NEA, GNEA, Phi Delta Kappa; AST; award: Provo Peak Scouting Award; publ: articles; civic: ldr neighborhood opposition to Cedarcrest Apt construction; pol: state conv del; mil: US Navy 1943-6; Appropriate Conduct, Pacific Theatre, Victory Medal; rel: LDS, bishop, h council, stake presidency; home: 1393 Apple; off: 210-D MCKB, BYU.

HARMON, RONDO S   asst prof Indian Ed; b: 14 June 1919; m: June R; p: Walter S & Laprele Tolman; c: Lynda Jane, Rondo Jr, Richard (Dick), Kent, Debra, Phillip; foster: Henry John Joe, Nora John Joe; ed: BS 1949 Masters 1952 BYU; grad work Stanford, U of Utah, U of Colorado; former: tchr; principal; sup church schools, Tongan Islands; chm BYU Indian Ed Dept; career: BYU Indian Student "Earned Your Feather Award" 1974; mem: Phi Delta Kappa; publ: *Biography of Joseph Byron Smith;* civic: mem of Power Board, Tongan Govt; mil: Field Artillery WW II; rel: LDS, bishopric, stake mission pres, h council; club: Lions; home: 631 S 1500 E; off: 137 BRMB, BYU.

HAROLDSEN, EDWIN OLIVER   prof of Communications BYU; b: 22 Apr 1918; m: Kathryn Baird; p: George Arthur & Catherine Smith; c: Mark O, Jon Scott, Suzanne, Jay B, Michelle; ed: BS econ 1943 high honors MS journalism 1956 U of Utah; PhD 1967 Iowa State U; Phi Kappa Phi; former: Chicago reg editor US News & World Report; econ editor, Iowa State U staff writer, SL Tribune, Deseret News, United Press Internatl; career: Natl Plant Food Award for Distinguished Agricultural Journalism 1966; mem: Soc of Professional Journalists; publ: co-auth

Roots of the Farm Problem; A Taxonomy of Concepts in Communication; magazine articles; civic: former board mem Utah Valley Chapter Amer Red Cross; Utah Valley Symphony; Utah County Beautification Com; mil: US Maritime Serv, WWII; rel: LDS, bishop, h council, dist pres, sunday school tchr; club: former Kiwanis Club; home: 2827 Arapahoe Ln; off: F-537 HFAC, BYU.

HARPER, KIMBALL TAYLOR   prof of Botany & Range Sci; b: 15 Feb 1931; m: Caroline Frances Stepp; p: John Mayo & Mary Ella Overson; c: Ruth Lynne, James Kimball, Gay Annette, Denise Caroline, Karla Diane, Steven Stepp; ed: BS 1958 MS 1960 BYU; PhD 1963 U of Wisconsin, Madison; grad BYU Very High Honors; Phi Kappa Phi; Natl Sci Found grad fellowship; former: range technician US Forest Serv 1957; range scientist US Forest Serv Intermtn Forest & Range Experiment Station 1958-9; asst & assoc prof of biology U of Utah 1963-73; dept chm BYU 1963-6; career: Karl G Maeser Distinguished Research Award 1979; mem: fellow Amer Assn for the Advancement of Sci; Botanical Soc of Amer; Sigma Xi Soc; Soc for Range Mgt; Ecological Soc of Amer; British Ecological Soc; Utah Acad of Sci, Arts & Letters; Soc for the Study of Evolution, Calif Botanical Soc; publ: 100 publ; pol: Republican; mil: US Army Signal Corps 1953-4, Korea; Cycle Scholastic Award; rel: LDS, h council, bishop; home: 410 S 300 E, Spanish Fork; off: 489 WIDB, BYU.

HARRIS, JAMES M   prof BYU; b: 29 Jul 1926; m: Delores Hug; p: Everett C & Clarabelle R; c: James G, Michael J, Susan Hansen, Linda, Steven, Leilani, Heidi; ed: BS 1952 Utah State U; MS 1953 Utah State U; PhD 1955 ed phych, Cornell U; Phi Beta Kappa, Utah State U 1952; former: school psychologist, Denver 1952; State Ed Psychologist, Hawaii 1969-70; dir Pupil Personnel Services, Clovis Schools, Calif 1975-6; mem: Phi Kappa Phi Natl Assn of School Psychologists; publ: *Building Your Child's Self-Esteem;* mil: 1st Lt US Air Force; Good Conduct, Sharpshooter; rel: LDS elder's quorum pres, clerk; home: 635 Sagewood Ave; off: 320-E MCKB, BYU.

HARRIS, MARILYN T   image consultant; owner Avedon Hair Specialists; b: 2 Aug 1938; m: Robert E; p: Blaine F

& Edna Starr Thorpe; c: Stuart, Roxanne, Lisa, Caren, Nathan, Kirt, Sara, Weston; ed: 1 yr BYU; scholarships on academic GPA; former: co-founder Success Perceptions Image Consultants; owner Merle Norman Cosmetic Studio, Univ Mall; owner fabric stores; 1st place Utah State Clairol Color Contest; mem: Natl Hair Dressers Assn; publ: book in progess on color & image; pol: image & advertising consul to Utah Senators, Congressmen & local candidates; rel: LDS, Sisters Personal Development, Board of Dir, MTC; club: former pres Utah Assn of Women, Provo Dist; home: 5366 N Edgewood Dr; off: 669 E 800 N.

HARRIS, R KELLY   asst VP Commercial Security Bank; b: 29 Jan 1956; m: Denise; p: Raymond & Joyce; c: Holly Anne 2; ed: BS marketing BYU; mem: Utah Industrial Development Executives Assn; award: Utah Jaycee of the Yr 1980-1; civic: VP Provo Chamber of Commerce; officer Utah County United Way; 1981 chm Red Cross Fundraiser; rel: Provo Community Church, diaconate board mem, church auditor; club: Provo Jaycees pres 1981-2; Cougar Club; home: 353 W 205 N; off: 207 N Univ Ave.

HARRIS, ROBERT E   Hearing Aid Audiologist; business owner; b: 15 Mar 1933; m: Marilyn T; p: Carl V & Norma B; c: Stuart, Roxanne, Lisa, Caren, Nathan, Kirt, Sara, Weston; ed: 3 yrs BYU; publ: produced 2 full-length hunting movies; mil: US Army 2 yrs Japan; rel: LDS, bishopric, branch pres Provo Boys School; club: Sertoma; home: 5366 N Edgewood Dr; off: 330 W Center.

HARRISON, B(ERTRAND) KENT   prof of Physics BYU; b: 21 Jul 1934; m: Janyce M(axfield); p: Bertrand F & Lorna J; c: Alan K, Neil B, Paul E, Mary Ellen; ed: BS 1955 BYU; MA 1957 PhD 1959 Princeton U; Valedictorian BYU 1955; Phi Kappa Phi; Phi Eta Sigma; NSF Predoctoral Fellow 1955-6; former: staff Los Alamos Sci Lab 1959-64; sr resident research assoc Jet Propulsion Lab 1968-70; career: Outstanding Tchr Award BYU Continuing Ed 1982; chm BYU Physics & Astronomy Dept 1972-9; chm BYU Faculty Advisory Council 1975-6; NSF research grants 1965-77, 80-2; mem: Amer Physical Soc; Utah Acad of Sci, Arts & Letters; New York Acad of Sci; Sigma Xi, pres-elect BYU chapter; award: Provo Peak

Award, Boy Scouts of Amer; Cubmaster's Key; publ: co-auth *Gravitational Theory and Gravitational Collapse;* 31 papers, abstracts, chapters in books, and book reviews; civic: 13 yrs serv in Cub and Boy Scouts; organizer & chm MX Concerned Citizens of Central Utah 1980-1; pres Provo Peak Scouters 1978-9; pol: Republican voting dist chm, county & state del; rel: LDS, stake missionary, 70s pres, stake clerk, h council, bishop; club: Provo Timp Lions; home: 380 E 4380 N; off: 285 ESC, BYU.

HARRISON, BETTY DODGE   Prof Ed Psychology BYU; b: 1 Nov 1928; p: Harold & Marion Holden Dodge; c: Rosemary, Brent; ed: BS MS PhD 1965 BYU; scholarships; magna cum laude; Phi Kappa Phi; former: initiator & coor Ed Center BYU; career: Outstanding Educators of Amer 1975; World Who's Who of Women 1973; Medallion Award ACLD; mem: Council for Exceptional Children; Assn for Children with Learning Disabilities; award: Reader's Digest Scholar 1946; publ: "Worry Children" workbook & video tapes; Dial-A-Skill; civic: pres Uintalands Board; Utah State Board of Ed Advisory Com for Handicapped; rel: LDS, stake sunday school board 12 yrs, Relief Soc tchr; club: AAUW; home: 1495 N 1880 W; off: 332-C MCKB, BYU.

HART, EDWARD LeROY   prof of English BYU; b: 28 Dec 1916; m: Eleanor Coleman; p: Alfred A & Sarah C; c: E Richard, Paul L, Barbara Dixon, Patricia; ed: BS 1939 U of Utah; MA 1941 U of Mich; PhD 1950 Oxford U; Rhodes Scholarship 1939; Phi Beta Kappa 1939; Phi Kappa Phi 1966; Charles Redd Award in Humanities, Utah Acad 1976; Coll of Human Disting Fac Award 1977; former: instr U of Utah 1946; asst prof U of Wash 1949-52; visiting prof U of Calif at Berkeley 1959-60; Ariz State, summer 1968; career: Amer Council of Learned Societies Fellow 1942; Utah Inst of Fine Arts Awards 1963, 73, 75; Fullbright Sr Lecturer in Pakistan 1973-4; Amer Philosophical Soc Fellow 1964; BYU Karl G Maeser Creative Arts Award 1968; Found for Economic Ed Fellowship 1956; P A Christensen Memorial Lecture 1982; listed in Who's Who in Amer 1982; mem: Modern Language Assn of Amer; Amer Soc for 18th Century Studies; Rocky Mtn Modern Language Assn; Utah Acad; publ: *Minor Lives; Instruction and Delight; Mormon In Motion; Jo*

Utah; Poems of Praise; other articles & poems; civic: mem of board Utah Arts Council 1977-84; pol: local Democratic activities; mil: Lt sg USNR 1942-6, Intelligence, Japanese language; Unit Citation; rel: LDS, bishop; home: 1401 Cherry Ln; off: A-230 JKBA, BYU.

HATCH, MARY GAY   dir Early Childhood Ed Prog; b: 6 Apr 1934; p: William Arthur & Mary Ellen Ott; ed: BS BYU; MA Arizona State U; post grad U of Utah; former: dist sup Provo School Dist; specialist State Board of Ed; instr U of Utah; tchr Jordan & Alpine School Dist; career: Professional Award 1975 Utah County Mental Health Assn; mem: Council for Exceptional Children; AAMD; NEA; UEA; PEA; ASH; Mental Health Assn; Utah Assn of Retarted Citizens; publ: TMR Guide and EMR Guide, State of Utah; civic: pres Utah Valley Care & Training Board of Dir; rel: LDS, sec to bishop, tchr, counselor, youth; club: Cougar Club; home: 1664 Lakewood Dr, Orem; off: 815 N 800 W.

HAWKINS, CLYDE WEST   asst mgr BYU Married Housing; b: 18 Apr 1945; m: Lorraine Hasler; p: O Earl & Ruby W; c: Claine H 9, Casey 8, Crystal 6, Cameron 3, Corey 1; ed: BS youth leadership 1970 BYU; former: dist exec Boy Scouts of Amer; award: Woodbadge BSA; civic: Lions Club; mil: Utah Natl Guard; rel: LDS, scoutmaster, activities dir; home: 556 N 500 E, Orem; off: C-141 ASB, BYU.

HAWKINS, LARAE K   ticket mgr Marriott Ctr BYU; b: 17 Mar 1935; m: Harold J; p: Odeal C & Hazel K; c: Anne, Lynne, Kim; ed: BS BYU; Scholastic Fraternity; former: sec US Govt in Iran; sec BYU; civic: United Fund Board of Dir 3 yrs; rel: LDS, YW pres 6 yrs, Relief Soc ldr 2 yrs, Sunday School sec 4 yrs; home: 1536 S 850 E, Orem; off: 2132 MC, BYU.

HAYES, DARWIN L   assoc prof of English; b: 2 Aug 1930; m: Loris E Johnson; p: Lyle & Mildred Egli; c: John Robert, Karl, Terri Anne, David Paul, Thomas, Jennifer Lynn; ed: BA MA English BYU; grad study N Carolina A&T State U; former: English tchr Montpelier Idaho; dir of English Composition BYU; dir & founder of Writing Lab BYU; sr author TICCIT English BYU; mem: Utah Folklore

80   Prominent Men & Women of Provo 1983

Soc; Natl Council of Tchrs of English; Rocky Mtn Modern Language Assn; Utah Acad of Sci, Arts & Letters; publ: *Review of Boontling: An American Lingo by CC Adams Folklore;* mil: US Army 1953-5; Good Conduct Medal; rel: LDS, bishopric, h council, branch pres; home: 29 S 400 E, Springville; off: A-286 JKBA, BYU.

HECKMANN, RICHARD A   prof of Zoology BYU; b: 7 Dec 1931; m: Karen Lynn Olsen; p: William C & Olivea A; c: Lisa 17, Nancy 15, Amy 13, Adam 8, Camille 5; ed: BS 1954 MS 1958 zoology Utah State U; U of Calif Davis; U of Pacific, Stockton; U of Hawaii; Natl Sci Found Inst, U of Washington; Natl Sci Found Inst, U of Calif Berkeley; PhD 1970 Montana State U; Carl Raymond Grey Scholarship; Pauley Res Fellowship; Natl Sci Found Fellowships, Traineeships & Res Grants; Faculty Res Awards; Utah Natural Resources Grant; former: acct prof Calif State U; consul Westinghouse, Central Utah Project, BLM, Vaughn Hansen Assoc, Niagara Chemical Co, Forest Serv, Nielsen, Maxwell & Wangsgaard Engineers, Noorlander Corp; dir Res Team to Guatemala; career: Outstanding Educators of Amer 1972; cert as Fisheries Scientist by Amer Fisheries Soc 1971; BYU Prof of the Month 1974; honored by Alpha Chapter PreDental Soc 1974; Amer Men of Sci Who's Who in the West; BYU Rank Advancement Com; mem: Amer Inst of Fishery Res Biologists; pres Fish Health Section AFS; Soc of Protozoologists; Soc of Parasitologists; Amer Fisheries Soc; Wildlife Disease Assn; Amer Inst of Fishery Res Biologists; World Mariculture Soc; Comparative Invertebrate Pathology Soc; publ: 67 publs; editorial board *Calif Fish & Game Magazine, Journal Wildlife Diseases,* two publ co, *Great Basin Naturalist,* Trans AFS; mil: US Army artillary 1st Lt; rel: LDS, bishop, h council, stake mission presidency; home: 603 E 4300 N; off: 153 WIDB, BYU.

HEINER, BARTA LEE   actress; tchr; dir; playwright; b: 7 Feb 1949; p: H Bartley & Laverne Farr; ed: BA BYU; MFA Amer Conservatory Theatre; former: faculty BYU Theatre Dept; assoc producer Sherwood Shakespeare Theatre; dir 3 plays for BYU & Utah Valley Repertory; career: Cameo & Best Supporting Actress WSC; 2 Best Actress BYU; Best Supporting & Best Actress, Glendale Centre Theatre; Upcomer's Award, Hollywood Forum

Club; mem: Screen Actor's Guild; Actor's Equity Assn; publ: *Diantha...A Pioneer Portait;* rel: LDS, tchr, Cultural Arts Rep; club: Theta Alpha Phi; DAR; home: 483 Canyon Rd, Ogden; off: BYU Theatre Dept.

HEINER, RONALD A   Prof of Economics BYU; b: 27 Nov 1950; m: Marilyn; p: Ralph & Mona; c: Jessica 6, Cameron 4, Laura 2, Daniel 1; ed: PhD economics UCLA; Elliot Jones Award, Western Economic Assn 1974; mem: Phi Beta Kappa; publ: "A Reformulation of the Law of Demand"; "The Collective Decision Problem and a Theory of Preference"; "Length & Cycle Equalization"; "The Necessity of Christ's Messianic Role"; "Theory of the Firm in Short Run Industry Equilibrium"; rel: LDS; home: 1054 E Dover Dr; off: 700 SWKT, BYU.

HEMINGWAY, MICHAEL F   Sr Producer KBYU-TV; pres Glenthorne Productions; b: 20 Feb 1951; m: Lee Ann W; p: D W Hemingway; c: 3 boys; ed: BA 1978 BYU; former: audio engineer Osmond Studios; freelance film production; rel: LDS, scoutmaster, sunday school tchr; home: 601 E 1000 S, PG; off: C-302 HFAC, BYU.

HENSTROM, RICHARD HENRY   assoc dean Div of Continuing Ed BYU; b: 26 Jun 1928; m: Martha C Adams; p: Henry Hamuel & Relia Strong Best; c: Shelley Leigh, David Richard, Alexander Paul, William Lee, Douglas Kimball, Michael James, Robyn Louise; ed: BFA U of Utah; MFA U of Utah; EdD BYU; former: KLUB Radio; KSL Radio TV; KLOR TV newcaster; 25 yrs with BYU admin; career: serv awards from AEA-USA, Mtn Plains AEA, ALTAH AEA; listed in Outstanding Educators in Amer, Men of Achievement, Dictionary of Internatl Biography, Leaders in Ed; mem: Adult Ed Assn of USA; Mtn Plains Adult Ed Assn; Utah Adult Ed Assn; Natl Univ Continuing Ed Assn; award: Freedoms Found Award; publ: articles & phamplets; civic: State of Utah Task Force on Vocational, Technical, Community Serv, Cont Ed 1975-80; pol: Republican county & state del; mil: US Army Chaplain 1953-5 Korean Serv; Army Reserves 6 yrs; serv awards; rel: LDS, bishop, stake clerk, h council, Church Adult Correlation & Review Coms; hom: 2466 N 930 E; off: 397 HCEB, BYU.

HEPPLER, THONE K   banker Zions First Natl Bank; b: 23

Sep 1948; m: Dessa Lee; c: Justin 5, Rhett 3, Heather 1; ed: BS business mgt BYU; Pacific Coast Banking School, Seattle, Wash; Academic & Ldrship Scholarship BYU; former: mgr Utah Natl Office, asst mgr University Office, Zions First Natl Bank; mem: Amer Inst of Bankers; Utah County Bankers; civic: pres elect Provo Chamber of Commerce; rel: LDS, bishop, clerk; home: 1038 E 680 N, Orem; off: 111 N 200 W.

HERLIN, WAYNE RICHARD   prof of Gen Studies BYU; b: 20 May 1928; m: Joan Isbell; p: M Arnold & Leone Elizabeth Hooper; c: Richard Kent, Kenneth Wayne, William Reed, Thomas Rex, Rebecca; ed: BA English; MA Education; PhD Ed Psychology; former: tchr, counselor, SLC schools; mem: Amer Personnel & Guidance Assn; Phi Delta Kappa; Internatl Reading Assn; Natl Reading Conf; Western College Reading Assn; publ: co-author: *Critical Reading; Successful Study Skills; Improving Reading Speed and Comprehension;* civic: scouting; pol: neighborhood dist ldr & state del; mil: US Army, Reserve, Tech Sgt; rel: LDS, bishop, stake mission pres, MTC branch pres; home: 526 E 900 S, Orem; off: 3126 HBLL, BYU.

HERMANSEN, MERRILL L   Admin Judge 3rd Dist Juvenile Court; b: 11 May 1922; m: Jean L Pehrson; p: Lawrence & Sarah Jane Allred; c: five; ed: Snow College; BS accounting 1951 JD 1953 U of Utah; tribune & v-dean Delta Theta Phi; Dale Carnegie course on human relations; former: tchr Malad Idaho High School; SLC court clerk; candidate Sanpete County Attorney; City Attorney for Manti, Redmond, Centerfield, Salina, Ephraim; Judge 4th Dist Juvenile Court; judge Orem City Court; presiding judge State Juvenile Court System; State Advisory Council on Child Abuse & Neglect; career: Cert of Merit for Outstanding Work on Traffic Court to Orem City by Amer Bar Assn; Award by Natl Assn of Municipal Judges; KSL Award for Traffic Safety; mem: pres Utah Council of Juvenile Court Judges; VP & sec Utah Council of City Court Judges; chm Standing Com on Legislation for Board of Juvenile Court Judges; chm Reg 4 Law Enforcement Planning Assn Council; Utah State Bar Assn; Amer Bar Assn; Amer Judicature Soc; sec Southern Bar Assn; Natl Council of Juvenile Court Judges; Utah County Bar Assn; Southern Utah Peace Officers Assn; Natl Ed

Assn; Idaho Ed Assn; civic: chm of board Utah Council of Drug Abuse Rehabilitation & Ed; chm Tri-County Council of Drug Abuse; Mtnland Assn of Govts Task Force; Children & Youth Advisory Council, Div of Mental Health; consultant Health & Welfare Commission State PTA; chm Sanpete County Polio March of Dimes; sec Ephraim Jr Chamber of Commerce; mil: Utah Natl Guard; Army Reserve Corp; rel: LDS; club: dir Ephraim Lions Club; pres Snow College Alumni Assn; Ephraim Sportsman Club; South Central Utah Knife & Fork Club; dir & pres Orem Kiwanis Club; home 734 S 590 E, Orem; off: Utah County Bldg.

HERNDON, DARLENE MONTEAUX   health counselor & instr BYU; coor health care with agcy PHS clinics; family nurse practitioner; b: 21 Sep 1934; c: Renee Ficklin, James Herndon; ed: BS nursing BYU 1977; masters work BYU; Dean's Scholarship Award 1976-7; career: Who's Who in Amer Colleges & Univ 1977; mem: Utah Nurses Assn; Amer Indian Nurses Assn; Phi Kappa Phi; civic: health workshops Indian Reservations; rel: LDS; home: 98 E 600 S No. 12; off: 160 BRMB, BYU.

HERRIN, C SELBY   research assoc & data processing mgr, ML Bean Museum BYU; b: 16 May 1939; m: Vila Jean; p: Charles Curtis & Wyllodeene Selby; c: Rebecca Kay 18, Michael Jay 16, ViAna Ruth 15, Lauralie 13, Deena Delaine 12, Daniel Selby 8, Thomas Curtis 7, Jeannie Mignon 4; ed: BS 1963 MS 1966 BYU; PhD 1969 Ohio State U; Predoctoral Acarology Traineeship, Ohio State U; former: research assoc U of Georga Dept of Entomology; research assoc Georgia Southern College Dept of Biology; research assoc & proj dir BYU; proj dir & special projs consul BYU Research Div & Computer Serv; mem: Acarological Soc of Amer; publ: sr author 13 papers; jr author 4 papers; rel: LDS, bishop, h council; home: 920 W 1020 S; off: 378 MLBM, BYU.

HESS, WILFORD M "BILL"   prof of Botany BYU, dir Electron Optics Lab; b: 18 Feb 1934; m: Carlene B Falkenburg; p: Lewis William & Arvilla M; c: Carl Zane 18, Carla Ann 13; ed: BS BYU; MS PhD Oregon State U; Purdue U; Oak Ridge Inst of Nuclear Studies; U of Texas; Swiss Fed Inst of Tech; Career Development Award,

Natl Inst of Health 1969-74; Karl G Maeser Research Award 1972; Sigma Xi Lectures 1974-5; pres BYU Phi Kappa Phi 1979-81; Faculty College Achievement Award 1979; former: research asst US Dept of Agriculture 1958 & Oregon State U 1959-62; asst prof BYU 1962-6; assoc prof BYU 1966-71; mem: Internatl Soc of Plant Pathology; Phi Kappa Phi; Sigma Xi; Amer Phytopathological Soc; Botanical Soc of Amer; Mycological Soc of Amer; Amer Assn for Adv of Sci; Amer Soc for Cell Biology; Electron Microscopy Soc of Amer; publ: over 100 sci papers, review articles, edited books & manuals; civic: Provo City Neighborhood com 10 yrs; scout & cub masters; mil: US Army 1957; rel: LDS, bishopric, stake & ward sunday school pres; high priest group ldr; home: 670 E 2780 N; off: 245 WIDB, BYU.

HICKMAN, DON RUE Brig Gen US Army (ret.); b: 16 Feb 1918; m: LoRee; p: Don F & Julia; c: DeAnn Giles, Mary Higbee, Pamela Norris, Judy Clark; ed: BA Northern Ariz U 1941, Grad Harvard Adv Mgt 1967; US Command & Gen Staff College, Ft Levenworth, Kansas; US Army War College; Advanced Infantry Officer Course, Ft Benning, GA; former: prof Mil Sci, Reno Nev High School; Chief of Plans Hqs, Ft MacArthur, Calif, Plans Officer, US Caribbean Command, Canal Zone; Career Mgt Div, Adjutant General's Office; Sr Adv Imperial Iranian Army Infantry Ctr, Shiraz, Iran; Chief, Mobilization Plans Branch, The Pentagon; Chief of Infantry Branch, The Pentagon; Deputy Chief of Staff, Personnel & Admin, Vietnam; Deputy Chief of Staff, Personnel Hqs, US Continental Army Command, Ft Monroe; mem: Dir, Utah Valley Bank; mil: 31 yrs US Army, Private to Brig Gen; 32 awards, incl Distinguished Service medal, Legion of Merit, 2 Silver Stars, 4 Bronze Stars, 6 air medals; rel: LDS, h council, bishopric, dist pres; club: Kiwanis; former pres, Cougar Club; home: 2891 Iroquois Dr; off: 750 N 200 W.

HILL, DEBRA L coach BYU Women's Gymnastics Team; b: 27 Jun 1952; m: Rodney C; p: Robert & Alberta Stark; c: Rodney C Jr 16, Troy Rodney 6, Lara Lee Marguerite 3; former: owner & coach Denver School of Gymnastics for Girls 10 yrs; career: All Amer in Gymnastics 1970; Most Inspirational Athlete in Colorado 1977; Outstanding Gymnast by Rocky Mtn AAU 1971; Outstanding

Contribution to Colorado Gymnastics 1974; mem: 1970 US Worlds Games Team; 1972 US Olympic Team; 1973 US Pre-Worlds Games Team; US Natl Team 1970-4; rel: LDS, tchr; home: 491 E 1090 N, Orem; off: 105 RB, BYU.

HILL, GARTH A   assoc prof Industrial Ed; b: 4 Apr 1933; m: Harriet B; p: F LeRoy; c: Ron, Roxann, David, Lynette, Gordon, Justin; ed: BS MS BYU; PhD Colorado State Univ; former: Industrial Arts Trade & Industrial Specialist, Utah State Board of Ed; career: Industrial Arts Tchr of the Year 1967-8; UVA Service Award 1971-5; AVA Region V Service Award 1978; mem: life mem Amer Vocational Assn; Amer Industrial Arts Assn; Utah Vocational Assn; Phi Delta Kappan; Iota Lumba Sigma; Utah Industrial Ed Assn; civic: Salem City Council 4 yrs; scoutmaster 4 yrs; scouting 25 yrs; mil: US Army; rel: LDS, bishop, h council; home: 55 W Lake View Dr, Salem; off: 230 SNLB, BYU.

HILL, MAX W   prof of Physics & Astronomy BYU; b: 20 May 1930; m: Donna Marie Parkinson; p: Wilmer S & Edna Andrus; c: Douglas, James, Sharon, David, Kent, Mark, Greg; ed: BA 1954 BYU; PhD 1959 U of Calif at Berkeley; Elk's & Knight scholarships to BYU; Willard D Thompson Memorial Scholarship & Univ Fellow at U of Calif; former: teaching & res asst, U of Calif; mem: Phi Eta Sigma; Phi Kappa Phi; Sigma Xi; award: Eagle Scout; Scouter's Key; Scouter's Training Award; On My Honor Award; 5 LDS Fitness Awards; 4 1000-mile Club Trophies, BYU Joggers Awards; publ: 38 journal articles; civic: asst Cub Scout Dist Commissioner, BSA; rel: LDS, ward clerk, bishop, h council; ome: 1745 Lambert Ln; off: 283 ESC, BYU.

HILL, RODNEY C   coach BYU; writer; b: 22 Nov 1935; m: Debra; p: Cecil A & Marguerite; c: Velvet, Lorena, Ty, Rod Jr, Troy, Lara; ed: Notre Dame 2 yrs; Oklahoma 1 yr; BS 1961 U Nevada Reno; former: tchr Sparks, Nev 7 yrs; owner Denver School of Gymnastics for Girls 10 yrs; coach BYU Girls Gymnastics 4 yrs; career: Youth Serv Award, Sertoma Club; mem: 1970 Worlds Games Team; 1972 US Olympic Team; 1975 Pan Amer Games Team; 1974 US Jr Team to Japan; 1976 US Olympic Team; mem US Olympic Com 1972-6; USGF Technical Com 1972-77;

publ: *I Want Gold; Gymnastics With Laurie;* magazine articles; mil: US Marine Corps sgt; rel: LDS high priest ldr, sunday school pres, tchr; home: 491 E 1090 N, Orem; off: 105 RB, BYU.

HINTZE, LEHI F   prof of Geology BYU: b: 14 Apr 1921; m: Ione Nelson; p: Ferdinand F & Henrietta J; c: Sharon, David, Paul, Wayne; ed: PhD 1951 Columbia NY; Sigma Xi Annual Lecturer 1974; former: assoc prof of Geology, Oregon State U; career: Internatl Field Excursion Switzerland 1962; pres Utah Geological Soc 1964; pres Sigma Xi 1970; mem: fellow of Geological Soc of Amer; Amer Assn of Petroleum Geologists; publ: *Geological Maps of Utah 1963, 75, 80; Geological History of Utah* 1973; civic: chm Utah County Earthquake Awareness Com; mil: Lt Capt US Army 1942-6; Japanese Occupation Troops; rel: LDS, h council, bishopric, exec sec; club: Beta Theta Pi; home: 1835 N 1450 E; off: Geology Dept, BYU.

HIRSCHE, BLAYNE L   plastic surgeon; b: 27 Feb 1942; m: Sandra; p: Lynn A; c: Leslie 15, Blayne Lynn 12, Nicole 10, Alexia 8, Cyril 5, Christinia 2; ed: BS MD Univ of Alberta, Edmonton Alberta, Canada; Alpha Omega Alpha Med Honor Soc; Gold Key Soc Award for Distinguished Service; Silver Ring Award for Exceptional Service; Tanner Trophy for Campus Activity, Med Rep to Student's Council, U of Alberta; pres Med Undergrad Soc; VP Assn of Fellows, Mayo Grad School of Med; career: certification, Amer Board of Surgery 1978; Mayo Foundation, Fellow in Transplantation Res; mem: Alpha Omega Alpha Med Honor Soc; Minn Med Soc; Amer Med Soc; Utah State Med Assn; publ: *Use of Bovine Carotid Grafts for Hemodialysis and Hyperalimentation,* Experience with Elective Surgery in Renal Allograft Recipients, *Five-day Perfusion of Canine Kidneys: A Postulated Effect of Steroids;* rel: LDS; home: 4157 Imperial Way; off: 2230 N Cotton Tree Sq No. 5.

HOLLAND, JEFFREY R   pres BYU; b: 3 Dec 1940; m: Patricia Terry; p: Frank & Alice; c: Matthew 16, Mary Alice 13, David 9; ed: Bachelors 1965 Masters 1966 BYU; PhD Amer Studies 1973 Yale Univ; ES Hinckley Scholar; Phi Kappa Phi; Yale Univ Fellow; former: Church Comissioner of Ed; dean Rel Instruction BYU; Institute

instr & dir; career: Distinguished Alumni Serv Award
BYU; governing boards of Deseret News Publ Co, LDS
Hospital & Intermtn Health Care Inc, Polynesian Cultural
Ctr; mem: dir Amer Assn of Presidents of Independent
Colleges & Univs; publ: 40 articles & addresses; rel: LDS,
h council, bishop, stake presidency, dir Mel Priest Church
MIA prog, chm Church Young Adult Com; home:
President's Home, BYU; off: D-346 ASB, BYU.

HOLLAND, JENA V   educator; b: 24 Apr 1904; m:
William LeGrand Holland; c: William Hal, Dr John Lee;
ed: bachelor, masters, doctoral work at BYU; attended 5
other univ; magna cum laude scholarship student; US Dept
of State ed grad scholarship to U of Michigan; Utah Ed
Certs in admin & supvr, secondary sr & jr high school
teaching, elementary school teaching; special ed cert for
teaching handicapped students; Fulbright Ed Grant US
State Dept 1956 to lecture on amer ed & demonstrate ed
teaching procedures in the Orient 1 yr; Studentbody VP U
of Utah; former: principal; supvr; tchr trainer; univ &
adult ed; Provo City school tchr; tchr in LDS Church
School, Hawaii; Utah State Supvr of Preschools;
Recreation Supvr for women's & children's rec Los
Angeles City Rec Dept; organized & supervized Provo
City Women's & Children's Recreation Prog; career:
Professional Tchr Award 1954 Utah Ed Assn; 46 yrs supvr
& teaching in education & recreation positions in US and
abroad; mem: Provo City Recreation Board 4 yrs; Provo
School Dist PTA Council; Natl Ed Assn; Utah Ed Assn;
award: LDS Church Poetry Award 1918; publ: articles on
recreation and ed, incl cover-page recognition in natl ed
magazines, some syndicated; religious articles; editor
Play School magazine for Utah State Recreation Dept;
civic: co-organized first Cub Scout groups in Provo;
leading roles in operas; rel: LDS, Church Activities Prog,
Sunday School board mem, MIA presidency, tchr all ages
in religion classes, Primary, Sunday School, MIA, Relief
Soc; club: Provo Soroptimist Club; BYU Women; home:
125 E 600 N.

HOLLEY, MACK   Utah County Sheriff; b: 3 Aug 1921; m:
Wanda C; p: John I & Wilda; c: Dennis M, Peggy Sanford,
Patricia Barney, Brenda Oberhansley, Linda Anthony; ed:
BYU; BS Weber State; former: Chief Deputy Sheriff; dept

store part owner-mgr; livestock feeder; career: Exchange Club Outstanding Policeman Award; Innovative Jail Program Award, Utah Correctional Assn; Utah Assn of Counties Outstanding County Official nominee; mem: former chm Utah State Peace Officer Standards & Training Council; award: Spanish Fork Jaycee Distinguished Serv Award; civic: Squaw Peak Footprinters Assn; pol: former republican precinct chm; rel: LDS, h council, bishopric; club: Timpanogos Knife & Fork Club; home: 315 N 400 E, Spanish Fork; off: 1775 S Dakota Ln.

HOLMES, BLAIR RALPH   assoc prof History BYU; b: 29 Jun 1942; m: Margie Green; p: Harold H & Muriel B; c: Brian 13, Steven 10, Christopher 8, Karin 5, Robert 3, Richard 1; ed: BA 1966 BYU; MA 1968 PhD 1972 U Colorado; cert of completion Newberry Summer Inst on Quantitative History 1977; high honors & cum laude BYU 1966; NDEA Fellowship 1966-8 U Colorado; former: part-time faculty U Colorado & Metropolitan State; mem: Institut fuer Oesterreichkunde; W Assn for German Studies; Mormon History Assn; Conf Group on E European History; Amer Assn Advancement Slavic Studies; award: Eagle Scout 6 palms; Silver Award Explorer; rel awards; Scouter Training Award; Natl Jamboree Competition Medal; publ: journal articles; civic: Boy Scouts of Amer; pol: dist offices; county del Democrat; rel: LDS; home: 1203 N 1270 W; off: 406 KMB, BYU.

HOLTKAMP, JAMES A   attorney, partner Van Cott, Bagley, Cornwall & McCarthy; adjunct Prof of Law BYU; b: 4 Apr 1949; m: Marianne Coltrin; p: Clarence J & Karyl Roberts; c: Ariane 7, Brent 6, Rachel 2, Allison 1; ed: BA 1972 BYU; JD 1975 George Washington U; articles editor George Washington Law Review; former: atty US Dept of the Interior; staff US Senate Watergate Com; career: Distinguished Serv Award, Energy & Natural Resources Sect, Utah State Bar 1981; former chm environmental Law Com, Utah State Bar; mem: Utah State Bar; Amer Bar Assn; Rocky Mtn Mineral Law Found; Utah Mining Assn; publ: co-author *Utah Environmental & Land Use Permits & Approvals Manual* 1981; pol: vice chm voting dist; rel: LDS; home: 7983 Davinci Dr, SLC; off: JRCB, BYU.

HOOPES, MARGARET ANN HOWARD   prof Family Sci BYU (Marriage & Family Therapy); b: 12 May 1927; p: James P & Elizabeth Joyce Howard; ed: BS English 1953 Ricks College; MS counseling & guidance 1962 BYU; PhD counseling psychology 1969 U of Minnesota; post doctoral Philadelphia Child Guidance Clinic & Bach Inst; grad with honors; Phi Beta Kappa; research grants; licensed psychologist & marriage & family therapist; former: instr & asst prof U of Minnesota; elem, jr high, high school tchr; career: listed in Natl Register of Health Serv Providers in Psychology; mem: Amer & Utah Assns for Marriage & Family Therapists; Natl & Utah Councils of Family Relations; Utah Psychological Assn; publ: co-auth *Ordinal Position Shame and Guilt, and Family Systems;* co-auth *Family Facilitation Programs: Structured Enrichment, Education, and Treatment for Individuals, Couples, and Families;* co-auth *Readings in Ethical & Professional Issues for Marital and Family Therapists; Who's Who in Marriage & Family Therapy;* 17 journal articles, book chapters, and reviews; 2 training films; rel: LDS, Relief Soc gen board special com, stake family relations com; home: 3532 N Piute Dr; off: 257 CCB, BYU.

HOOPES, SHIRLENE G   homemaker, Provo City PTA Council pres; b: 19 Jan 1932; m: Keith H Hoopes; p: Melvin Pratt & Lois D Griffeth; c: Robert, Sherry, Ben, Dan, Jim, Shirley; ed: BS Utah State U; former: home econ tchr 2 yrs; adult ed tchr; PTA officer Edgemont Elem; rel: LDS, primary pres & tchr, sunday school & Relief Soc tchr; club: Pro Libris Literary; home: 3356 Cherokee Ln.

HOPKINS, THEODORE R   physician, obstetrics & gynecology; b: 4 Aug 1920; m: Bobbie N; p: Dr & Mrs Ira Jay; c: James R, Jay M, David B; ed: BS Stanford U 1947, MD George Washington U 1951; mem: Amer Med Assn; UMA; Utah gyn Soc; award: Eagle Scout; pol: republican; mil: WW II Lt. Cmdr USNR; combat area awards; Unit Citation; rel: LDS, bishopric, stake mission; home: 2248 N 650 E; off: 777 N 500 W.

HORSLEY, RICHARD B   tchr, counselor, researcher, writer of family histories; b: 27 Sep 1931; m: Shirley Snow; p: Rulon & Patricia Brown Hayes; c: Michelle, Teri,

Raelone, Todd, Ricky, Matthew; ed: BS BYU; MEd UCLA; PhD work rel ed BYU; scholarship BYU; former: English Dept head Mapusaga Hig School, Amer Samoa; BYU instr; mem: UEA; Sons of Utah Pioneers; award: all-state basketball & tennis player; Eagle Scout; publ: co-auth *Brief History of the Natl Soc of the Sons of Utah Pioneers; Who's Who Among the Mormons* in progress; pol: state & county rep voting dist 34 Republican; mil: US Army asst chaplain; rel: LDS, elders pres, bishop, h council; home: 1141 N 750 W; off: 1355 Riverside Ave.

HORTIN, LARRY L   library director; b: 13 Jul 1934; m: Carol; p: Glen & Lucille; c: Lesley, Kristen, John, Melinda, Michael; ed: BS BYU; MS U of Oregon; former: order supvr BYU; school librarian, Boulder City, Nev; career: Adult Ed for Service; mem: Utah Library Assn; Amer Library Assn; Adult Ed Assn; civic: cubmaster; mil: US Army; Good Conduct; rel: LDS, ward clerk, h council, bishopric; club: Rotary Internatl; home: 3675 N 500 E; off 13 N 100 E.

HOWARD, JANET   instr BYU; b: 9 Sep 1933; p: Benjamin Franklin Methvin & Orelia Grappe; c: Kim, Ben James, Steve Dawson; ed: bachelor & master Northwestern State U, Louis; doctoral work BYU; former: exec sec; instr Northwestern State U; career: Outstanding Tchr, School of mgt; Prof of Month, BYU; mem: Internatl Information Word Processing; publ: article *Teaching Proofreading for Information/Word Processing* Business Ed Forum; civic: seminars & workshops; rel: LDS; stake Sunday School sec; home: 876 S 550 E, Orem; off: 50 JKB, BYU.

HOWELL, ROBERT JAMES   clinical & forensic psychologist; prof & dir of Clinical Training, BYU Dept of Psychology; b: 13 Sep 1925; m: Mary Raiford; p: Elmer V & Myrtle Knight; c: Carol, Peggy, Bruce; ed: Washington State U; BA 1948 MA 1949 PhD 1951 U of Utah; Phi Chi; Phi Kappa Phi; Sigma Xi; former: faculty Calif State U at Fresno; sr psychologist Utah State Hospital & Patton State Hospital; dir of Research Ctr for Training in Community Psychiatry, U of Calif LA; admin dir Timpanogos Mental Health Ctr; career: diplomate Clinical Psychology, Amer Board of Professional Psychology; diplomate Forensic Psychology, Amer Board of Forensic

Psychology; diplomate Clinical Hypnosis, Amer Board of Examiners in Psychological Hypnosis; mem: Utah Psychological Assn pres 1964; Amer Psychological Assn; Rocky Mtn Psychological Assn; Amer Psychology Law Soc; Amer Acad of Forensic Psychology pres 1981-2; Amer Board of Forensic Psychology pres 1981-2; civic: Miss Liberty Bell Pageant Com, 4th of July Pageant; mil: US Air Force 1943-6; rel: LDS; home: 2761 Iroquis Dr; off: 285 CCB, BYU.

HOWELLS, JOYCE WILTBANK   sr cataloger, HB Lee Library, BYU; b: 22 Apr 1938; m: Samuel J Howells; p: William Ellis Wiltbank Jr & Mary Alta Udall; c: Yvette Marie 18, Amyjo 13; ed: BS 1960 BYU; MLS 1968 BYU; former: home econ tchr, Park City High School, Snowflake Union High School; mem: Phi Kappa Phi; Omicron Nu; publ: *Vocations in Biography and Fiction: a Selected List for Young People;* rel: LDS, Primary counslelor; home: 460 E 3050 N; off: 6380 HBLL, BYU.

HUBBARD, ERNEST DEE   prof of accounting BYU; b: 6 Feb 1929; m: Patricia Hurren; p: Ernest B & Pearl J; c: Jeff, Heidi, Brian, Daniel; ed: BS Utah State U; MBA U of Utah; PhD U of Washington; AAA Fellowship; former: cost accountant, construction; career: Distinguished Serv Award IPA BYU; mem: Natl Assn of Accountants; Amer Accounting Assn; publ: articles; civic: mem of board & sec Marrcrest Homeowners Assn; pol: dist v-chm; mil: Korean conflict 1st Lt Quartermaster Corps; rel: LDS, bishopric, h council, clerk, h priest grp ldr; home: 2785 Marrcrest East; off: 324 JKB, BYU.

HUBER, CLAYTON S   dept chm Food Sci & Nutrition BYU b: 28 Feb 1938; m: Beth; p: LeRoy & Vera; c: Kerry 16, Philip 14, Lanae 12, Douglas 9, LeAnn 7, Brad 5, Kevin 2; ed: BS MA Utah State U; PhD Purdue U; Valedictorian; Who's Who; Borden Award, NDEA Fellowship; former: sr scientist Kraft Co; mgr food sci Tech Inc; career: Snoopy Award (Astronaut Office), NASA's Sci & Tech Award, Virginia Cutler Lecture; mem: Inst of Food Technologists; Amer Dairy Sci Assn; Poultry Sci Assn; Phi Kappa Phi; Sigma Xi; publ: over 30 tech papers; civic: dist chm Boy Scouts of Amer, Pony League pres; pol: voting dist chm, natl com chm, county & state del; mil: Lt US Army;

Commendation Medal; rel: LDS, bishop, h council, stake presidency; home: 189 E 4380 N; off: 2218 SFLC, BYU.

HUGHES, BRENWYN G   biochemist; b: 5 Nov 1944; p: Lowell & Helen B; ed: BS MS PhD BYU; Phi Kappa Phi; honors prog grad with high honors; NDEA Title IV Fellowship; Harvard Sci-Ed Fellowship nominee; former: research assoc BYU Cancer Research Ctr; mem: NY Acad of Sci; Amer Assn for the Adv of Sci; Amer Chemical Soc; publ: 15; rel: LDS, Relief Soc stake board, ward pres; stake YA & YSI co-chm; tchr devel tchr; home: 1998 N 700 W; off: 680 WIDB, BYU.

HUGO, CHARLES V   Chief Bldg Official; b: 22 Feb 1944; m: Nancy Kay Everett; p: LeRoy & Gladys; c: Chet 12, Mikel 10, Lillian 9, Lydia 7, Della 5, Carrie 2; ed: BS 1970 BYU; former: Construction Analyst; Residential Plans Examiner; career: Internatl Conf of Bldg Officials Certified Inspector for bldg, mechanical, plumbing, combination; Plans Examiner, Council of Amer Bldg Officials Certified Solar Specialist; mem: Internatl Conf of Bldg Officials; Internatl Assn of Plumbing & Mechanical Officials; civic: officer in Utah County Mtn Rescue Team; Dist Commissioner BSA; rel: LDS, 70s pres, h council, bishopric; home: 370 S 300 W; off: Box 1849.

HUNGERFORD, CURTISS R   prof Ed Admin BYU; b: 1 Aug 1930; m: Darleen; p: Samuel S & Evelyn McKenna; c: Mary Hungerford Lund; ed: BA theater & philosophy Stanford; MA communications PhD higher ed admin & communications U of S Calif; Mothers Club Award, Stanford; former: Dean of Academic Affairs, W New Mexico U; Asst Dean Continuing Ed USC; Asst to Chancellor, Alumni Field Sec USC; Dir of Pub Affairs Calif State U LA; career: Excellence in Ed Award BYU 1981; mem: AAHE; ASTD; Smithsonian; Amer Acad of Pol & Soc Sci; Phi Delta Kappa; Pi Kappa Phi; Alpha Epsilon Rho; award: VSC Telecommunications Award; publ: Toward A New Scenario for ation I's of Management"; "Nature of Learning"; civic: chm Bi-Cultural Univ Alliance; chm LA Mayor's Com on Sr Cit Ed; Governor's Commission on Impr Quality of Life in New Mexico; mil: 6th Army Public Info Officer 1952-4; Army Reserve Pictorial Officer 1954-64; 6th Army Commanders Merit

Award; rel: LDS, stake Sunday School pres, elders quorum pres, tchr devel & ins dir; home: 3000 Iroquois Dr; off: 310-C MCKB, BYU.

HUNSAKER, RUTH P   owner Wedding House Fashions; tchr BYU Ed; tchr Girls Acad; costumer BYU Ballet; b: 4 Jan 1924; m: Melvin J Pulsipher; c: Darlene, Allen J, Stan M, Scott L, Drew J, Nathan R; ed: 2.5 yrs college USAC; grad LDS Inst USAC; former: asst mgr House of Fabrics; mgr Nortons Clothing; mgr Geraldines Bridal; award: Home Arts Sweepstakes Utah State Fair 1973; Best of Show Award, Fine Arts Dept Utah State Fair 1976; trophy 25 yrs costuming Colleen Collins Smith Ballet; civic: Chamber of Commerce; Mini Mall Chm of 1st place float 4th of July parade 1973; area rep Cancer Drive; Home Arts Dept County Fair Div Chm; costumer Panarama Productions; costumer Utah Valley Opera Assn; costumer Provo City Queen Floats; pol: voting judge, registrar at polls; mil: WAC 1944-6 Medical Technician; WW II Victory Medal; Good Conduct; Amer Campaign; rel: LDS, tchr or sec in all orgs, Cub Scout Den Mother 15 yrs; home: 815 E 2780 N.

HUNTER, BYRON A   adjunct prof of chemistry BYU; b: 15 Oct 1910; m: Margaret Oleson; p: Daniel & Mary Calderwodd; c: Shirley, James, Robert, Margaret, Wendy, Sharman, Heather, Deborah; ed: BS 1933 MA 1937 U of Utah; PhD 1941 Iowa State College; Sigma Xi; Phi Lambda Epsilon; former: sr research assoc Uniroyal Chemical; career: research grants Uniroyal Chemical 1979-82; Distinguished Alumnus 1978 U of Utah; mem: Amer Chemical Soc, ACS Rubber Div; publ: 52 patents; 13 publs; rel: LDS, branch pres, h council, HP group ldr; home: 352 E 426 N, Alpine; off: ESC, BYU.

HUNTINGTON, SHARON   editor, writer World Inst for Computer Assisted Teaching (WICAT); b: 3 Aug 1951; p: John R & Bonnie S; ed: BA 1974 magna cum laude U of Utah; academic scholarship; Phi Kappa Phi; former: asst dir BYU Development Communications 1975-81; career: 1981 Young Career Woman of the Year, Provo Chapter of Business & Professional Women; top 20 in 1977 Writer's Digest natl short story contest; award: 2nd deg black belt karate; publ: freelance articles in natl & local publs;

civic: 1978 Provo Freedom Festival Com; BYU Cougar
Club; editor Cougar Club newsletter; former volunteer U
of Utah Helpline; Provo Civil Air Patrol; pol: Provo
Chapter Natl Org for Women; rel: First Church of Christ,
Scientist; Second Reader, sunday school pianist, treasurer,
chm usher com; club: past honored queen Internatl Order
of Job's Daughters; home: 2090 N 940 W; off: 931 W 300 N.

HURLEY, D RICHARD   prof of Health Sci BYU; b: 9 Mar
1935; m: Sandra; p: Frank & Rachel; c: Don 20, Kathy 19,
Julie 16, Cindy 15, Daniel 6, David 4, Lori 3; ed: BS MS
BYU; PhD S Illinois U; research fellowship S Illinois U;
research grant BYU; former: tchr & coach Granite School
Dist & Nampa Idaho Public Schools; lecturer S Illinois U;
career: Public Serv Award, Dugway Proving Grounds;
mem: Utah Assn of Health, PE & Recreation, Southwest
Dist, Amer Allaince of Health Educators; award: Public
Serv Award, Jaycees; publ: *Health Promotion Mgt & Self
Care; Adolescent Health; Preventive Health*; pol: former
precinct com; mil: US Navy AK3; rel: LDS, bishop, h
council; club: former Jaycee; Cougar Club; home: 1609 W
1000 N; off: 229-D RB, BYU.

INFANGER,   CARLTON   ADOLPH   agricultural
economist, educator; b: 25 Jan 1923; m: Abbie Lucille
Whiting; p: William Henry & Emma Vogel; c: Rex, Dale
Marie Peterson, Mark, Amy, Joni; ed: BS 1955 Mont State
College; MS 1956; PhD 1964; postgrad U of Calif at
Berkeley & U Mo; Phi Kappa Phi; Alpha Zeta; former: asst
specialist U of Calif 1956-7, exec sec Mont Taxation Edn
Com 1957-9, assoc economist Wash State U 1960-1, asst
prof & research assoc Mont State College 1961-4, asst
prof BYU 1964-6, assoc prof & dept chm 1966-70, prof
1972-5, dept chm 1975-7, mem Presidents Adv Council
1973-6, prof & head agrl econs U Nebr, mem Diplomatic
Exchange to Latin Amer USIA 1975; agrl economist AID,
Washington 1977-9; career: listed in Who's Who in the
World; mem: Western Amer Agrl Econs Assn; mil: USNR
1944-6; off: 473 WIDB, BYU.

INGRAM, CREGG F   assoc prof Dept of Ed Psychology
BYU; dir Ed Assessment Clinic BYU; consul Utah Valley
Psychiatric Out-Patient Clinic; b: 31 Aug 1942; m:
JoAnne Sullivan; p: George & Lucille; c: Jilleen 14,
Danielle 11, Erin 8, Matthew 5; ed: BS elementary ed &

special ed 1968 MS special ed 1970 U of Utah; DeD
special ed 1974 U of Kentucky; dr assistantship U of
Kentucky 1972; former: asst prof U of Louisville; Dir of
Special Ed for the SW Ed Development Ctr; public school
tchr; mem: pres Canyonlands Chapter of CEC; VP Student
CEC, U of Utah; SCEC; Phi Delta Kappa; Assn of Tchr
Educators; Council for Exceptional Children; consul &
com positions with State Learning Disabilities Prog Utah
State Board of Ed, Southwest Residential & Ed Ctr, Cedar
City, Council for Exceptional Children Special Projs Div;
Utah State Dept Evaluation team; Utah State Dept of Ed
Textbook Adoption Com; publ: *Jundamentals of Ed
Assessment; A Self Contained Instructional Module on
Using Project Vision-Up Materials;* writer for Biological
Sci Curriculum Study; 3 chapters in books; 15 articles; 15
presentations; civic: Elkridge Utah City Council; Park &
Recreation Councilman & Roads Commissioner; dir
personal Ed Assessment; pol: City Councilman; mil: US
Army 3 yrs; Utah Natl Guard 19th Special Forces Group
15 yrs; Commendation for serv rendered to 19th Special
Forces Group; Good Conduct; Expert Infantry; EIB;
Master Parachutist; rel: LDS, stake dir athletic officials;
home: 507 E Lakeview Dr, Eldridge; off: 322-E MCKB,
BYU.

IVIE, EVAN LEON   prof Computer Sci BYU; b: 15 May
1931; m: Betty Jo Beck; p: H Leon & Ruth Ashby; c:
Dynette, Mark, Joseph, Robert, Ruthann, Rebecca, John,
James, Mette, Emily, Peter; ed: BS 1956 BES 1956 BYU;
MS 1957 Stanford U; PhD 1966 Mass Inst Tech; NSF
Fellow; former: dep dir programming sect USAF
Intelligence Agcy, Washington 1957-60; instr & research
asst Mass Inst Tech 1960-6; Bell Telephone Labs 1966-79;
Whippany, Piscataway & Murray Hill, NJ 1969-79; process
admin Whippany 1969-71; vis sr lectr Stevens Inst Tech
1969-79; mem: Assn Computing Machiners; IEEE; publ:
articles; civic: BSA; founder NJ Br Geneal Library 1969;
mil: US Air Force 1957-60; rel: LDS, h council, bishopric;
home: 1131 Dover Dr; off: Dept Comp Sci, BYU.

JACKMAN, FRED   MD general surgeon; b: 17 Aug 1925;
m: Travis; p: Victor A & Gladys F; c: Rick, Rod, Robin,
Randy, Rebecca; ed: MD U of Utah 1950; internship SL
county; 4 yr residency U of Utah; former: Utah Valley
Hospital; Amer Fork Community; mem: Fellow Amer

College of Surgeons; board certified Amer Board Surgery; civic: Boy Scouts 20 yrs; mil: PT boat commander WW II, S Pacific Ensign USNR 10 yrs; returned to active duty 144th Evac Hospital 1960; current chief of surgery 328th Gen Hospital; rel: LDS, youth; club: barbershop quartets; Kiwanis; home: 746 Sunny Ln, Orem; off: 930 N 500 W.

JACOBS, DAVID K   motion picture producer, director, writer; b: 13 Aug 1937; m: Gail W; p: Heber G & Erma U; c: David Wade 7, Caroline 4, Jeffrey 2; ed: BS MA BYU; PhD theatre & cinema directing U of Utah; Phi Kappa Phi; Blue Key; Outstanding Man at Weber College 1957; Block "W" Award; former: casting dir BYU Motion Picture Studio; drama dir Church College of Hawaii; career: George Washington Honor Medal 1980 for film Uncle Ben include Cine Golden Eagle 1977, Gold Camera Award 1978, Gold Cindy 1978, Best of the Year from Learning Mag 1979; mem: Amer Film Inst; Associated Latter-day Media Artists; films dir: *The First Vision; The Church in Action 1971-80;* civic: judges chm 6 yrs Miss Utah Pageant for Miss America; pol: Republican state del; rel: LDS, bishop, h council, mission presidency; home: 305 W 1600 S, Orem; off: Media Production Studio, BYU.

JACOBSEN, VIRGIL E   Evening School Principal, Provo Canyon Shool; art educator, Apline School Dist; b: 11 Aug 1947; m: Jacqueline Ovard; p: Charles & Sara Darrah; c: Johnathan Virgil 8, Joseph Ovard 2; ed: LA Harbor College; Church College Hawaii; BS 1973 MIE 1976 EdS 1981 BYU; grad scholarships; res assistantships; former: coor for Alpine School Dist Art Inservice; Wax Artisan for Wasatch Bronze Works, Lehi; career: recognition as outstanding art tchr & community artist liaison by Alpine School Dist; addressed Opening Inst of Alpine School Dist Aug 1979; Ed Evaluation Team, State Office Of Ed; certified Utah Professional Tchr, Utah Admin/Supvr; mem: Utah Ed Assn; Utah Art Ed Assn; Natl Ed Assn; Natl Art Ed Assn; Alpine Ed Assn; award: grants to work with local artists from Utah Arts Council & Natl Endowment for the Arts; adv com BYU Dept of Ed Admin; publ: Masters Field Proj at BYU in ceramic instr; civic: Utah Youth Soccer Assn coach; Pleasant Grove Swim Team; rel: LDS, bishopric; home: 731 Cherry Hill Cr, PG; 765 N 600 W, Orem.

JACOBSON, JESTON O   real estate broker; b: 12 Jul 1915; m: Maurine Meservy; p: William M & Emma Peay; c: Kathy, Karl, Kay, Laura, Nanci, Reed, David, Gordon, Brian; ed: BYU; career: pres Utah Co Board of Realtors; chm Utah Real Estate Ed Found; VP Central Utah Real Estate Exchangers; mem: NAREB; Utah Co Board of Realtors; Natl Assn of Realtors; CURE; mil: Staff Sgt Supply WW II New Guinea 1943-4; rel: LDS, bishopic, h council; home: 881 E 2730 N; off: 972 W Center.

JACOBSON, PHYLLIS COLLEEN   chm Dept of Physical Ed Dance; b: 4 Sep 1929; p: Lathen & Eva; ed: BS MS Utah State U; grad study Penn State U; PhD U of Utah; Phi Kappa Phi Scholastic Recognition Award; former: prof of physical ed; chm Dept of Physical Ed Women Sports & Dance; school tchr; career: BYU Master Teacher; Outstanding Educators of Amer; Karl G Maeser Distinguished Teaching Award; Honor & Service Award UAHPER; listed in Who's Who of Amer Women; listed in Personalities of the West and Midwest; listed in Notable Personalities of Amer; speaker consul; mem: Amer Alliance, Southwest Alliance, and Utah Alliance for HPERD; Western Soc Physical Ed; Natl Assn for Physical Ed & Higher Ed; Phi Kappa Phi; Smithsonian Inst; US Rep to Internatl Olympic Acad 1978, Olympia, Greece; Internatl Stud U of Mexico 1981; award: Physical Fitness Prog, LDS Welfare Serv; mem YWMIA Gen Board 1962-73; Young Women's Gen Board 1975-9; publ: *Fitness Manual for Lady Missionaries—A Sensible Course in Physical Fitness, Physical Fitness Awards Program 1979*, co-auth: *Move It! Proven Exercises for Family Health & Fitness; Fundamental Skills in Physical Education;* civic: Governor's Physical Fitness Council; Natl Olympic Acad Planning Com; physical fitness workshops & clinics; rel: LDS; home: 3532 N Piute Ln; off: 296 RB, BYU.

JAMES, DAVID (BOWLER, CLARK)   News Dir KEYY Radio; b: 28 Mar 1938; c: Darci 14, Dena 12, Shauri 11; former: ABC Radio Network, Los Angeles; entertainment dir, Las Vegas; radio prog dir, SLC; radio station mgr, Idaho; disk jockey, Utah, Colo, New York, Ariz, Wash; career: Gold Mike Award; News Reporting Award, Associated Press; serv award: March of Dimes; Veterans of Foreign Wars; Utah Alcohol Found; Voice of

Democracy; Arthritis Found; Girl Scouts; Muscular Dystrophy; publ: David James Trivia TV-Facts magazine; civic: March of Dimes; Arthritis Assn; pol: advisor for consumer groups; mil: US Army; rel: LDS, sunday school, MIA; home: 911 E 100 N; off: 307 S 1600 W.

JEFFS, M DAYLE   lawyer; b: 7 Mar 1930; m: Janice; p: Alvin W & Melvina Payne; c: David, James, Robert, Bill; ed: BYU 4 yrs; JD 1957 U of Utah; former: Utah County Attorney 1966-70; career: Commissioner Utah State Bar Assn; Master of the Bench & Treas Amer Inn of Court I; mem: Central Utah Bar Assn; Utah State Bar Assn; civic: chm Provo Freedom Festival 1966; mil: US Army Counter Intelligence 1952-4; rel: LDS, bishop, h council, ward clerk, scoutmaster; club: lifetime Sertoma; home: 160 E 4320 N; off: 90 N 100 E.

JENKINS, JEAN REESE   prof Theatre & Cinematic Arts BYU; b: 3 Aug 1926; m: Glen L (deceased); p: David & Bessie Johnson Reese; c: Kathryn J (Frandsen), Martin Glen; ed: BA, MA, LIB, Honorary Doctorate; Teacher of the Month, BYU; consul STM Exec Recruiters; Board of Frandsen Assoc; consul in dialects and langs; career: Poet of the Year, South & West, Int; Amer Assn of Univ Women Woman of the Year; mem: Speech Communication Assn, Amer Theatre Assn; Natl Fed of State Poetry Soc, Inc; Amer Assn of Univ Women; award: listed in: Int Who's Who in Poetry, Community Leaders & Noteworthy Americans, The World Who's Who of Women, Who's Who in the West, Int Blue Book, World Who's Who of Women in Ed; Northwest Rep, editorial board of South & West, Inc; publ: *The More For Loving; Relationship of Speech and Poetry; Trends in Modern Poetry; Poetry is Therapy; Stage Fright; Voice, Diction, and Interpretation; Jen Times Happy Me;* numerous poetry and articles in magazines; civic: Utah Acad of Arts, Sci, Letters; rel: LDS; club: Theta Alpha Phi; home: 452 W 800 S, Orem; off: F-422 HFAC, BYU.

JENSEN, CLAYNE R   dean College of Physical Ed BYU; chm BYU Athletic Council; b: 17 Mar 1930; m: Elouise Henrie; p: Alton & Arvilla; c: Craig, Mike, Blake, Chris; ed: BS 1952 Masters 1956 U of Utah; Doctorate 1963 Indiana U; Phi Kappa Phi; former: visiting prof N Illinois

U; assoc prof Utah State U; US del to Internatl Olympic
Acad, Olympia, Greece, 1980; US Olympic Acad
Participant 1979-81; BYU Faculty Athletic Rep; career:
Special Events Advisory Com; Dean's Council; Univ
Curriculum Council; Univ Public Relations Coor Council;
Stadium Expansion Exec Com; listed in Who's Who in
Amer 1982, Who's Who in Amer Ed 1967-, Who's Who in
the West 1969-, Outstanding Educators of Amer 1970,2,
Internatl Biographies 1970-, Creative Personalities of the
World 1970-, Leaders in Ed 1970-, Contemporary Authors
1965-, Writer's Directory 1973-, Men of Achievement
1973-, Personalities of the West & Midwest 1973-,
Community Leaders & Noteworthy Americans 1974-,
Dictionary of Internatl Biographies 1974-, Internatl
Authors & Writers Who's Who 1981; special citation for
outstanding contributions to recreation & park
development in Utah 1964; mem: Amer Alliance of
Health, Physical Ed, Recreation & Dance; Natl
Recreation & Parks Assn; Natl Assn of Athletic
Administrators; Alumni of the Intermtn Olympic Acad; alt
US rep to CIOFF; Southwest Dist Assn of Health, Physical
Ed, Recreation & dance; Utah Ed Assn; Utah Assn for
Health, Physical Ed, Recreation & Dance; award:
Breitbard Found Athletic Excellence Award; lettered in
athletics 4 yrs U of Utah 1949-52; numerous athletic
records; publ: 10 college textbooks; 6 books; 24 articles &
reports; editor *Utah Journal of Health, Physical Ed, &
Recreation;* civic: chm Natl Conf on Outdoor Recreation
& Ed 1969; exec council Amer Assn for Health, Physical
Ed, Recreation & Athletics 1966-7; various positions Natl
& Utah Recreation & Parks Assn; mil: US Marine Corps
Captain; coached 2 All-Marine Champ teams track &
field; rel: LDS, h council; club: Kiwanis; home: 1900 Oak
Ln; off: 212 RB, BYU.

JENSEN, JERRY LEE coor Non-Major Advisement Ctr;
instr Career Ed Dept BYU; b: 22 May 1936; m: Edith
Myrlene Fish; p: Peter L & Floy Arney; c: Raelene Jensen
Dewitt, Ingrid R, Erin Colleen, Robert W, Denya Myrlene;
ed: BS BYU, U of Calif at Berkeley; MS U of Calif at
Berkeley; Fullride Defense Dept Scholarship thru grad
school; former: instr U of Calif at Berkeley & Princeton
U; mem: Natl Committeeman in Natl Academic Advising
Assn; Assn of Mormon Conselors & Psychotherapists;

Amer Assn of Collegiate Registrars & Admissions Officers; award: Lifetime Master in Rifle & Pistol, Natl Rifle Assn; publ: co-auth article in New England Med Journal 1964; pol: Republican; mil: Capt Special Forces, SE Asia, 8 yrs active duty; Major US Army Reserve 4 yrs; Bronze Star; Natl Defense Medal; Amer Expeditionary; Good Conduct Medal; Purple Heart; Master Jump Wing; Expert Rifleman Medal; rel: LDS, h council, elders quorum pres; club: Natl Rifle Assn; home: 460 Ridge Ln; off: 128-b SWKT, BYU.

JENSEN, MICHAEL "K"   owner Sound Concepts; b: 15 Mar 1950; m: Karen A; p: Kaye L & Iown; c: Joy 4, Julie 2, Jason 3 mo; ed: BYU; former: VP DLR Corp; co-founder Wisdom House & Patriots United for Freedom; mem: Freemen Inst; pol: advisor Found for Economic Stability; rel: LDS, elders quorum pres; home: PO Box 1326; off: 108 W Center.

JOHNSON, ALLEN CARL   physician, anesthesiologist; chm Dept of Anesthesia Utah Valley Hospital; b: 12 Feb 1948; m: Cheryl Dawn; p: Alma Carl & Irene Robinson; c: Katherine Ann 5, Bradley Carl 3, Heidi Marie 2; ed: Duke U; BS 1972 MD 1975 U of Utah; internship Virginia Mason Hospital, Seattle; residency Mass Gen Hospital, Boston; fellowship Hospital for Sick Children, Toronto; mem: Amer Med Assn; Utah County & Utah State Med Soc; Amer Soc of Anesthesiologists; award: Eagle Scout; rel: LDS, elders presidency; home: 1084 E Hillside Dr; off: 1034 N 500 W.

JOHNSON, CLARK V   assoc prof of Church History BYU; b: 29 May 1938; m: Cheryl Geddes; p: Voris E; c: Janette 19, Paul C 18, Duane C 17, Chamane 14, James E 11; ed: BA 1963 Utah State U; MA 1969 PhD 1977 BYU; former: seminary instr & principal at Malad, Idaho 1963-7; inst instr & dir at San Jose State U 1967-71; career: 1st recipient Charles Redd Fellowship for work on Mormon pioneers 1980-1; mem: Mormon History Assn; Conservative Historians Forum; award: Special Serv Award, Tendoy Council, Boy Scouts of Amer 1967; rel: LDS, scoutmaster; h council, bishopric, Church curriculum writer 6 yrs; home: 845 N 950 W; off: 78 JSB, BYU.

JOHNSON, EDITH   admin aid BYU Cancer Research Ctr; b: 5 Nov 1919; p: John Johnson & Ivy A W Johnson; former: exec sec & office mgr 1965-78 to Ernest Wilkinson, pres BYU; office mgr Nielson & Psarras CPAs, SLC; sec to pres Consolidated Dairy Products Co 1951-5; sec Amer Airlines 1947-50; sec & head clerk James Madison Jr High 1940-6; pol: Republican county del; rel: LDS, youth leader; home: 1637 N Woodland Dr; off: 687 WIDB, BYU.

JONES, KENNETH HAROLD   VP Mfg, owner, Jones Paint & Glass; b: 10 May 1940; m: Judith Robinson; p: Harold B & Fay Knight; c: David K 20, Gary R 18, Kendra 13, Brian H 12; ed: Provo High School; 2 yrs BYU; career: Cert of Achievement in Sales; Carlite Golden Circle Award for outstanding sales, Ford Motor Co; award: Eagle Scout; civic: Industrial Development Com; pol: neighborhood chm, Provo City; mil: 1st sgt, sgt maj Utah Natl Guard; Achievement Ribbon; Bronze Beehive Device; rel: LDS, bishopric, exec sec, scoutmaster, h council; club: BYU Cougar Club; home: 1265 N Oquirrh Dr; off: 1250 W 100 N.

JONSSON, JENS J   prof of electrical engineering; chm Electrical Engr Dept BYU; b: 4 Apr 1922; m: Hellen Broadbent; p: John F & Catharina Latare; c: Craig, Diane, Karen, Catherine, Eric; ed: BSGE 1940 U of Utah; grad US Navy Electronics Tech School1945; BSEE 1947 U of Utah; MSEE 1948 PhD 1951 Purdue; postdoct fellowship Polytechnic Inst of Brooklyn 1960-1; Cert of Recognition for Outstanding Engr Contribution in Ed, Utah Engr Council 1965; Western Electric Fund Award 1968-9; HKN Elec Engr Honorary Soc; Theta Tau; Sigma Xi; registered in Utah as licensed engineer 1954-; former: prof of Elect Engr BYU 1953-; chm Engr Sci Dept BYU 1954-5; dir Engr Analysis Ctr 1964-74; "Computers in Engr Design Ed" prog U of Michigan; staff NASA/Stanford Summer Design Proj Prog 1966; UNESCO Field Expert, Middle East Tech Univ, Turkey 1967-8; UNESCO Chief Tech Advisor, Polytechnic Inst of Bucharest, Romania 1974-6, 77, 79; career: listed in Who's Who in Amer, Who's Who in Computer Ed Research, Engineers of Distinction; mem: Utah Acad of Sci, Arts & Letters; Natl Soc of Prof Engrs; Amer Assn of U Professors; Amer Soc of Engr Ed; Inst of

Elect & Electronics Engrs; Utah Conf on Higher Ed; award: Eagle Scout BSA 1940; publ: 3 tech reports; 20 journal & symposia articles; 9 research papers; civic: Community Serv Award, Inst of Electrical & Electronics Engrs 1973; chm Provo Cancer Drive 3 yrs; pol: voting dist; mil: US Navy 1944-6; rel: LDS, branch pres, bishop, stake presidency; club: Great Books; home: 1710 N Lambert Ln; off: 459 CB, BYU.

KARREN, KEITH JOHN   assoc prof Health Sci BYU; b: 23 Aug 1943; m: Diane Johnson; p: Clinton & Joyce; c: Scott 13, Holli 11, Jamie 7, Brady 5, Mandy 1; ed: BS MS BYU; PhD Oregon State U; former: prof Ricks Jr College & Oregon State U; instr Utah Emergency Medical Technician Prog; instr & trainer Amer Red Cross; instr Basic Life Support, Amer Heart Assn; instr BYU Youth Survival Prog; First Aid Coor BYU; developed BYU Advanced Life Support, Ambulance Attendant Prog, and other workshops; consultant to LDS Church Health Office; advisor BYU Emergency Unit & BYU Hockey Team; career: registered EMT-A Natl Registry of Emergency Medical Technicians; mem: Amer School Health Assn; Utah Public Health Assn; board of dir Eta Sigma Gamma; advisor Health Sci Student Org; former VP Utah Alliance for Health, Physical Ed & Recreation; Amer Alliance for Health, Physical Ed & Recreation; publ: *Emergency First Aid Workbook; God's Special Children; Teaching Health in Elementary School; Surviving Health Emergencies & Disasters; Prehospital Emergency Medical Care & Crisis Intervention;* co-author *Health and the Elementary Teacher; The Will to Win; Basic Skills Manual for First Aid & Emergency Care; The First Responder;* articles; civic: Utah County Board of Health; SAVERS, Springville Utah Voluntary Ambulance Assn; rel: LDS, bishop; home: 515 E 4750 N; off: 229F RB, BYU.

KAY, GERALDINE   office supvr X-Ray Dept Utah Valley Hospital; b: 1 May 1932; m: LeRoy Kay; p: Vivian Foutin & Emma Jean Foutin; c: Vincent L, Valerie, Ronald, Becky; career: 15 yr serv award, Utah Valley Hospital, Employee of Month, award: 1st place bowling league 1979, 81; civic: pres Lions Club 1980-1; rel: LDS, youth tchr, activity counselor 15 yrs; club: BPOE; home: 1410 W 900 N; off: 1034 N 500 W.

KEARNEY, WAYNE ORBAN   Dean of Student Servs
UTC; psychologist; b: 5 Oct 1944; m: Connie Wright; p:
Orban John & Margaret Irene Wellman; c: Shawnna Rae
Goodrich, Cauleen Jo, Michele M Gillman, Steven Wayne,
Tina Dell, Jeffery Orban, Charleen May; ed: BS
psychology EdD psychology & counseling psychology BYU;
Grad Student of the Month; Dean's List; former: counselor
Job Corps; counselor Disadvantaged Youth USES; Retired
State Employee Service; career: presented research to
vocational orgs; mem: NAFSA; NASPA; UACRAO; ATEA;
Western Deans Assn; APGA; award: Refugee Serv Award;
Cert   of   Recognition   US   Catholic   Conf   &
Migration-Refugee Serv; Eagle Scout; publ: research
1979; reg editor NASPA publs; civic: VP Utah Co Mental
Health Assn; Utah Co Vietnamies Relocation Com; United
Way; BSA 30 yrs; teaches mountaineering to
disadvantaged youth for Mtn Lands Assn of Govts; Utah
County Vocational Improvement Com; pol: Republican;
mil: US Marine Corps; 3 meritious promotions;
Leatherneck Award; Platoon Honorman; Series Honorman;
rel: LDS, mission presidency, elders pres, 70 pres, youth
ldr; home: 1475 S 75 W, Orem; off: UTC, Box 1609.

KELLER, BETTY JEAN   computer operator, off coord; b:
17 Feb 1931; m: Ernest V; p: Arthur D & Clara L
Longworth; c: Audrey Anne Ashbey Merkley, Stephen R
Ashbey, Arthur C Ashbey, Michael J Keller; civic: PTA;
pol: mem community Republican neighborhood area,
Orem, sec, Payson Election com; rel: LDS; home: 590 E
2950 N; off: 685 E 1700 N Rm 143 GSRB.

KELLING, HANS-WILHELM   chm BYU Dept of Germanic
& Slavic Langs; prof of German; b: 15 Aug 1932; m: Joyce
Kay Coy; p: Wilhelm & Emma; c: Sven 20, Kareen 17,
Kirsten 11, Kerryl Anna 10; ed: BA German 1958 BYU;
MA German lit 1960 PhD German lit 1967 Stanford U;
Woodrow Wilson Fellow; DAAD Fellow; former: dir BYU
Study Abroad Progs; career: Karl G Maeser Distinguished
Teaching Award 1980; mem: Modern Language Assn;
Rocky Mtn Modern Language Assn; Assn of Tchrs of
German; Western Assn Of German Studies; publ: 5 books,
4 articles, 2 reviews; rel: LDS, bishopric, stake
presidency, h council, mission pres; home: 2840 Apache
Ln; off: 270 MSRB, BYU.

KENNEY, SUSAN HOBSON asst prof BYU; b: 11 Nov 1942; m: Scott Glenn Kenney; p: George Glen Hobson & Louise Kimball Hobson Clark; c: Meghan Ann 3, Erica Louise 1; ed: BS elementary ed 1966 U of Utah; MA music ed 1977 BYU; grad cum laude; former: elementary school tchr & music specialist; career: Outstanding Elementary Music Tchr of Utah 1978-9 by UMEA; listed in Outstanding Young Women of Amer; mem: UMEA, MENC; Utah rep to natl seminar on music for handicapped U of Kansas; VP UMEA 1976-9; Natl Ex Comm Council for Gen Music of MENC; civic: com to write Utah State Course of Study for Vocal & Gen Music in Utah 1976-7; Utah State Music Curriculum Adv Com 1975-9; rel: LDS, Relief Soc pres, church music com; home: 2302 Snow Mtn Dr, Sandy; off: C-550 HFAC, BYU.

KNUDSEN, J GORDON Circuit Court Judge, 8th Circuit Court; b: 3 Jan 1928; m: Erla M Call; p: N William & Julia A Brown; c: Debra K Free, Michell, Jonathan; ed: BS 1952 BYU; JD 1959 U of Utah; Phi Kappa Phi BYU 1952; former: private practice attorney; Provo City Judge; mem: Utah State Bar; Circuit Court Judges Assn; mil: enlisted US Air Force 1952-6; rel: LDS, bishop, h council; home: 1665 W 1050 N; off: 48 S 300 W.

KNUDSON, GOLDBURN gen contractor; b: 10 Oct 1903; m: Helen & Margeret; p: Mathias & Julia; c: Paula, Mark, Bruce; ed: 3 yrs BYU; former: fruit farmer; sheep rancher; built 536 homes & commercial bldgs in Utah 1932-1980; publ: personal history by BYU; civic: chm com Lions & Elks; mil: US Air Force; rel: LDS; home: 667 N 500 W.

KUHNI, RALPH J pres & gen mgr John Kuhni Sons Inc; b: 14 Jul 1919; m: Gloria C; p: John H & Nettie W; c: Claudia, Rosemary, Candace, Hans R; ed: BYU Trade Tech; career: pres Utah Feed Manufactures & Dealers Assn 1964-5; pres Downtown Coaches Club 1967-8; civic: Provo Chamber of Commerce; former chm of highways & roads; mil: US Air Force 1942-6; rel: LDS; pres sunday school, MIA, h priest ldrshp; club: Cougar Club; Riverside Country Club; home: 2085 N 150 E; off: 1750 S Kuhni Rd Box 1606.

LAMBERT, MICHAEL J   assoc prof Psychology BYU; b: 17 Jul 1944; m: Linda Pizza; c: 5; ed: BS 1967 MS 1968 PhD 1971 U of Utah; licensed psychologist State of Utah 1971, Marriage & Family Counselor State of Utah 1975; former: psychologist Primary Children's Hospital 1971-4; instr Weber State College 1975; visiting asst prof U of Houston 1975; designated examiner State of Utah Civil Commitment proceedings 1976-8; BYU Counseling Ctr 1971-6; BYU Inst for Studies in Values & Human Behavior; mem: exec sec/treas Soc for Psychotherapy Research 1980-; State of Utah Psychology Licensing Board 1979-; exec sec/treas Utah Psychological Assn 1975-80; board of dir Utah County Mental Health Assn 1975-8; Amer Psychological Assn; Western Psychological Assn; Assn for Humanistic Psychology; publ: *The Effects of Psychotherapy;* co-auth *Bibliography of Behavior Change Research: 1968-1978;* journal articles civic: board of dir, pres, Alpine House 1975-9; home: 930 N 1260 E.

LAMSON, MERLE E   Rare Books Cataloger BYU; b: 10 Aug 1930; m: Norma R; p: Wm E & Elfleda E; c: Steven 16, Merlene 15; ed: AAS 1953 Yakima Valley Jr College; BS 1955 BYU; Colorado College; MS 1960 Columbia U; U of S Calif; BYU; PhD 1975 U of Utah; George Washington Found Scholarship; Natl Sci Found Scholarship; NDEA Title II-B Fellowship; Sigma Pi Sigma; former: librarian & cataloger Carnegie Free Library, Columbia U, S Puget Sound Reg Library, BYU, U of Utah; electronics & math instr Weber County High School; asst & assoc prof BYU Library School; math sci tchr Provo Canyon School; mem: Amer Library Assn; Assn of Amer Library Schools; chm research com Utah Library Assn; Utah Acad Sci, Arts & letters; Phi Delta Kappa; Amer Assn of Univ Profs; Soc of Ed & Scholars; faculty advisor Beta Theta Chapter Beta Phi Mu; coor Re-accreditation Com; Asst to dir Library School; Univ Curriculum Com; publ: *Classification: An Introduction; Formatting Catalog Cards: Samples;* 2 journal articles; civic: board of dir Oakridge Development Co; rel: LDS, clerk, high priest grp ldr, elders quorum pres; home: PO Box 498, Woodland Hills; off: 6446 HBLL, BYU.

LARSEN, J ELMO   retired Interviewer & Employment, USS Geneva Works; b: 1 Dec 1906; m: Genevieve; p:

Hyrum M & Hentietta; c: Carol Ann Jackson, James E; ed:
BS BYU; career: Outstanding Serv Award, Geneva Works
& BYU Athletic Dept; rel: LDS, bishopric, clerk, exec sec;
club: treas Provo Jr Chamber of Commerce; treas Provo
Exchange Club; home: 654 E 500 N; off: 528 S 100 W.

LARSEN, KENNETH M   prof of Mathematics BYU; b: 26
Jun 1927; m: Merlee M Smith; p: Mrs H Martin Larsen; c:
Debra, Joseph, Rebecca, Paul, John, Peter, James, Mark,
Rachel; ed: BA 1950 U of Utah; MA 1956 BYU; PhD 1964
UCLA; Phi Beta Kappa; Phi Kappa Phi; former: tching
asst UCLA; assoc engineer Lockheed Aircraft Corp; mem:
Amer Math Soc; Math Assn of Amer; Soc for Industrial &
Applied Math; Amer Physical Soc; Sigma Xi; publ: 2
papers; mil: US Army 1946-7, 50-1; rel: LDS, asst ward
clerk; home: 2270 N 300 E; off: 348 TMCB, BYU.

LARSON, JERRY W   asst prof Spanish, dir Language
Testing; b: 15 Oct 1945; m: Janet M; p: Arnold W & May S
Darrington; c: Jill 12, Jason 11, Jeneil 9, Jeffrey 7, Jodi
4, Justin 2, Jami 5 mo; ed: BA Utah State U; MA BYU;
PhD U of Minnesota; NDEA Fellowship; former: asst prof
Spanish, Northern Arizona U; instr U of Minnesota; mem:
Amer Council on the Teaching of Foreign Languages;
Amer Assn of Teachers of Spanish & Portuguese; Utah
Foreign Language Assn; award: Phi Kappa Phi Honor Soc;
Sigma Delta Pi Spanish Honor Soc; publ: *Espanol a lo vivo;*
civic: Boy Scout Com; YBA Basketball coach; mil:
honorable discharge Army Security Agcy 1972;
Distinguished Grad, Defense Language Inst, Monterey,
Calif; rel: LDS, bishopric; home: 85 E 1600 N, Orem; off:
240 B-34, BYU.

LAUN, GERHARD, THE REVD   rector, St. Mary's
Episcopal Church, Anglican Clergyman; b: 17 Jan 1941; m:
Georgia Marcelino; p: Hermann & Luise; c: John Thomas
13; ed: MA cum laude U of Frankfurt, W Germany;
Nashotah House; Canterbury & Durham, England; former:
asst to dean St. Paul's Cathedral, Okla City; Vicar of St.
Raphael's Church, Yukon, Okla; instr Bishop's School of
Theology, Diocese of Okla; mem: various clergy assn;
publ: *Anglican – Roman Catholic Relations: The Influence
of the Anglo-Catholic Revival on Relations between the
Anglican and Roman Catholic Communions, 1967;*

rel: Anglican – Episcopalian; mem Standing Com of the Diocese of Utah; alternate to Gen Conv of Episcopal Church, Utah; club: Rotary Internatl; home: 275 E 200 S, Orem; off: 50 W 200 N.

LAYCOCK, HAROLD R   prof Music BYU; b: 14 Nov 1916; m: Lois Evelyn Peterson; p: George Elijah & Fern Redd; c: Christopher, Grant, Rosemary; ed: BA 1937 MA 1947 BYU; DMA 1961 U of S Calif; Karl G Maeser Distinguished Tching Award 1981; former: tchr SLC schools 1940–2; mem: Utah Acad of Sci, Arts & Letters; Music Educators Natl Conf; Amer Musicological Soc; publ: co-auth *First-Year Music Theory;* civic: former Utah State Symphony Orchestra; Utah Valley Symphony Orchestra 4 yrs; pol: Republican county & state del; mil: Infantry & Ordnance Battalions AUS 1943–6, Guam 1945–6; rel: LDS, bishop, stake presidency; home: 734 N 440 W; off: E–546 HFAC, BYU.

LAYCOCK, RALPH GEORGE   Prof of Music & Dir of Orchestras BYU; b: 11 Feb 1920; m: Lucy Tanner; p: George Elijah & Fern Redd; c: Jo Lane, Linda Joyce, Claudia, Elizabeth, Kathryn; ed: BA music 1941 BYU; MS orchestral conducting 1948 Juilliard School; DMA conducting 1970 USC; high honors BYU; honors Juilliard School; former: asst prof of Music Drake U 1949–53; career: Master Tchr ASBYU 1971; Distinguished Faculty Lecturer BYU 1971; mem: Music Educators Natl Conf; Utah music Educators Assn; Pi Kappa Lambda; Phi Mu Alpha; Salt Lake Fed Musicians; Provo Fed Musicians; publ: *Conductor's Corner The Instrumentalist; Music For The Home; Simplified Accompaniments for the LDS Hymns;* musical arrangements for Oakland Temple Pageant; civic: dir Provo Municipal Band; musical dir & conductor Utah Valley Symphony Orchestra; mil: Royal Canadian Air Force 33 mo; bandmaster 1 yr; rel: LDS, branch pres, 70s pres; home: 508 E 600 S, Orem; off: E–464 HFAC, BYU.

LEE, J CRAIG   asst dir BYU Public Affairs; b: 9 Sept 1953; m: Bertha Hiskey; p: Bertha Craig; c: Brandon 4, Rachele 2, Stacey 2; ed: BA interpersonal communication BYU 1978; former: asst dir Performance Scheduling BYU 1977–80; mem: Public Relations Soc of Amer; Council for

Adv & Support of Ed; civic: chm Retail Merchants Com; Orem Chamber of Commerce; board mem Utah Valley Industrial Assn; Hillcrest Park Com; rel: LDS, bishopric, elders quorum pres; club: Orem Gun Club; BYU Cougar Club; off: Hosting Ctr, Thomas House, BYU.

LEWIS, JAMES PAUL   manufacturing mgt consultant; b: 6 Mar 1921; m: Betty Jo Stone; p: James Allen & Anna Lynn Haas; c: Nancy Lynn Bartlett, James Paul Jr, Robert Carl; ed: Long Beach City College; UCLA extension 2 yr course; former: mgr & gen supvr, Fabrication Planning, McDonnell Douglas Aircraft Corp, Long Beach, CA 35 yrs; VP gen mgr Fiber Technology Corp 1978-81; civic: gun safety instr Calif Dept of Fish & Game 1956-76; mil: US Air Force WWII; rel: LDS, bishopric, ward clerk; club: former pres Douglas Long Beach Rod & Gun Club; home: 3007 Iroquois Dr; off: 765 S 100 E.

LIMBURG, NEVIN   exec VP Provo Area Chamber of Commerce; b: 1 Aug 1948; m: Darlene Rose; p: John M & Beverly Standing; c: Matthew 8, Heidi 6, Lauralee 5, Rebecca 1; ed: BA U of Utah; MA U of Redlands, Calif; Owl & Key, U of Utah; former: accountant Peat, Marwick, Mitchell & Co; auditor JC Penney Co; career: Inst for Org Mgt 6 yr grad; mem: Amer Chamber of Commerce Exec Assn; Natl Assn of Development Cos; award: Award of Merit, Boy Scouts of Amer; publ: writer, columnist *The Daily Herald* 1980-; civic: board of dir Utah State Chamber of Commerce; Utah County Travel Council; v-chm United Way; RSVP Advisory Board; board of dir UVIDA; pol: state & county del, voting dist chm; mil: US Army Reserve 2nd Lt 1973-81; Dist Mil Grad, U of Utah; rel: LDS, stake presidency, bishopric, h council; club: Provo Rotary; BYU Cougar Club; home: 1394 E 640 S; off: 10 E 300 N.

LIND, CHARLENE   assoc prof of Clothing & Textiles BYU; b: 6 Dec 1932; p: Leslie A Lind; ed: BA Utah State U; MA U of Maryland; PhD U of Wisc, Madison; Ellen H Richards Scholarship 1971 Amer Home Econ Assn; Natl 4-H Fellowship 1959-60; Phi Kappa Phi; Omicron Nu; Phi Upsilon Omicron; former: chm BYU Clothing & Textiles Dept 1972-81; County Extension Agent 4-H in Multnomah Co Oregon; County Home Agent, Carbon Co Utah; career:

natl sec Assn of College Prof of Text & Clo; VP Utah Home Econ Assn; reviewer for Journal of Home Econ; mem: Assn of College Profs of Textiles & Clothing; Amer & Utah Home Econ Assn; Amer Handweavers Guild; Costume Soc of Amer; Atwater Handweavers Guild; pol: Republican dist vice-chm; rel: LDS, YWMIA pres, tchr; home: 2974 N 320 E; off: 2251-C SFLC, BYU.

LITTLEFIELD, MAX   Capt, Deputy Chief of Police, Patrol Div Commander; b: 22 Jan 1928; m: Colleen Adamson; p: John R & Eva B; c: Stanley M, Robert A, Mark C, Carolyn; ed: FBI Natl Acad; US Army X-ray Tech School, Munich, Germany; BYU; Northwestern Traffic Inst; former: patrolman, Sgt & Lt; career: 20-30 Club Internatl Serv to Community Award 1963; Footprinters Outstanding Peace Officer 1964; Provo Exchange Club Outstanding Serv Award 1968; KSL Radio & TV Outstanding Serv Award 1970; Utah Motor Safety Award 1963-4; mem: Utah Peace Officers Assn; Central Utah Police Officers Assn, FBI Natl Acad Associates; Internatl Chiefs of Police Assn; civic: PTA Safety Chm; Natl Safety Council Traffic Safety Coor; mil: US Army; rel: LDS, bishopric; club: Utah Lake Lions Club; home: 1237 S 1100 W; off: PO Box 1849.

LOSEE, BLAIR I   family dentist; b: 26 Jun 1953; m: Sandra; p: Cecil Dee & Ava Bishop; c: Justin 2, Natalie 1; ed: BS zoology BYU; DMD Washington U; BYU cum laude; OKU Honor Soc Washington U top 10% dental school class; former: dental resident Illinois Masonic Medical Ctr; mem: Amer Dental Assn; Utah Dental Assn; Provo Dist Dental Soc; award: Eagle Scout; rel: LDS, elders quorum presidency, bishopric; home: 1711 S 450 W; off: 1275 N University No. 5.

LOSEE, REX L   Dept Coor Electrica & Automation UTC; b: 27 Oct 1926; m: Diane Holt; p: Ardella Anderson & Andrew Fredrick; c: Greg, Kurt, Kerri Kopinsky, Todd, Michelle; ed: BYU; U of Utah; Utah State U; Assoc of Applied Sci UTC; former: instr UTC; apprentice trainer US Steel Corp; career: Tchr of the Year UTC 1978; Regents Award for Excellence in Teaching 1978; mem: Instrument Soc of Amer; Amer Vocational Assn; Utah Vocatinal Assn; UPEA Assn; award: Instrument & Process

Control Training Course, Power Plants; Mine Cert Preparation; mil: Chief Electrician, US Maritime; rel: LDS, seventy; club: 2 Gold Medals Skills Olympics, Vocational Industrial Clubs of Amer; home: 390 N 300 E, Lehi; off: UTC 1395 N 150 E.

LUCIDO, BONNIE RAE instr & clinical supvr Ed Psychology BYU; b: 18 Aug 1934; m: Joseph G; p: Arthur P & Mary Young Wilson; c: Clifton E, Starla Kay Blackburn, Lori Henry, Scott, Fara Mary; ed: BS cum laude MS speech pathology BYU; PhD in progress U of Iowa; former: public school speech clinician; asst development dir central Utah communication centered prog; coord public school Communication & Hearing Conservation prog; dir Preschool Handicapped Ed Prog; dept head Utah State Training School Communicative Disorders Dept; inservice instr Utah State Training School; mem: Amer Speech Language & Hearing Assn; Utah County Assn for Retarded Citizens; Amer Assn for Mental Deficiency; civic: board Utah County Assn for Retarded Citizens; Headstart Health Policy Board; rel: LDS, primary & Relief Soc tchr; home: 6182 W 10550 N, Highland; off: 138 CCB, BYU.

LUTHY, MELVIN J prof of English & Linguistics; b: 15 Nov 1936; m: Anne-Maj Savstrand; p: August & Frieda; c: Michael 15, Melanie 12, Annette 8, Michelle 6; ed: PhD Indiana U 1967 Linguistics & Finno-Ugric Studies; Fulbright Award to Finland; Phi Kappa Phi; Title VI Language Awards; former: asst prof U of Wisconsin-Oshkosh; tch assoc Indiana U; mem: Linguistic Soc of Amer; Soc of Advancement of Scandinavian Studies; ITESOL; Deseret Lang & Linguistic Soc; publ: book on colloquial Finnish; articles on language, teaching materials for Finnish; pol: del to state convention; campaign worker; mil: capt, Army Military Intelligence; Bronze Star; rel: LDS, bishopric, h council, branch pres; home: 551 E 4380 N; off: A-290 JKBA, BYU.

LYNN, SHARON REDFORD part owner, mgr Fabric Mill; b: 8 Mar 1947; m: David Lynn; p: Rex & Carol; c: Josh 6, Jeffrey 5, Justin 3, Jeremy 1; ed: Bachelors BYU social work; MS; former: social worker Canadan Dept of Social Development 1971-3; child protection worker;

adoption placement worker; lifeguard & instr Royal Lifesaving Soc; award: Award of Merit Royal Lifesaving Soc; Royal Conservatory of Music Grade 10, piano tchr; rel: LDS, Relief Soc presidency; home: 2098 W 300 N; off: 250 W Center.

LYON, THOMAS EDGAR "TED"   prof & chm Dept Spanish & Portuguese BYU; b: 13 May 1939; m: Cheryl Larsen; p: T Edgar & Hermana Forsberg; c: Thomas Rex 16, Ann Marie 14, Jennifer 12, Gregory 4, Peter 4; ed: BA 1963 U of Utah; PhD 1967 UCLA; Phi Beta Kappa; Fulbright Grant to Chile; ACLS grant to Chile; Natl Endowment to Humanities Summer Fellow; former: prof UCLA, U of Oklahoma, U of Wisconsin, U of Glasgow; career: Who's Who in the West; Internatl Scholars Directory; Dictionary of Internatl Bibliography; Outstanding Educators of Amer 1975; mem: Modern Lang Assn; publ: 2 books, 26 articles; civic: Lions Club; Big Brothers of Amer; pol: Republican Associates; mil: 6 mo active; 7.5 yrs US Army Reserve artillery; rel: LDS, bishoprics, youth; home: 3008 N 175 E; off: 164 FOB, BYU.

McDONALD, DEAN M   educator; b: 5 Sep 1918; m: Arlene Redd; p: Lloyd C & Myrtle Peterson; c: Joy, Lynette, Marian, Michael, Julie; ed: BS MS Utah State U; EdD BYU; former: Dean of Students, Treasure Valley Community College, Ontario, OR; pres College of Eastern Utah, Price, UT; publ: *The Comprensive Community College – Problems & Prospects;* civic: pres Carbon Co Chamber of Commerce; Ldrship Acad Orem Chamber; pol: Republican; mil: US Air Force 1942-5; rel: LDS, bishop, h council; club: Rotary; Kiwanis; home: Rt 1 Box 36B, Genola; off: UTC, 1395 N 150 E.

McMULLIN, E CURTIS   realtor associate; b: 23 Jun 1910; m: Ruth Fisher; p: John Edwin & Edna Mae Dayton; c: Cpt Michael USAF, Kathleen Peterson; ed: BYU music 1924-5; Weber College economics & music; Amer Inst of Banking; grad U of Washington Grad School of Banking; scholarships at Weber College & U of Washington; former: banker with Bank of Amer & United Calif Bank; career: Real Estate Sales Trainer Acad; RE Classified Advertising Workshop; mem: Utah County Board of Realtors; former commander Amer Legion Post 13; award: Special Citation for volunteer serv with Utah Div Amer Cancer Soc; publ: *Industrialization of the San Jernando Valley;* civic: exec com Provo Amer Legion Post 13; former reg dir S Utah Div Amer Cancer Soc; mil: US Army Finance Div assigned to USAF WW II; Good Conduct Medal; Marksmanship M-1 Rifle & auto weapons; rel: LDS, bishop, h council; club: former pres Commonwealth Club of San Francisco; Rotary; Kiwanis; Optimist; home: 255 S 700 E, Orem; off: 215 W 940 N.

McNAMARA, DELBERT HAROLD   prof of Physics & Astronomy; b: 28 Jun 1923; m: Elmeda; p: Delbert H & Florence; c: Marilyn, Susan, Jay; ed: BS PhD U of Calif at Berkeley; Lick Observatory Fellow; former: research asst U of Calif at Berkeley; research astronomer Space Sci Lab N Amer Aviation; career: Distinguished Faculty Lecture BYU 1966; Maeser Research Award 1964; mem: Amer Astronomical Soc; Astronomical Soc of the Pacific; Internatl Astronomical Union; Sigma Psi; publ: articles in Variable Stars, Stellar Evolution, Interstellar Reddening; editor, Publications Astronomical Soc of the Pacific; mil: Lt jg USNR Pacific Theatre WW II; Purple Heart; rel: LDS, h council; home 1880 N 1500 E; off: 408 ESC, BYU.

MADSEN, HAROLD STANLEY   prof of Linguistics BYU; b: 23 Apr 1926; m: Mona Eloise Darton; p: Harold Johannes & Helen Anna Sanders; c: Suzanne Garoufalias, Larry Wayne, Debra Puckett, Denise Williams, Marcia Hansen, Harold Jay; ed: BA MA PhD; Karl G. Maesar Research & Creative Arts Award; U of Colorado Academic Award; Ford Found Research Award; former: Haile Sellassie I Univ Ethiopia; Amer Univ in Cairo Egypt; mem: Tchrs of English to Speakers of Other Languages; publ: *Adaptation in Languge Jeaching;* 30 articles & chapters; civic: board of governors Amer Community School, Ethiopia; pol: county chm, state board, Young Republicans; mil: US Army WWII European Theatre; rel: LDS, branch pres, h council, bishopric; home: 720 Sunny Ln, Orem; off 157 FB, BYU.

MADSEN, RONALD ANDERSEN   dir Provo City Redevelopment Agency & Housing Authority; b: 16 Oct 1943; m: Sharon King; p: Carl D & Jneil A; c: Andrus 12, Julie 11, Kristie 9, Laura Marie 3, Amy 2; ed: BA 1969 MS public admin 1970 BYU; former: Rehabilitation Coord, Planning Aid, Admin Asst, Property Mgt, Advertising Business; mem: pres state chapter Natl Assn of Housing & Redevelopment Officials, regional & natl com for Development and Economic Development; mil: US Army Reserve 8 yrs; rel: LDS, bishopric, tchr, clerk; home: 2030 W 1550 N; off: 351 W Center.

MANGUM, JOHN HARVEY   prof of Chemistry & Biochemistry BYU; b: 16 Apr 1933; m: Sandra; p: Milton & Vera; c: Michele, Marcia, Leslie, Bryan; ed: BS MS BYU; PhD U of Wash; NIH Predoctoral Fellowship; career: NIH Career Development Award; Karl G Maeser Research Award 1976; mem: Amer Chem Soc; Amer Soc of Biological Chemists; Amer Soc of Pharmacognosy; publ: 50 articles & abstracts; pol: Amer Chem Soc Scientific Counselor to Sens Garn & Hatch; rel: LDS, scoutmaster; home: 692 S 450 E, Orem; off: 647 WIDB, BYU.

MANNING, EUGENE   gen mgr K-96/KDOT Radio; b: 6 Jun 1932; m: Joellyn; p: Walter J & Ada Grace Jenkins; c: David, Maureen, Shannon, Sean; ed: MA communications 1973 BYU; Earl J Glade Award for Outstanding Sr in Broadcasting 1968; former: Broadcast Serv Dept BYU 1963-73; mem: chm board of dir Better Business Bureau of Utah County; Handshakers; PR Div Provo Chamber of Commerce; board of dir Utah County Chapter Amer Cancer Soc; pol: asst area dir to elect Ray Beckham to US Congress; mil: US Navy 1951-5; rel: LDS, bishop, h council, stake mission pres, temple worker; club: Exchange Club of Utah County; home: 142 N 600 W; off: PO Box 960.

MARSHALL, DONALD RAY   prof of Humanities BYU; b: 25 Nov 1934; m: Jean Stockseth; p: Wilford Earl & Eva Daly; c: Robin 13, Jordan 11, Reagan 6; ed: BA art 1960 MA English 1965 BYU; PhD Amer Lit 1971 U of Conn; mem: Amer Film Inst; British Film Inst; award: 1st place Best Musical Score 1960; 1st place Choral Music Composition 1959; 1st place Best Fiction, Dialogue 1974; 2nd place Best Collection of Short Stories, Utah Fine Arts 1976; numerous 1st place awards for color photography; publ: short story collections: *The Rummage Sale* and *Frost in the Orchard;* TV/screen play: *Christmas Snows,*

Christmas Winds; civic: Utah Arts Council Lit Board; mil: US Army & Natl Guard; rel: LDS, bishop; home: 2765 Oneida Ln; off: A-261 JKB, BYU.

MATSON, REX C   pres Security Title & Abstract Co; b: 17 Mar 1920; m: Jeannine Frandsen; p: Joseph & Hannah M; c: Larry, Kenneth, Mary Lynne, Peter; ed: BYU 3 yrs; mem: Amer Land Title Assn; Utah Land Title Assn; civic: VP Jr Chamber of Commerce; pres Exchange Club of Provo; mil: Captain artillery, 5 yrs WW II, 2 yrs Korea; Purple Heart; Bronze Star; re: LDS, bishopric; club: Riverside Country Club; home: 1180 E 560 N; off: 55 E Center.

MAYFIELD, CRAIG KIMBALL   BYU prof; b: 17 Mar 1927; m: Elaine Ward; p: John B & Doris Niess; c: Dean, Rene, Jan; ed: bachelor & masters U of Oregon; doctors BYU; post doctorate work U of Illinois; Ford Found Fellowship; former: BYU-Hawaii; San Jose State U; U of Illinois; career: 2 natl awards from Natl Univ Extension Assn; Outstanding Teaching Award, US Coast Guard; mem: Internatl Reading Assn; Western College Reading Assn; award: Who's Who in the West; Leaders in Ed; Amer Men in Sci; Men of Achievement; publ: *Reading Skills for Law Students; Physician's Electro-Diagnostic Handbook; Successful Study Skills; Improving Reading Speed and Comprehension; Critical Reading;* 18 journal articles; civic: regional Boy Scout Com; mil: Sgt US Army; Meritorious Sev Award, 4th Replacement Depot, Japan; rel: LDS bishop, stake presidency, temple officiator; home: 4026 N 800 E; off: 3126 HBLL, BYU.

MCALLISTER, E CRAIG   lawyer; b: 17 Nov 1951; m: AnnaRae; p: Dale A & Faye C; c: Melinda 7, Marsha 6, Mary 5, Michael 3, Martin 1; ed: BS business mgt & accounting magna cum laude 1975 JD 1978 BYU; Phi Kappa Phi; former: inst UTC; research asst BYU; mem: Amer Inn of Court; Utah State Bar Assn; civic: dir Provo Chamber of Commerce, Provo Handshaker, Legislative Action Com, law tchr Utah Continuing Ed, guest lecturer Amer Inst of Medical Technology, former pres, sec & treas, Orem Jaycees; pol: county del; Legislative Action Com Provo Chamber of Commerce; rel: LDS, sunday school pres, youth ldr, choir dir; club: Orem Jaycees; home: 369 W 700 S, Orem; off: 8 W Center.

MCDONOUGH, MICHAEL L recording engineer, producer; b: 17 Dec 1951; m: Marilyn; p: Robert & Betty; ed: BA communications BYU; former: head engineer AT&T Recording, Hollywood; career: awards for producing *Illustrated Man, Kaleidoscope, The Man, A Sound of Thunder, The Halloween Tree*; awards for directing *The First Vision, The Deserter;* mem: Audio Engineering Soc; rel: LDS; home: 1448 S 280 E, Orem; off 135 MPS, BYU.

MCMURTREY, GLENN JAY admin asst to dean College of Fine Arts & Communications; coor Mormon Festival of Arts; b: 15 Apr 1949; m: Mary L; p: Lawrence Jay & Dolly; c: Jennifer 7, Michael Jay 5, Stephen Jay 3, Nathan Jay 2; ed: BA English; BS finance; Master of Ed Admin; Master of Public Admin; Charles C Mott Found Fellowship; former:BYU Traffic Court Judge; career: 1981 memo commendation from Pres of BYU for audit com; 1981 Golden Cup IABC Intermtn Excellence in Special Publs; 1981 Silver Cup IABC Intermtn Merit in newsletters; 1981 Distinguished Achievement in special topics NSPRA; mem: Internatl Assn of Business Communicators; award: 1979 Outstanding Young Man of the Year, Jaycees; 2-time 1st place softball champ BYU; Intramural Fencing Champ; publ: exec editor *Focus, Mormon Festival of Arts, Bridges,* and performance publs; rel: LDS, stake 70 pres; home: 1330 N 1520 W, PG.

MEECHAM, ANAGENE D Provo City Councilmember; b: 28 Dec 1925; m: Elmo V; p: Thomas C & Alice B; c: Christine, Susan, Thomas G; ed: BYU; former: Provo School District; Provo City Commissioner 1978-81; career: USEA Outstanding Sec of the Year Award 1975; Civic Serv Award 1980; service awards, Handicapped Awareness Inc & UTC; mem: Amer Public Works Assn; Utah State Peace Officer Assn; Utah State Parks & Rec Assoc; Natl Assn of Housing & Redevelopment Officials; Utah Library Assn; civic: Metropolitan Water Board; Provo Library Trustee; Ladies Chamber of Commerce; Pink Lady at Utah Valley Hospital; PTA 20 yrs; Neighborhood Prog; board mem Provo Jordan Parkway Authority; Natl Cougar Club, Utah State Fireman Training Adv Com & Fire Prevention Com; chm Gen Adv Com UTC; UTC Foundation Com; Utah State Adv Council for Vocational & Technical Ed; United Way of Utah County board; former chm Provo Housing Authority Board & Mountainland's Community Action Agcy; Resolution Com Utah League of Cities & Towns; rel: LDS, typist Provo Temple; club: Lady Lions; home: 786 W 1020 S; off: PO Box 1849.

MELBY, ALAN K   asst prof Linguistics BYU; consultant Mgt Accounting Inc; ed: BS mathematics magna cum laude 1973 MA linguistics 1974 PhD computational linguistics 1976 BYU; coursework Notre Dame, Purdue, U of Neuchatel Switzerland; mem: Linguistic Soc of Amer; Linguistic Assn of Canada & US; Assn for Computational Linguistics; Amer Translators Assn; Assn for Computing Machinery; Acoustical Soc of Amer; Deseret Language & Linguistics Soc; Amer Assn for Applied Linguistics; award: Outstanding Young Men of Amer; Who's Who in the West; publ: 6 articles; 18 papers; off: Linguistics Dept, BYU.

MELDRUM, NORTON R   lead custodian BYU; b: 17 Aug 1947; m: Keri; p: Jack & Louise; c: Christopher 6, Blake 3, Rebecca 1; ed: Associate degree; former: auto mechanic; truck driver; award: Scouters Training Award; Scouters Key; Den Leaders Training Award; Scouting 2nd Miler Award for Outstanding Service; Scouting Unit Commissioner; Training Com; rel: LDS; home: 573 Nb 500 W, Orem; off: 248 JRCB, BYU.

MELENDEZ, GLORIA SCHAFFER   Asst Prof of Spanish; b: 23 Jan 1932; m: Mario Melendez; p: Dr Jay Maitland Schaffer & Hazel Stocks Davila; c: Bunny, Mark, Terry, Holly Sue, Patsi; ed: BA 1955 U of Utah; PhD 1980 BYU; 1st Woman Fullbright Scholar in Latin Amer; Natl Sci Found Scholarship; former: tchr Spanish & English, Farrer Jr High School 1967-72; mem: ACTFL; UFLA, Fullbright Alumni Assn; publ: on computerized teaching, Aztec medicinal herbs; Mexican-Amer proverbs; rel: LDS; home: 1110 S 150 W, Orem; off: 164 FOB, BYU.

MEMMOTT, MARCUS   business mgr Plumbers & Steamfitters Local 466; b: 6 Apr 1948; m: Susan Lloyd; p: Byron & Zelma; c: Angela 3; ed: Snow College 1 yr; Utah Pipe Trades Prog grad 4 yrs; Academic Scholarship to

Snow College; Future Farmers of Amer Awards; former: local union officer, Pipefitter & Plumber Local 466; mem: officer United Assn of Journeymen & Apprentices of the Plumbing & Pipefitting Industry of the US & Canada; civic: town councilman, Cedar Hills; community committees; pol: political action coms; mil: US Army; Lehi Natl Guard 8 yrs; rel: LDS; club: BPOE Lodge 849; home: 10137 N Maple Court, Cedar Hills; off: 605 E 600 S.

MERRITT, LAVERE B   BYU prof, civil engineer; b: 11 Mar 1936; m: Jackie Call; p: Joseph M & Lera B; c: Teri F, Lynn T; ed: BS MS U of Utah; PhD 1970 U of Wash; BYU Faculty Advisory Council 1981-4; former: civil engineer US Forest Serv; career: Sigma Xi Natl Res Soc; Amer Acad of Environmental Engineers; mem: Amer Soc of Civil Engrs, natl dir 1982-5; Amer Soc for Eng Educators; Amer Water Works Assn; Assn Env Eng Professors; publ: 13 tech papers; 42 research reports; 16 conf presentations; civic: pres Utah Water Pollution Cont Assn 1978-9; natl dir Water Pollution Cont Fed 1981-4; chm Provo Metro Water Board 1976-; rel: LDS, elders pres, scouting ldr, bishop; home: 3035 N 600 E; off: 368-R CB, BYU.

MILLER, CHUCK   news dir K-96 Radio; b: 6 Sep 1954; m: Karen; p: Jimmy & Delores; c: Christopher 4, Benjamin 3; ed: college; A Honor Roll; A-B Honor Roll; former: news dir KFTN Radio; Air Personality on KFTN; career: 3 Intermtn Network News Awards; rel: LDS, asst ward clerk, organist, sunday school tchr; home: 59 E 600 N, Orem; off: PO Box 960.

MILLER, DONALD LEROY   bldg construction instr UTC; pres Sol-A-Terra Co; b: 14 Sep 1927; m: Kathleen Shirley; p: Herman & Florence; c: Nancy, Timothy, Theresa, Robert, Mary, Patricia, Susan; ed: 3 yrs at Colorado State U and U of SD; former: Bldg Const Dept Chm at UTC and Mitchell Area Voc-Tech School; career: certified bldg inspector Internatl Conf of Bldg Officials; publ: article in Modern Builder; weekly column "Plumb & Square" in Daily Republic, Mitchell, SD; mil: US Army WW II European Theatre of Operations 3 yrs; Victory Medal; rel: catholic; home: 686 W 1285 N, Orem; off: UTC PO Box 1609.

MINER, M VINSON   Head Basketball Coach, professional staff UTC; b: 30 Apr 1950; m: Patty; p: J Edwin; c: Mekette 4, Tierra 1; ed: MA; home: 2350 N Geneva Rd, PO Box 441; off: Box 1609.

MOAKE, GLORIA GEHRING   owner Moake Trailer Sales, Rentals, Parts, Serv; b: 20 May 1927; m: Charles R Moake; p: Paul H & Belva Gehring; c: Marilyn, Marjorie, Steven, Connie, Karen, Todd; ed: S High School, SLC; former: inventory control clerk Federal Govt; civic: PTA pres Lincoln Elem; rel: LDS, Relief Soc presidency, youth & child tchr; home: 1582 W 1000 N; off: 550 S 500 W.

MONTROSE, CELESTIA   diet counselor; pres Diet Center Inc; b: 15 Sep 1932; m: John L Montrose Jr; p: Barney & Hattie Vaughn; c: Steven, Bonnie, Leslie, John III, Doug; ed: college 2 yrs; LDS Business College 1 yr given by Daughters of Amer Revolution; former: bank accountant; career: Diet Counselor Cert; mem: Diet Counselors of Utah County; rel: LDS, Relief Soc tchr & librarian, pres YWMIA; home: 290 E 260 S, Orem; off: 201 E Center.

MOON, HAROLD KAY   prof of Spanish BYU; b: 24 Jul 1932; m: Mayva Anne Magleby; p: Harold K & Ellen DeWitt; c: Anne, Jacqueline, Kelly, Todd, Leslie, Shawn, Kristen, Elaine, Karen; ed: BA MA PhD; former: instr Syracuse Univ; tchr Apline School Dist; publ: *Alejandro Casona, Playwight; Spanish Literature, A Critical Approach;* 11 articles; 1 book review; 4 papers; 1 play; 7 short stories; 2 books in progress; rel: LDS; home: 764 W Center, Orem; off: 168 FOB, BYU.

MOORE, HAL G   mathematician, BYU prof; b: 14 Aug 1929; m: D'On Empey; p: Lewis Henry & Nora Gillman; c: David Claudius, Nora D'On, Alison; ed: BS 1952 MS 1957 U of Utah; PhD 1967 U of Calif Santa Barbara; former: tchr SLC Public Schools 1952-3; instr Carbon Jr College & Carbon High School 1953-5; instr & admin asst Purdue U 1957-60; asst prof BYU 1961-7; exec asst to chm BYU Dept of Math 1961-4; assoc in math U of Calif Santa Barbara; assoc prof BYU 1967-71; prof of math BYU 1971-; undergrad coor Dept of Math BYU 1975-9; career: Natl Sci Found Sci Faculty Fellow 1964-6; BYU Research Fellow 1968-9, 71-2; BYU Summer Research 1970, 81;

MAA (NSF) Summer Seminar 1973; Prof of Month 1977; listed in Amer Men & Women of Sci, Who's Who in the West, Who's Who in Amer; mem: Amer Math Soc; Math Assn of Amer, 1st v-chm & prog chm of Intermtn Sec; Sigma Xi, pres; Utah Acad of Sci, Arts & Letters; Amer Assn for the Adv of Sci; publ: co-auth *University Calculus, with Analytic Geometry and Linear Algebra;* auth *Precalculus Mathematics* & instr manual; *Syllabus for Math 111; Elementary Linear Algebra with Applications;* 15 articles & papers; civic: Boy Scouts of Amer, asst dist commissioner 1968-72, committeeman 1972-7; Utah County Council on Drug Abuse Rehabilitation board mem; pol: Republican dist chm, state conv del; rel: LDS, bishop, h council; home: 631 W 650 S, Orem; off: 324 TMCB, BYU.

MORRIS, ARTHUR GRAY   pres Standard Office Supply, Inc; b: 23 Jan 1928; p: William G & Leona Steele; c: Kathleen 16, Cynthia 14, former: dist sales mgr Gillette Co, Paper Mate Div; career: Natl Salesman of the Yr 1965-67; President's Cup Winner & Sales Mgr of the Yr 1970; mem: Natl Office Products Assn; Natl Office Machine Dealers Assn; civic: Provo Chamber of Commerce 1981; pol: Republican Natl Com; finance chm pro-tem Farnsworth for US Congress com; mil: US Navy WWII Hospital Corpsman; rel: LDS, h council, elders pres; club: Provo Rotary Club board of dir 1981-2; home: 1313 E 580 S; off: 120 N Univ Ave.

MORRIS, CARLA DEE   reference librarian Provo Public Library; b: 6 Apr 1953; m: Steven Ross Morris; p: Don Carlton Mittelstadt & Leeola Jean; ed: BA 1975 MLS 1977 BYU; mem: Utah Library Assn; Amer Library Assn; rel: LDS, sunday school stake board, Relief Soc presidency; home: 1200 N Terrace Dr; off: 13 N 100 E.

MOSES, GORDON WOODRUFF   educator UTC; b: 24 Jun 1922; m: Mary Ellen Norsworthy; p: Elmer W & Alice M; c: Laura, Gordon, Donald, Darin, John; ed: BE engineering U S Calif at LA; MA ed admin U of Utah; doctoral candidate ed admin BYU; also 2 yrs electronic engr Utah State U, U of Paris France, grad engr course U Calif San Diego; engr & ed San Diego State, Mesa College, San Diego City College; honor roll; former: sr design & proj

engr Gen Dynamics – Astronautics, San Diego and at
Convair, Fort Worth, Texas; secondary ed instr BYU; tchr
Culver High School; electronics instr UTC SLC; electronic
technician US Forest Serv; radio engr & announcer KVNU
Logan; installed missile tracking station at Cape
Canaveral; developed mtn home bldg lots; built, owned &
operated rental units; career: div chm Gen Ed at UTC;
mem: AIEE, Phi Delta Kappa, UEA, UVA, UPEA, Convair
Mgt Club; UTC Faculty Senate; board mem Educare &
ANALAC; publ: 60 one–hr ed TV progs in electronics;
civic: board mem Upper Whittemore Property Owners
Assn & Water Co; mem & treas Sertoma; candidate for
Board of Ed; mil: US Navy commissioned officer in charge
of naval radar station WW II; Lt JG Destroyer USS
McGowan DD–678 Korea; Bat Commander Midshipman
Officer; V–12 prog at U S Calif; certs of training for
fighter direction, communications, training officer,
midshipman school; rel: LDS, branch & dist pres, 70s pres,
stake dir tchr training; club: Lambda Delta Sigma pres at
UTC, VP at Utah State U; Amateur Radio Club; Aviation
Club; home: 3749 N 500 E; off: 1395 N 150 E.

MOSS, J JOEL   prof Family Sci BYU; b: 17 Aug 1922; m:
Audra Lucile Call; p: John W & Zelma Bell; c: Kevin,
Lani, Katheryn, Shauna, David, Janine; ed: PhD 1953 U of
N Carolina; Sigma Psi; Phi Kappa Phi; former: assoc prof
W Virginia U, U of Nebraska, prof S Illinois U; career:
Osborne Award for Distinguished Teaching, Natl Council
of Family Relations 1970; one of 5 Home Economists of
the Year 1963, Amer Home Econ Assn for TV
Programming on Marriage; mem: Natl Council on Family
Relationships; Amer Home Econ Assn Utah Council on
family Relations; Utah Home Econ Assn; publ: *Moss on
Marriage* booklet; journal articles; civic: public speaking;
pol: former dist chm; mil: mstr sgt ETO WW II 16 mo; rel:
LDS, Sunday School tchr; home: 751 S 500 E, Orem; off:
1054 SWKT, BYU.

MOTT, GLORIA   pres Glo–Ver Enterprises; b: 3 Jul 1927;
m: LaVerl V; p: LeRoy & Ethel Ferguson; c: Peggy,
Richard, Rebecca Anne; ed: BYU, U of Wisc; Cert
Advertising Specialist; former: Provo City Welcome
Wagon Hostess; career: Outstanding Business Woman in
Provo; Business Woman of Month in Orem; SAAI Award

for Marketing Development Seminar; mem: ASI; Specialty Advertising Assn Internatl; Orem Ambassadors; Salt Lake Valley Convention & Visitors Bureau; civic: Orem Chamber of Commerce; Provo Chamber of Commerce; rel: LDS, stake Relief Soc board 5 yrs; club: Or-Lin Club; home: 740 N 1000 E; off: 215 W 940 N Suite 1.

MURPHY, LONETA   Women's   Rights   Woman; homemaker; b: 30 May 1924; m: Joseph Robison Murphy; p: Roy & Agness Mangus; c: Joel, Gayle, Robert, David, Philip; ed: BYU; former: pres League of Women Voters of Provo, Utah County, Chair Public Relations League Women Voters of Utah, Women's Rights Chair for the League Women of Utah; mem: Natl Org for Women; Natl Women's Party; League Women Voters; Mormons for ERA; public relations Alice Louise Reynolds Forum; publ: "The Voice of Womankind: An Historical Perspective of Equality in Utah"; Equal Rights a Forgotten Part of Utah Heritage at Provo Canyon School; Change in Utah County & Provo City Govt Coms; pol: Voting Judge 6 yrs; Democrat; advocate of Equal Rights Amendment; rel: LDS, pres & tchr of Primary, MIA, Relief Soc; club: BYU Women; home: 2806 N 650 E.

NAYLOR, CLYDE R   Utah County Engr; m: Fae; p: John R & Rosella Wright; c: Janice, Shari, Lisa, Bret, Jerry, Becky; ed: MS civil engineering 1962 BYU; Most Outstanding Student in Civil Engineering 1960; former: consulting engr; part-time tchr BYU; mem: ASCE; NSPE; ACSM; UCLS; USPE; NACE; ARTBA; pres elect Utah Soc of Professional Engrs; award: Eagle Scout; publ: *Use of State Coordinates* Utah County; pol: elected county surveyor; rel: LDS, bishop, h council; home: 189 E 1864 S, Orem; off: 160 E Center.

NAYLOR, JAY H   chm Dept of Recreation Mgt & Youth Ldrship BYU; b: 5 Oct 1934; m: Ruth Ann Romney; p: Thomas C & Caroline; c: Judy, Michael, David, Wendy, Barbara; ed: BS 1958 MS 1959 BYU; EdD 1973 U of Utah; Phi Kappa Phi; former: dir of intramurals BYU; dir Pacific Palisades Youth Ctr, Calif; career: former board of dir AALR; adv board Amer Camps Internatl; mem: AAHPERD; NRPA; URPA; UAHPERD; publ: textbook

Managing Neighborhood Parks & Centers; co-auth *Careers in Recreation;* civic: rec chair Provo River Parkway; chm Provo City Rec & Parks Adv Board; Provo City Youth Adv Board; rel: LDS, stake presidency, h council, bishopric; home: 495 E 4300 N; of: 273 RB, BYU.

NELSON, DAVID G   baseball coach UTC; b: 28 Oct 1950; m: Zeffie Sheriff; p: David & Kathalee; c: DG 7, Kimberlee 6, Mattie 4, Breck 3, Kamron 5 mo; ed: BS BYU; civic: basketball referee; rel: LDS; home: 218 N 300 W, Orem; off:
PO Box 1609.

NELSON, DONALD TRACY   pres Deseret Charities Inc; b: 29 Sep 1934; m: Elaine Duke; p: James Henry & Margie Jacobs; c: Tracy 20, Mark 16, Daniel 11, Chris 11; BS MPA BYU; Amer Legion Scholastic Award; Dean's List; former: personnel consul; personnel dir; career: Dist VII Case Award for serving as dist conf chm; mem: Council for the Adv & Support of Ed; Amer Mgt Assn; Provo Jordon Parkway Found; award: athletic scholarships; mem Canadian Natl Football Champ Team; publ: articles on fundraising, personnel; upcoming book on fundraising; civic: Kiwanis; mil: batal communications officer, exec off in line rifle co; rel: LDS, bishop, h council, stake presidency; home: 3790 N 850 E; off: A-384 ASB, BYU.

NELSON, K LEROI   prof of chemistry BYU; b: 4 Apr 1926; m: Ina Shepherd; p: Parley LeRoi & Margaret; c: Marlene, Alan, Ronald, Harold, Karalee, David; ed: BS 1948 Utah State U; PhD 1952 Purdue U; post doct 1953 UCLA; former: instr 1953-4 Purdue U; asst prof 1954-6 Wayne State U; assoc prof 1956 prof 1961 BYU; career: visiting prof Oregon State 1951-2; mem: Amer Chemical Soc; Sigma Xi; British Chemical Soc; Amer Assn for Advancement of Sci; AAVP; Phi Kappa Phi; publ: "Laboratory Projects in Organic Chemistry, Correlated Organic Laboratory Experiments"; civic: Boy Scouts of Amer scoutmaster, explorer advisor; mil: US Army Air Force 1944-5; rel: LDS, stake MIA supt, bishop, YM pres, asst ward clerk; club: Kiwanis; Pi Kappa Alpha; home: 2010 N Oak Ln; off: 222 ESC, BYU.

NELSON, MARGARET R   Deputy Utah County Attorney;

b: 27 May 1952; p: V Pershing & Hattie Jones Nelson; ed:
BA English BYU magna cum laude 1973; Dean's List; Phi
Kappa Phi; JD charter class BYU 1976; BYU Law Honor
Soc; Board of Advocates; former: secondary student tchr;
law clerk; private attorney 1977–; law tchr UTC; mem:
Utah Legal Serv Advisory Board 1977–8; Central Utah Bar
Assn sec-treas 1979; Amer Bar Assn; Utah Statewide Assn
of Prosecutors; Natl Dist Attorney's Assn; Utah Trial
Lawyers Assn; Assn of Trial Lawyers of Amer; Amer
Judicature Soc; Amer Inn of Court I; Ad Hoc Com to
Revise Juvenile Court Rules of Practice & Procedure;
Women Lawyers of Utah; pol: Utah County campaign chm
Republican; rel: LDS, stake inservice ldr, sunday school
tchr & sec, Relief Soc tchr; home: 210 W 800 S, Orem;
off: PO Box 357.

NELSON, SHELDON DOUGLAS assoc prof of Agronomy
BYU; b: 12 Aug 1943; m: Cheryl Hunter; p: Adrian D &
June Clifford; c: Shaughn 16, Shad 14, Chanin 14, Cherae
8, Shayne 5; ed: PhD soil physics U of Calif Riverside;
Salutatorian College of Biological & Agricultural Sci;
former: research soil sci Agricultural Research Serv
USDA; career: Tchr of Month; mem: Phi Kappa Phi; Sigma
Xi; Amer Soc of Agronomy; Internatl Soil Sci Soc; Utah
Acad of Sci; award: Eagle Scout; publ: *Some Practical &
Theoretical Aspects of Subsurface Irrigation;* pol:
Republican county & state del; rel: LDS, bishopric, stake
exec sec, scoutmaster, YMMIA pres; club: Utah Valley Fly
Rodders; home: 1180 E 700 S; off: 253 WIDB, BYU.

NEWMAN, PARLEY WRIGHT prog chm Communicative
Disorders; b: 27 Oct 1923; m: Jeanette Wilkinson; ed: BS
1950 MS 1951 Utah State U; PhD 1954 U of Iowa; former:
coor BYU Special Ed; chm BYU Dept of Speech &
Dramatic Arts; prof of Speech Pathology BYU; assoc sec
Amer Speech & Hearing Assoc, Wash DC; assoc prof of
Speech Utah State U; consul Cache County Board of Ed &
Nebo School Dist; visiting prof to U of Utah, U of Iowa,
Utah State U, Div of Handicapped Children & Youth, US
Off of Ed, Dept HEW; career: Advanced Clinical Cert in
Speech & Cert of Clinical Competence in Speech
Pathology by Amer Speech & Hearing Assn; site visitor
for accreditation functions Ed & Training Board of Amer
Boards of Examiners in Speech Pathology & Audiology;

Presidential Citation Div of Handicapped Children & Youth US Off of Ed; President's Com on Employment of the Handicapped; consul Neurological & Sensory Disease Control Prog, Natl Ctr for Chronic Disease Control Public Health Serv; BYU Master Tchr Award 1971; mem: former pres Utah Speech & Hearing Assn; fellow of Amer Speech & Hearing Assn; Council for Exceptional Children; Amer Psychological Assn; board mem Interprofessional Res Commission on Pupil Personnel Serv; pres Natl Council of Grad Progs in Speech-Language Pathology & Audiology; publ: asst ed, book reviewer, assoc ed *ASHA;* asst ed & book abstractor *DSH Abstracts;* ed consul *Journal of Speech & Hearing Disorders;* over 27 publ; rel: LDS, stake presidency, bishop; home: 581 E 3460 N; off: 135 CCB, BYU.

NGUYEN, THE dir Exerciser Internatl; translator LDS Church; b: 18 Jan 1943; m: Lien My Le; p: Duong Van Nguyen & Oi Thi Trinh; c: Vu 10, Huy 9, Linh 7; ed: 1 yr college; former: English language instr; mil: 1st Lieutenant, Platoon Ldr, Company Commander, English Language Instr, S Vietnamese Army; rel: LDS, branch pres in Vietnam & Utah Valley Vietnamese Branch, h council; home: 1682 S 400 W; off: 275 E 800 S.

NIBLEY, REID N Prof of Music, Pianist in Residence BYU; conductor, composer; b: 5 Jan 1923; m: Marjorie McBride; p: Alex & Agnes Sloan; c: Stephen, Breta, Richard, Michael, Virginia, Jonathan; ed: BFA 1950 MA 1953 U of Utah; DMA 1963 U of Michigan; Park Scholarship; Danforth Study Grant; Rackham Grad Scholarship; former: faculty U of Utah, U of Mich, Natl Music Camp, Interlaken, Mich; career: Community Serv Award SLC 1956; Teacher of the Month BYU 1982; mem: Music Tchrs Natl Assn; Utah Mustic Tchrs Assn; Amer Liszt Soc; publ: piano pieces & choral works; co-auth beginning piano method; civic: Utah Symphony 10 yrs; rel: LDS, ward choir dir; home: 1875 N 650 E; off: E-466 HFAC, BYU.

NIELSEN, DOUGLAS KRAIG Budget & Finance Officer, USDA Forest Service Service, Uinta Forest; b: 7 Jul 1943; m: Jeanne LaVon Merrell; p: Harold Kalmar & Laraine Jones; c: Diane 13, Wendy 11, Michael Merrell 8, Mark

Errell 3; AS Ricks College 1966; BS BYU 1968; former: Admin Officer, Bureau of Land Mgt; mem: former mem & officer Jaycees; Football, Basketball and Baseball Officials Assns; award: Eagle Scout; civic: Loaned Exec to United Way 1978; VP Fed Group of United Way 1980-1; rel: LDS, bishopric; home: 36 S 1000 E, Orem; off: 88 W 100 N, Box 1428.

NIELSEN, SWEN C   Chief of Police; b: 16 Mar 1935; m: Shirlene Jones; p: Arnold C & Anna K; c: Richard, Bradley, Eric, Claudia; ed: BS 1961 Calif State Los Angeles; MS 1970 BYU; former: Chief Security Officer BYU 1961-74; Special Investigator Los Angeles Police Dept 1958-1961; career: Law Enforcement Commendation Medal 1981 by Sons of Amer Revolution; mem: Internatl Assn of Chiefs of Police, mem Small Dept Com; Natl District Attorneys Assn; former pres Utah Police Chiefs Assn; publ: *General Administrative and Organization Concepts for University Police;* mil: US Army paratooper 1954-6; Parachutist Wings; Good Conduct Medal; Amer Defense Medal; rel: LDS, bishop, h council; home: 1202 E 700 S; off: PO Box 1849.

NISH, DALE L   prof Industrial Ed BYU; b: 18 Apr 1932; m: Norene; p: Ray & May; c: Deanna, Randall, Don, Darrel, Brian, Karen; ed: BS MS BYU; EdD Washington State U; former: coor Instructional Systems, Washinton State U; career: Educator of the Yr 1972; College Eng Sci & Tech Award of Excellence 1982; mem: Internatl Wood Collectors Soc; Amer Wood Carvers Assn; The Ward Found; publ: *Creative Woodturning; Artistic Woodturning;* article Harvesting Green Wood Woodworking Magazine 1979; rel: LDS; home: 3107 Foothill Dr; off: 230 SNLB, BYU.

NOBLE, NANCY   asst mgr Aspen Grove Family Camp; b: 11 Dec 1952; p: Cleon Ernest & Catherine Bowen Noble; ed: BS youth ldrship MA recreation mgt BYU; grad banquet student speaker; former: public rel clerk BSA; ldrship training dir YMCA; mem: Amer Camping Assn; Amer Red Cross; Utah Valley Symphony; N Fork Special Serv Dist Board of Dir Sec; award: Amer Red Cross 50 Mile Swim Award; Run for your Life Award; rel: LDS, Relief Soc pres, Activities chm of LDS Lamanite Day

Camps; club: Daughters of the Utah Pioneers; home: 851 N 600 W No. 6; off: 262 ALUM, BYU.

NORDGREN, QUENTIN RICHARDS   prof of music, asst chm, grad coord, Dept of Music BYU; b: 4 July 1920; m: Grace M; p: Nephi & Lilly Richards; c: Mark, Sandra Rupper, Bruce, Brent, Gary; ed: BA 1942 MA 1950 BYU; PhD Indiana U; Honor Soc Phi Kappa Phi; Honor Music Soc Pi Kappa Lamba; former: instr Dixie College; mem: Soc of Music Theory; publ: co-author, *First-year Music Theory;* several articles in Amer Music Tchr and Journal of Music Theory; gen editor of Dept of Music Grad Handbook; mil: Army Airforce, WW II; rel: LDS, branch pres, bishopric, exec sec, clerk; home: 2127 N 250 E; off: C-550 HFAC, BYU.

NORDMEYER, FRANCIS   chemist, educator; b: 1 Feb 1940; m: Jerry Lou Joiner; p: Raymond & Astrid; c: Gregg, Susan, Trent, Kimberly, Kristjane, Becky; ed: BA 1961 Wabash College; MS 1963 Wesleyan Univ; PhD chemistry 1966 Stanford; former: asst prof chemistry U of Rochester 1967-72; mem: Amer Chemical Soc; publ: sci publs; rel: LDS, scoutmaster, bishopric, h council; home: 879 S 800 E, Orem; off: 125 ESC, BYU.

NORTON, H DON   exec VP & dir Far West Bank; b: 26 Jun 1945; m: Rhonda; p: C Blaine & Donna; c: Ali Rae 10, Jocelyn 7, Mauri 5, Jory 3, Ashlee 1; ed: design engineering BYU; Pacific Coast Banking School; Amer Inst of Banking Basic Cert; former: sec/treas Productos de Carretera, Inc, Puerto Rico, Subsidiary Syro Steel Co, mem: pres & former treas Utah County Bankers Assn; Provo Chamber of Commerce; sec Utah Chapter Western Independent Bankers Assn; civic: former treas Provo Freedom Festival 2 yrs; mil: US Army; rel: LDS, h council, bishopric, YM pres; club: Cougar Club; home: 3664 N 700 E; off: 201 E Center.

NORTON, M BRENT   sales mgr; b: 20 Nov 1953; m: Robin; p: C B Norton & R B Greenwood; c: Keri 6, Eric 3, Melissa 1; ed: BYU grad 1977 public relations; honor roll; rel: LDS, exec sec; club: Jaycees; home: 3735 N 500 E; off: PO Box 103.

NORTON, MERRITT RONALD   corp pres Norton Fruit
Co & Norton Food Ctrs; rancher of 400 acres; b: 16 Aug
1913; m: Lael Scott; p: Merritt L & Eliza Ann; c: M
Ronald, A Dennis, Scott Lee, Shauna N Hatch; ed: BYU 1
yr; career: Mark of Distinction Business Character Award
1977 from Red Book; mem: Utah Retail Grocers; United
Fresh Fruit & Produce Assn; awards: Boss of the Year by
TI-UTC Chapter of Amer Business Women's Assn 1978;
civic: Jr Chamber of Commerce; dir Provo Chamber of
Commerce; Provo Industrial Development Corp; rel: LDS;
club: former dir Rotary Club; Jaycee Oldtimers; Elks;
Riverside Country Club; home: 1170 N Birch Ln; off: 290
W 600 S.

OAKS, CLINTON L   prof of Business Mgt BYU; b: 31 May
1923; m: Elaine Waddoups; p: L Weston & Jessie Nelson; c:
Barbara, Ruth Wood, Connie Baker, Carrie Thompson,
Michael, John, Shirly; ed: BA 1948 BYU; MBA 1950 PhD
1955 Stanford; Chamber of Commerce Efficiency Award
for Outstanding Sr 1948; Henry Newell Scholarship 1953;
Lane Publishing Fellowship 1954; former: asst prof U of
Utah 1950-4; asst prof U of Washington 1955-6; asst prof
Stanford Grad School of Business 1956-7; career: Karl G
Maeser Award for Teaching Excellence 1967; BYU Mgt
Soc Distinguished Achievement Award 1980; mem: Acad
of Mgt; Amer Marketing Assn; Beta Gamma Sigma; Phi
Kappa Phi; publ: *Managing Suburban Branches of
Department Stores;* civic: chm Utah State Money Mgt
Council; mil: US Army 1942-6; US Army Reserve officer
1950-4; rel: LDS, bishop, stake presidency, temple sealing
officiator; home: 325 E 4750 N; off: 393 JKB, BYU.

OLSEN, ROYDON S   linguist; gen mgr Automated
Language Processing Sys Inc; b: 21 Dec 1944; m: Elisabeth
Toronto; p: John W & Ellen B; c: John, Joshua, Daniel,
Elisabeth, Leif, Joseph, Kirsten, Meredith; ed: U of Utah,
Stanford U, BYU BA MA; NDEA Fellow, Stanford;
academic scholarship BYU; honor roll; BA & MA cum
laude; former: staff linguist Language Training Mission;
prog dir Internatl Linguistics Found, Brazil; asst dir
Translation Sci Inst BYU; career: accredited by Brazilian
Ministry of Ed; accredited by Amer Translators Assn; 2
Commendation Awards for Journalism; Sine Cera Award,
Warner Enterprises; mem: Amer Translators Assn;

Internatl Fed of Translators; Natl Geographic Soc; award:
1st place, 2nd place for song compositions, Porto Alegre
Brazil Music Festival; publ: papers, articles, language
textbooks, training manuals; civic: PTA; Little League;
pol: Republican; local political milieu; mil: Infantry 82nd
Airborne Dic, Vietnam 1969-70; Combat Infantry Badge;
Campaign Ribbon; 3 Commendation Medals; rel: LDS,
bishop, branch pres; home: 525 S 800 E, Spanish Fork; off:
750 N 200 W.

ORD, JOHN E   prof Elementary Ed BYU; b: 1 Jan 1917;
m: Faun M; p: George V & Loretta Russell; c: Craig,
Sandra, Bonnie, Mary; ed: BS Utah State U; MS U of Utah;
EdD Stanford; former: elementary ed tchr; principal, sup,
consul; award: Phi Delta Kappa, Natl Council for the
Social Studies, Natl and State Assns of Tchr Ed; publ:
*Elementary School Social Studies for Today's Children;
Utah History Program - An Individualized Approach;
Barbershoppers Chorus;* magazine articles; pol:
republican; mil: physical trg instr US Air Force WW II; rel:
LDS, pres stake YMMIA, bishop, h council; home: 2220 N
Oakcrest Ln; off: 247 MCKB, BYU.

OSGUTHORPE, RUSSELL T   instructional scientist,
assoc prof Ed Psychology, David O McKay Inst of Ed BYU;
b: 4 Dec 1946; ed: U of Utah; BS 1971 MS 1973 PhD 1975
BYU; former: research assoc & asst prof Natl Technical
Inst for the Deaf, NY; instr psychologist intern
Courseware Inc, BYU Div of Instr Res, Development &
Evaluation; school psychologist Provo City School Dist;
consultant to school dists; psychological examiner
Behavioral Consultants Inc; dir reg workshop Natl
Technical Inst for the Deaf & Seattle Community College;
co-dir Equity Ed Faculty Workshops BYU; publ: 19 instr
products; 10 journal articles; 4 tech reports; 30 papers;
rel: LDS; home: 476 W 1000 S, Orem; off: 216 KMB, BYU.

OTTLEY, VICKIE RANAE   med sec Utah Valley Hospital;
b: 18 Mar 1951; m: John Randall; p: R Melvin Johnson &
Estelle Johnson Skousen; c: Krista RaNae 4, Matthew
Leonard & Tracy Rae 2; ed: AA Phoenix College; former:
office mgr LDS Social Serv; mem: board of dir Birthright
1976-7; rel: LDS, Young Adult rep, tchr; club: Utah Valley
Mothers of Twins Club, pres 1981-2; home: 341 N 400 W.

OVESON, MELVIN JARVIS Furnishings & Bldg Supervision BYU; b: 25 Nov 1919; m: Edith Clark; p: David Patten; c: Cady Joy Gleave, Judy Brooks, David, Janet Pickup, Mork; ed: BYU 3 yrs; former: buyer Dixon, Taylor, Russell Co Home Furnishings; civic: scoutmaster Boy Scouts of Amer; pol: Democrat & Republican del; mil: US Army Field Artillery WWII S Pacific & Japan 3 yrs; Good Conduct Award; rel: LDS, sunday school tchr & pres, ward clerk, h council, bishopric, elders quorum; home: 790 E 200 N; off: Aux Maint, BYU.

PACE, H JOHN mgr BYU Residential Housing; b: 24 Jun 1949; m: Maryann; p: Heber J & Oara C; c: Tabatha 8, Jared 6, Lisa 4, Spencer 1; ed: BA BYU; MPA work; former: asst mgr BYU Residential Housing 1974–81; civic: pres William Pace - Ruth Lambert Soc; rel: LDS, bishopric; home: 996 N 475 E, Orem; off: 110 GSRB, BYU.

PACE, R WAYNE prof Organizational Communication BYU; exec dir Organizational Associates; b: 15 May 1931; m: Gae Tueller; p: Ralph W & Elda F; c: Michael, Rebecca, Lucinda, Gregory, Angela, Lavinia; ed: BS 1953 U of Utah; MS 1957 BYU; PhD 1960 Purdue U; Creative Problem Solving Inst SUNY 1961; Dept Chm's Inst WICHE 1967; Meritorious Serv Award BYU 1976; Faculty Sponsor Award Internatl Soc Gen Semantics 1973; former: chm & prof Speech Communications Dept U of New Mexico 1972-8, U of Montana 1966-72; faculty Calif State U at Fresno & Parsons College, Iowa; consul city, state, fed agencies, private business; career: fellow Amer Assn for the Advancement of Sci; listed in Who's Who in Amer, Directory of Amer Scholars, Who's Who in the West, Amer Men of Sci: Social & Behavioral Sci, Personalities of the West & Midwest, Internatl Scholars Directory, Community Ldrs of Amer, Dictionary of Internatl Biography; mem: exec sec Natl Soc for the Study of Communication; Speech Assn of Amer; pres Montana Speech Communication Assn; chm Western Speech Communication Assn; pres Internatl Communication Assn; pres New Mexico Communication Assn; pres Western Speech Communication Assn; fellow Amer Assn for Advancement of Sci; Internatl Soc for Gen Semantics; Amer Forensic Assn; Central States Speech Assn; publ: *Communicating Interpersonally: A Reader; The Human*

Transaction: Facets, Functions and Forms of Interpersonal Communications; Communication Probes; Communication Behavior: A Scientific Approach; Communication Experiments: A Manual for Conducting Experiments; Techniques for Effective Communication; theses;, monographs; articles; book reviews; papers; civic: board of dir Rotary Club; board of dir Kiwanis Club; mil: US Army 1953-5; rel: LDS, Sunday School pres, elders pres, h council; club: Sons of Utah Pioneers; home: 95 N Paradise Dr, Orem; off: BYU.

PALMER, GARY K   asst prof Dept of Recreation Mgt & Youth Ldrship BYU; ed: BS 1966 MREd 1967 EdD 1981 BYU; former: dir Extramural Sports; asst to dean College of Physical Ed; activities dir Explorer Conf; faculty advisor Student Recreation Club; dir BYU Summer Fun Festa children's recreation progs; sports dir BYU Housing; mem: pres Utah Recreation & Parks Assn; NRPA Southwest Reg Board; VP of recreation, Utah Assn for Health, Physical Ed & Recreation; constitutional chm Natl Intramural Assn; civic: Provo Freedom Festival Com 1969; dist com mem Boy Scouts of Amer; basketball coach YBA; Family Life Conf; youth conf speaker; rel: LDS, bishop, h council, youth ldr; off: 273-K RB, BYU.

PALMER, SPENCER JOHN   prof of History & Religion BYU; dir World Religions, Religious Studies Ctr BYU; assoc dir Ctr for Internatl & Area Studies BYU; b: 4 Oct 1927; m: Shirley Ann Hadley; p: John Leroy & Eliza Elizabeth Motes; c: Dwight, Jennette, James; ed: cert from Eastern Arizona at Thatcher 1947; BA Fine Arts 1948 BYU; MA East Asiatic Studies 1958 PhD Asian History 1964 U of Calif at Berkeley; Karl G Maeser Res Award 1976; former: dir BYU Jerusalem Study Abroad 1980; dir Ctr for Internatl & Area Studies; coor Asian Studies 1968-75; mem board of dir Research Inst Korean Affairs; project dir Asian Ed Resources; mem: organizer, 1st pres Western Conf of the Natl Assn of Asian Studies; board of dir & publ chm Royal Asiatic Soc Korea Branch; publ: 13 books, incl *The Expanding Church* and *Wisdom and Wit: Favorite quotes, poetry, and prose;* 27 articles, incl "Where in the World Are We Going?" BYU Sesquicentenial Lectures; assoc editor of encyclopedia proj for Greenwood Press, Conn; mil: US Army Chaplain

1st Lt, Korea, Japan, Ft MacArthur; rel: LDS, bishop, mission pres, stake presidency, reg rep, Mel Priesthood writing com; home: 1159 E Mtn Ridge Rd; off: 156 JSB, BYU.

PARKER, VIRGIL JON MD, spec internal medicine; b: 2 Feb 1925; m: Jacquelyn Abraham; p: Virgil & Ann Harnsworth; c: Heather, Holly, Matthew, Paul; ed: BA French lit 1954 U of Utah; MD 1957 U of Utah; career: former pres staff Utah Valley Hospital; mem: former pres AMA; Utah Diabetes Assn; founder Camp Utada; award: several one-man art shows; dramatic reading of "Enoch Arden" by Tennyson; civic: mem board of dir United Fund; Utah County Mental Health; mil: WW II S Pacific Theatre; rel: LDS, MTC branch pres, bishop, pres Belguim Brussels Mission; home: 787 W 650 S, Orem; off: 1055 N 500 W.

PATEL, RAMESH dist governor Friendship Inns; b: 11 Feb 1933; m: Pushpa; p: Manibhai Patel & Maniben Patel; c: Neeti Patel 20, Dhirein Patel 18; ed: Commerce grad with accountancy major; former: credit mgr, London, England; career: Friendship Inns Internatl 5 Stars (1981) and President's Award (1982); mem: honorable mem Chamber of Commerce Com; rel: Hindu; club: Moose; home 150 W 300 S; off: 160 W 300 S.

PAXMAN, MONROE J prof of Justice Admin BYU; b: 7 Apr 1919; m: Shirley Brockbank; p: W Monroe & Achsa Eggertsen;; c: John Monroe, Carolyn P Bentley, David B; Nancy P Thomas, Annette P Bowen, Mary P McGee, Susan P Hatch; ed: JD 1949 U of Utah; 2 Fulbright Sr Scholar Awards 1974, 78 lecturing at U of Freiburg, W Germany; former: Judge, 3rd Dist Juvenile Court 1953–69; exec dir Natl Council of Juvenile Court Judges 1969, 72; career: BYU Distinguished Public Serv Award 1972; lectures for US Dept of State in 9 European countries and in Jamaica; mem: Amer Bar Assn; chm Juvenile Justice Com; Legal Ed Com; dean Natl College of Juvenile Justice; award: finalist in 1960 All Amer Family Award, Florida; remodeled attic won grand prize in Better Homes & Gardens 1962 Natl Home Improvement Contest; publ: *Law enforcement Supervision;* co-auth with wife on 7 books; legal articles; civic: chm Utah County Red Cross 1959–63; pol: chm Utah County Young Republicans 1950-2, vice chm Utah Young Republicans 1952-3; dist chm & del; rel: LDS, branch pres, bishopric, h council; club: Provo Kiwanis 1962-5; home: 135 E 200 N; off: 764 SWKT, BYU.

PAXMAN, SHIRLEY BROCKBANK dir & owner McCurdy Historical Doll Museum; b: 10 Dec 1919; m: Monroe J Paxman; p: Isaac E & Elsie B Brockbank; c: John M, Carolyn P Bentley, David B, Nancy P Thomas, Annette P Bowen, Mary P McGee, Susan P Hatch; ed: BS BYU; RN Holy Cross Hospital; MS BYU; Phi Beta Kappa; former: instr child devel BYU; instr nursing UTC; career: Museum Excellence, Utah State Historical Soc; Museum Restoration, Utah Heritage Found; award: Family of the Yr natl award; Better Homes & Gardens 1st place for interior decorating; publ: *Jo Bed, Jo Bed the Doctor Said; Homespun; Jamily Night Jun; Jamily Jaith and Jun;* magazine articles; civic: Provo School Board 8 yrs; Governors School Study Com 2 yrs; rel: LDS, stake & ward primary, Relief Soc; home: 135 E 200 N; off: 246 N 100 E.

PEARSON, DALE FRANCIS asst prof & dir Undergrad Social Work Ed BYU; b: 1 Jan 1928; m: Ver Lynne Freebairn; p: R Vance & Maude Lindsay; c: Randall, Bradley, Sherilyn, Lynnette, Ryan; ed: BS 1957 sociology MSW 1959 social work U of Utah; PhD 1981 counseling BYU; licensed Marriage & Family Counselor, State of Utah; licensed Clinical Social Worker, State of Utah; former: coor Sr Field Practicum 1973-80; prog dir LDS Social Serv Day Camp, Orem 1973; instr Utah State Hospital 1971-3; special consul Central Utah Community Mental Health Ctr, Provo 1967-70; chief psychiatric social worker San Jose Community Mental Health Ctr 1966-7; private practice Individual, Marriage & Family Counseling 1965-; psychiatric social worker El Camino Hospital, Calif 1964-6; research social worker Stanford Med Ctr 1960-3; probation officer San Mateo County Probation Dept 1963-4; clinical social worker Veterans Admin Hospital, SLC 1960; probation officer 2nd Dist Juvenile Court, SLC 1959-60; career: Karl G Maeser Distinguished Teaching Award Com; chm BYU College of Social Sci Convocation Com; mem: Amer Assn for Marriage & Family Therapy; Amer Assn of Psychiatric Serv for Children; Amer Assn for Sex Educators, Counselors & Therapists; Assn of Mormon Counselors &

Psychotherapists; Council on Social Work Ed; publ: *Hints for Helpers; Creating the Empathic Relationship; The Practice of Social Work;* 8 other publs; 7 papers; civic: BYU United Way Rep; pres Central Utah Branch of NASW 1968-9, 75-6; community speaker; mil: Sgt, Cadre & class instr, US Army 1952-4; Amer Spirit of Honor Medal; rel: LDS, h council, bishop, state Social Serv Com, sunday school pres, elders pres, seminary instr; home: 747 E 2680 N; off: 842 SWKT, BYU.

PERKINS, MICHAEL W   prof of Physics & Math UTC; b: 12 Apr 1940; m: Claudia V; p: WW & Jessie Pierce; c: Deborah Jean 16, David Michael 15, Jennie 13, Daniel Joseph 9, Rebekah 7; ed: BS chemistry Utah State U; MA physics BYU; Sigma Phi Sigma; former: research chemist Battalle Northwest, Richland, Wash; career: Outstanding Tchr of the Yr UTC; 2 Natl Sci Found Fellowships; mem: Amer Chemical Soc; Amer Inst of Physics; rel: LDS, bishop, h council, gen church writtng com; home: 294 E 1800 S, Orem; off: UTC, 1395 N Univ Ave.

PERRY, DEVERN J   prof of Business Ed BYU; b: 3 July 1937; m: Connie Pierson; p: H Eugene & Elva Perry; c: Julie 17, J Michael 16, Bradley P 12, Amy 5; ed: BS 1958 MS 1962 BYU; EdD 1968 U of N Dakota; 4.0 GPA in doctoral prog at N Dakota; former: instr Weber State College; grad instr U of N Dakota; visiting prof Calif State U LA, Southern Ill U, Northern Ill U; workshops in shorthand methodology at 12 colleges & univ; career: 1st grant given for res by Delta Pi Epsilon Res Foundation 1981; mem: Utah Business Ed Assn; Natl Business Ed Assn; Western Business Ed Assn; publ: *Word Studies, College Vocabulary Building, 6,000 Most-Used Century 21 Shorthand Outlines, Word Division Manual,* 4 sets of tape scripts for typewriting & shorthand, 13 articles in professional publ; rel: LDS, exec sec, bishop, h council; home: 789 E 2730 N; off: 361 JKB, BYU.

PERRY, JAMES V JR   co-owner Provo Paint & Art Center; b: 18 Aug 1925; m: Norma R; p: James V Jr & Ann; c: Linda Ann Perry Walton; ed: high school; civic: Chamber of Commerce; Better Business Bureau; mil: US Coast Guard; club: Elks Club; Ducks Unlimited; home: 281 E 3860 N; off: 201 W Center.

PETERMAN, ROY S superintendent; b: 10 Apr 1947; m: LaDonna Winn; p: Kenneth L & Zelma Whittaker; c: Randall Lee 10, Julianna 9, Christopher 7, Roy Daniel 6, Jana Lee (deceased), Kasilynn 2, Casandra 1; ed: BS personnel psychology; career: Professional Ground Maintenance Honor Award, Professional Grounds Mgt Soc & Park Maintenance Mag; mem: Professional Grounds Mgt Soc; Natl Inst on Parks & Grounds Mgt; publ: "Athletic Field Maintenance" in *Park Maintenance* Mag; rel: LDS, h council, bishop, scoutmaster; home: 1453 E 800 S; off: Grounds BPPB, BYU.

PETERSEN, J LADELL bldg contractor; b: 3 Apr 1921; m: Mary Penrod; p: Parley & Edna Ellen Smith; c: Mary Ellen, Brent, Kevin, Becky Jo, Robyn; ed: Snow College; trade college San Diego; career: has built over 150 custom homes & sm bus bldgs; civic: Provo Municipal Water Board; mil: WWII Pacific area Iwo Jima; rel: LDS, bishop, HP group ldr; home: 2151 N Oakcrest Ln.

PETERSEN, ROBERT J physician; b: 13 May 1928; m: Bernice; p: Arthur & Julia; c: Sandy, Linda, Julia, John, Joslyn, Eric; ed: AB Grinnel Collese; MS Illinois; MD Washington Univ, St Louis; special ears, nose, throat, allergy, cosmetic facial surgery, vertigo; mem: Amer Acad Facial Plastic Surgery; Amer Acad of Otolaryngology & Head & Neck Surgery; publ: Sinus Puncture Therapy articles; civic: Contrabass Utah Valley Symphony; mil: Capt US Air Force Hospital Scott AFB Illinois 1961-3; rel: LDS, stake presidency; club: Civil War Skirmishers; home: 2880 N Chippewa Way; off: 1275 N University.

PETERSON, H DONL prof of Ancient Scripture BYU; b: 17 Feb 1930; m: Mary Lou Schenk; p: Harry C & Mada Peck; c: Terry, Diane, Jacqueline, Scott, James, Michael; ed: BS 1954 MeD 1960 BYU; EdD 1965 Wash State U; former: seminary principal, institute dir; career: Semester Abroad Dir 1973 Jerusalem; chm BYU Standards Com; dir tours to Middle East, Mexico, Guatemala; Book of Mormon & Pearl of Great Price coor; mem: Mormon History Assn; Lambda Delta Sigma; Phi Delta Kappa; publ: *A Study Guide for the Pearl of Great Price;* articles in church publ; civic: YBA basketball coach; pol: county &

state del Republican; rel: LDS, Church Writing Com; h council, bishop; home: 321 S 400 E, Orem; off: 220-C JSB, BYU.

PHILLIPS, RICHARD T   pres Golden West Computers Inc; b: 21 May 1953; m: Melody Susan Pay; p: Terry Harvey & Harriet; c: Heidi Ann 4, Julie Rochelle 2; ed: AA elect Snow College; honor student; Electronics Club pres; studentbody council; former: computer developer, store owner, electronic tech; mem: UPEA; NESDA; rel: LDS, bishopric, Sunday School presidency, scout advisor; home: 315 S 500 E, Mt Pleasant; off: 60 N 300 W.

PIERCE, ARTHUR C   exec dir Housing Authority of Utah County ret; b: 23 Jun 1916; m: Mary Joiner; p: Arwell Lee & Mary B Done; c: Nancy Searle, Mary Lee Parkes, Sabra Young, Arthur C Jr, Lourena Bangerter, Arwella Curtis; ed: BA 1942 BYU; grad study U of Arizona; lic Nursing Home Administrator in Utah; former: controller Ecotek Natl Corp; gen mgrRamada Inn; dir Dept Social Serv SL County; controller Richland Homes Inc; chm of board, pres, dir, gen mgr Inter-Amer Life Ins Co; pres, gen mgr Interstate Lumber & Development Co; pres & gen mgr Bellavista farms Inc; controller Compania Maderera Bellavista SA & Maderera Juarez SA; career: state pres & reg VP Natl Assn of Housing & Redevelopment; pol: voting dist chm; rel: LDS, scoutmaster 20 yrs, dist councilman, exec sec, pres MIA, pres sunday school, pres 70s, mission pres; club: pres Exchange Club; pres elect Kiwanis Club; home: PO Box 403, Jensen, UT 84035.

POLVE, JAMES H   prof Mechanican Engineering BYU; b: 7 Feb 1921; m: Dorothy Tregeagle; p: D V & Jennie Blackham; c: James Craig, Constance, Cindy; ed: BSME ME U of Utah; MSAC aeronatical Princeton U; PhD aerospace U of Arizona; Karl G Maeser Distinguished Teaching Award BYU 1981; mem: assoc fellow AIAA; ASME, ASEE, Tau Beta Pi; Theta Tau; awards: honorary mem Aventurers Club, Los Angeles; publ: *Theoretical Investigation and Optimization of an Airplane Gust Alleviation System;* civic: Provo City Airport Board, former chm Aviation Com, Provo Chamber of Commerce; mil: US Air Force colonel; dir Flight Test Engineering; command pilot; fighter pilot; test pilot; Air Force

Meritorious Serv Medal; Air Medal; rel: LDS, branch pres, stake presidency, h council; home: 1660 N 1500 E; off: 242-K CB, BYU.

PORTER, BLAINE R   univ prof & admin; b: 24 Feb 1922; m: Elizabeth Taylor (dec), Barbara Duessler; p: Brigham Ernest & Edna Brough; c: Claudia Black, Roger B, David T, Particia Ann Hintze, Corinna; ed: BS 1947 MS 1949 BYU; PhD 1952 Cornell U; former: chm Dept Human Development & Family Relations 1955–65; dean College of Family Living BYU 1966–80; career: Fullbright Research Scholar & Visiting Prof U of London 1965–6; Prof of Yr 1964; mem: Natl Council& Family Relations, pres 1963–4; Amer Psychological Assn; Amer Sociological Assn; Amer Assn of Marriage & Family Therapists; Phi Kappa Phi, pres BYU chapter 1970–2; publ: *The Latter-day Saint Family;* journal articles; civic: pres Family Living Council of Utah County 1973–80; mil: US Air Force pilot WWII; rel: LDS, bishop, stake presidency, h council, gen sunday school board; club: Provo Kiwanis Club; home: 1675 Pine Ln; off: 2240-A SFLC, BYU.

PORTER, SHERRON H; Dir Business   Affairs & Support Serv, Provo City School Dist; b: 16 Dec 1935; m: Cynthia M Bishop; p: E Harold & Lexie Virginia Denning; c: Sonja 20, Patricia 19, Becky 17, Wayne 14, Benton 11, Susan 10, Cheryl 5, David 1; ed: BS 1960 BYU; MS 1968 Oregon State U; former: math tchr; coord of data processing; mem: Phi Delta Kappa; Natl Assn of School Business Officials; pres Utah Assn of School Business Officials; publ: "School Business Affairs", *Utah Ed Journal;* pol: voting dist chm Republican; county & state del; rel: LDS, bishop, h council, stake sunday school pres; home: 363 S 1410 E; off: 280 W 940 N.

POWERS, TIMOTHY JOHN   Head Men's Swimming Coach BYU; b: 16 Aug 1945; m: Patricia; p: Les & Eileen; c: Jennifer 12, Emily 5; foster: Tanya Lilly 12; ed: BS 1968 U of Montana; MA 1973 San Jose State U; Commander's Trophy for Outstanding Cadet & Distinguished Military Student, U of Montana; former: swimming coach West Valley Aquatic Teams, Calif; swimming coach & aquatic dir Los Gatos High School, Calif; career: coached 1979 WAC Conf Men Champs; coached 1980 Intermtn Athletic

Conf Swim Women Champs; only BYU coach of both men & women to conf champs; coached swimmers to 11 All Amer citations; coached a nationally or world ranked swim for ea of 12 yrs of coaching; coached 61 high school All Americans; Swim Coach of 1976 Olympics for El Salvador; mem: College Swim Coaches Assn; award: 2 All Amer citations as swimmer; natl age–group record holder; Big Sky Conf Champ; U of Montana Team Capt; publ: "The Spirit of Sport" in *Natl Olympic Academy 999* 1979; civic: coach Swimming Utah Special Olympics; Utah Valley Dolphins head coach 5 yrs; mil: Capt US Army; Bronze Star & Air Medals, Rep of Vietnam 1969–70; rel: LDS, sunday school tchr; home: 177 S 200 E, Orem; 151 RB, BYU.

POWLEY, E HARRISON   prof of Music BYU; b: 10 Jan 1943; m: Ellen; p: Edward H & Elizabeth M Jr; c: William 13, Barrett 11, Martha 10, Edward 9, Philip 7, Julianne 7, Sarah 4; ed: BM MA PhD Eastman School of Music, U of Rochester; Fulbright Fellowship to Vienna, Austria; NDEA Title IV Grant for grad school; former: instr percussion Eastman School of Music; percussionist Rochester Philharmonic; mem: chm Natl Research Com for Percussive Arts Soc; Amer Musicological Soc; Sonneck Soc; College Music Soc; Music Library Assn; publ: editorial board *Percussionist Journal;* articles; civic: timpanist Utah Valley Symphony 1970–7; pol: Republican dist chm 1978–82; rel: LDS, bishop, h council, 70s pres; home: 2220 N 1400 E, off: E–221 HFAC, BYU.

PRATLEY, BRENT M   orthopedic surgeon, team physican BYU; b: 29 Sep 1935; m: Sue; p: Henry Hart & Gladys Cooper; c: Heather 12, Brooke 10, Jaron 8, Gretchen 7, Jordan 2, ed: BA 1961 BYU; MD 1966 U of Calif Irvine; mem: Utah Med Soc; LA County Med Assn; civic: cancer funds; pol: Republican; mil: US Navy Med Officer 1968–70; rel: LDS; home: 3917 N Quail Run Dr; off: 2300 University Parkway 6B.

PRATT FERGUSON, HELAMAN ROLFE   prof of Math BYU; b: 11 Aug 1940; m: Claire Marilyn Eising; p: Helaman & Jeanne Louise Reinhardt Pratt; Samuel & Dora Call Ferguson; c: Helaman David 17, Samuel Lehi 15, Benjamin Nathan 14, Sarah Noelle 12, Jonathan Daniel

8, Alexander James 4, Michael Paul 1; ed: AB 1962 Hamilton College; MS 1966 BYU; PhD 1971 U of Washington; NSF Fellow; awards for Seminar in Algebraic Groups, Bowdoin College; Seminar on Algebraic Geometry, Universite de Montreal; AMS Inst on Algebraic Geometry, Arcata; Automorphic Forms, Corvallis; former: inst U of Washington; career: Who's Who in the West; Amer Men & Women of Sci; mem: Amer Math Soc; Math Soc of Amer; Soc of Industrial & Applied Mathematicians; Sigma Xi; Phi Kappa Phi; publ: US Patent 4,235,668; journal articles; rel: LDS, 70s pres, h council; home: 848 S 100 W, Orem; off: 314 TMCB, BYU.

PRIEST, D JEFFLYN   pres Spotlight Serv, Inc; writer; producer; consultant; lyricist; b: 10 Apr 1943; p: William Henry & E E Schmitt; ed: masters in journalism U of Chicago; former: pres Summit Entertainment; consultant Natl Endowment for the Arts; career: Women in Media Arts, Outstanding Accomplishment Award 1981; New England Bicentennial Writing Award 1976; Northeastern Region Producer of Merit Award 1980; Cert of Distinction, Stage Producers Soc of Amer 1982; mem: board of dir Natl Prog for Women in the Arts; board of dir Utah Ecology Council; vice-chm board of consultants; Internatl Soc for Arts Communication; publ: TV script on stage life of Samuel Clemens (Mark Twain); articles; 2 books; book in progress; rel: LDS, sunday school tchr, Relief Soc counselor, MIA; off: KBYU, BYU.

PRITCHARD, VERNON DWIGHT   forester US Forest Serv, Reg 4; b: 13 May 1926; m: Lylan E; p: Vernon Leon & Buelah I; c: Vernon Ross, Carolyn Ruth Curtis, Jonothan Scott, Nancy Louis; ed: BS agriculture Washington State U; former: dist ranger US Forest Service 16 yrs on 3 natl forests; career: cash award for leadership 1976; US Dept of Agriculture Superior Serv Award 1978; Cert of Merit 1981; mem: Soc of Amer Foresters; Soc of Range Mgt; Amer Forestry Assn; The Wildlife Soc for Utah; Natl Wildlife Fed; civic: Kiwanis Internatl; mil: US Navy WWII Asiatic Pacific area, Petty Officer 2nd class; rel: Seventh-day Adventist, elder, sabbath school coord, Pathfinder dir, School Board & Finance Com; club: Trail Riders Assn Internatl Ltd; Oregon Equestrian Trails; home: Birdseye Star Rt 1, Box 472, Fairview; off: 88 W 100 N.

PRITCHETT, B MICHAEL economist, BYU School of Mgt; b: 3 Nov 1940; m: Patricia L; p: Melrose Jed & Lois Watson; c: Bruce M 16, Laura 15, Steven L 11; ed: BS 1965 BYU; MS 1967 PhD 1970 Purdue; NDEA Fellowship; Krannert Fellowship; grad with honors; former: instr Purdue U; mem: Amer Econ Assn; Western Econ Assn; publ: *A Study of Capital Mobilization;* home: 3996 N Quail Run Dr; off: 1305-B SFLC, BYU.

PURCELL, ALBERT E food chemist; b: 18 Nov 1921; m: Mary Talbot; p: Vaughn M & Margugrite Fort; c: Diane, Scott; ed: BS BYU; MS PhD Purdue; former: research chemist US Dept of Agric; prof Food Sci, NC State U; mem: Inst Food Technologist; Amer Chem Soc; Sigma Psi; publ: 100 publs; 3 book chapters; mil: US Army 1942-5; US Air Force 1951-3; rel: LDS, elders pres, h council, high priest grp ldr; home: 43 W 1070 N, Orem; off: Food Sci & Nutrition, BYU.

QUACKENBUSH, STANLEY FULTON asst to dean BYU School of Mgt; b: 2 Oct 1933; m: Virginia Marie; p: Claude Fulton & Anna Bernice Quackenbush; c: Catherine 18, Deborah 16, Cordell 14, Cynthia 12, Daniel 11, Charlotte 9, Christine 8, David 7; ed: PhD finance & investment U of Ill; NDEA Fellowship; Phi Kappa Phi; Omicron Delta Epsilon; Beta Gamma Sigma; former: realtor; assoc prof bus & finance; contractor; acct exec Bank of Amer; career: listed in Who's Who in Finance and Industry; mem: Amer Finance Assn; Financial Mgt Assn; Western Finance Assn; publ: 7 articles; civic: business ed panel; pol: finance chm Whitman County to re-elect Gov Evans, Washington; mil: US Air Force pilot 1955-8; rel: LDS, bishop, h council, branch pres; club: Kiwanis; home: 1625 W 11600 S, Payson; off: 240 JKB, BYU.

QUINN, D MICHAEL prof of Amer History BYU; b: 26 Mar 1944; m: Janice L Darley; p: Donald Pena & Joyce Workman; c: Mary 13, Lisa 11, Adam 7, Paul 5; ed: BA 1968 BYU; MA 1973 U of Utah; PhD 1976 Yale U; BYU Scholar; Yale Fellow; Whiting Dissertation Fellow; NEH Grantee; former: teaching fellow Yale U; career: Best Article Award 1974 Mormon History Assn; Egleston & Beinecke Dissertation Awards, Yale U 1976; mem: Amer Historical Assn; Org of Amer Historians; Western History

Assn; Utah State Historical Soc; Mormon History Assn; John Whitmer Historical Assn; publ: articles in books & several historical & religious publs; civic: speaker Inter-denominational Hiroshima Vigil, SLC, 6 Aug 1981; pol: Democratic pol campaigns 1978, 80; mil: US Military Intelligence 1968–71 Washington DC & Munich, Germany; rel: LDS, SL Temple Sq guide, temple worker, bishopric, h council; home: 923 Third Ave, SLC; off: Dept of History, BYU.

RAMAGE, THOMAS (TOM)   special teams coord & defensive line coach BYU football; b: 25 Aug 1935; m: Winona Prince; p: Tom & Romania; c: John, Lorrie, Rochele, Sheree, Dedra, Cory; ed: BS 1957 MS 1960 Utah State U; former: head coach Dixie Jr College; asst coach Weber State; asst coach Utah State; coach Bear River High School; career: Most Outstanding Multiple Sport Athlete, Utah State U 1956; All–Conf Football 1956; Honorable Mention All–Amer 1956 football; mem: Amer Football Coaches Assn; publ: *Forward Movement Time in 2,3,4 Point Football Stances, Off–Season Program, Injury Prevention;* civic: Orem softball sup; mil: capt US Army Reserve; rel: LDS; home: 61 N 700 E, Orem; off: 60 SFH, BYU.

RASBAND, JUDITH ANN   tchr, image consul, columnist, author, lecturer; b: 7 Oct 1942; m: S Neil Rasband; p: A L & Maxine Packard; c: Nanette 16, Matthew 12, Daniel 10; ed: Masters home econ ed; Phi Kappa Phi; Omicron Nu; Home Econ Grad Award 1964; former: jr & sr high school tchr; instr U of Utah & BYU; BYU Ed Week faculty; mem: Home Economists In Business; Amer Home Econ Assn; Utah Home Econ Assn; Assn College Profs of Textiles & Clothing; publ: *How To Clothe Your Family;* "Let's Face It" column; magazine & journal articles; civic: lecturer to civic orgs; pol: election judge; rel: LDS, tchr, counsl, pres YWMIA, Relief Soc & Primary chorister; club: BYU Women; home: 540 E Quail Rd, Orem; off: 3256 SFLC, BYU.

RASMUSSEN, REX   broker, Heritage Realty; b: 7 Aug 1951; m: Jane; p: DeArmond & Afton; c: Shane 7, Nathan 5; ed: BYU 3 yrs; career: Realtor of the Yr 1981, Million Dollar Club 1981; mem: Natl, state & local realtor assns;

chm loan com Realtors Credit Union; civic: charter pres
Orem Sertoma Club; chm telephone derby Amer Cancer
Soc; pol: asst Lee Farnsworth campaign; rel: LDS, scout
ldr, elders presidency, primary tchr; home: 735 E 2950 N;
off: 1900 N Canyon Rd.

RAUSCHENBACH, KONN (APOSTOL)   asst ticket mgr
BYU; b: 16 Jul 1952; m: Rory S; p: Chris J & Marva F; ed:
BYU 4 yrs; former: ticket clerk, office supvr, office mgr;
career: 5-yr Service Award; mem: Safety Comm; club:
pres Auno Service Club 1971-3; off: MC Ticket Off, BYU.

RAYNES, JOSEPH LINCOLN   principal Joaquin Elem;
dist dir Adult Ed; b: 21 Jun 1946; m: Alice Nielsen; p:
Lincoln F & Beth Milner; c: Janelle 11, Michelle 9, Denise
Grace 7, Alison 6, MelAnee Pearl 4, Stefanee Marie 2,
Jonathan Joseph 1; ed: BA MEd BYU; PhD in process
Texas A&M; Charles E Mott Fellowship; BYU Academic
Award; former: tchr Grandview School, admin asst Board
of Regents, BYU staff, long term internatl consultant &
technician US State Dept & Bolivian Ministry of Ed, short
term consultant World Bank, UNESCO & UNICEF; mem:
PEA; UEA; UAE, UCEA, NCEA, NAESP, Phi Delta Kappa;
state board of dir Community & Adult Ed; publ:
"Internships in Higher Ed in State of Utah"; civic: Provo
Freedom Festival Com; summer recreation dir Provo
School Dist; Utah State Ed Dir Partners of the Americas;
rel: LDS, bishopric, h council; home: 55 N 1000 E, Orem;
off: 550 N 600 E.

REDFORD, ROBERT   actor; Wildwood Enterprises Inc;
Sundance Ski Resort; b: 18 Aug; m: Lola Van Wagenen; p:
Charles Robert & Martha; c: Shauna, David James, Amy;
ed: U of Colorado 2 yrs; Acad Grand Chaumiere, Paris;
Scuola Bella Arte, Florence, Italy; Pratt Inst, Brooklyn
NY; Amer Acad of Dramatic Arts, NY; Baseball
scholarship; career: 5 broadway plays; 5 TV prods; motion
pictures: *Warhunt; Situation Hopeless, But Not Serious;
Inside Daisy Clover; The Chase; This Property is
Condemned; Barefoot in the Park; Tell Them Willie Boy is
Here; Butch Cassidy and the Sundance Kid; Downhill
Racer; Little Fauss, Big Halsey; Hot Rock; Jeremiah
Johnson; The Candidate; The Way We Were; The Sting;
The Great Gatsby; The Great Waldo Pepper; Three Days*

of the Condor; All the President's Men; A Bridge Joo Jar; The Electric Horseman; Brubaker; directed *Ordinary People* with 4 Acad Awards, incl Best Picture & Best Director; publ: *The Outlaw Trail;* civic: lobbied for Energy Conservation & Production Act; Solar Energy Sun Day; board of dir Environmental Defense Fund; board of dir Natl Resources Defense Council; board of dir The Solar Lobby; off: Sundance Ski Resort, Provo Canyon.

REEVES, DAVID   agency mgr Beneficial Life Ins Co; b: 26 Jul 1943; m: Vickie; p: Wayne & Madge; c: David Jr 14, Marc 12, Cynthia 11, Jeff 9 Steffani 7; ed: BS pol sci 1967 BYU; career: life & qualifying mem Million Dollar Round Table; 3 time winner Natl Mgt Award; 13 time recipient Natl Quality Award; Beneficial Life's Agency of Yr 1975, 82; mem: Natl Assn of Life Underwriters; Gen Agents & Mgrs Assn; award: mem 1966 Track & Field All Amer Team; Capt BYU Track Team 1967; civic: Cancer Soc volunteer; Little League Baseball; BSA; rel: LDS, bishopric, h council; home: 3579 N Littlerock Dr; off: 1675 N 200 W 2b.

REID, NINA B   Utah County Recorder; Utah County Boundary Commissioner; b: 7 Jul 1933; m: Omer Arthur Reid; p: Royal & Lillie M Barney; c: Terry, Kim, Wendy; ed: BYU; former: Deputy County Assessor; career: Natl Achievement Award for County Records Storage Prog 1978; Natl Achievement Award for Automated Land Records Mgt System 1980; Utah Assn of County Officials Cert of Recognition 1978, 81, 82; nominee Outstanding County Official UAC 1978, 81, 82; mem: Lady VP 1974-5, board of dir 1975-6, 80-, Utah Assn of Counties; pres Utah Assn of County Recorders 1980-; election com 1979-80, land records com 1979-, board of dir 1981-, Natl Assn of Counties; del, corresponding sec, Utah County Women's Legislative Council; chm Mtnlands Area Agcy Coor Council on Aging 1975-9; board of dir Amer Soc for Public Administrators 1978-; Utah County Insurance, Data Processing & Parking Coms; exec & admin sec to Board of Utah County Commissioners 1967-9; Utah State Human Resource Steering Com 1979-; board of dir Utah County Mental Health Assn 1980; Utah State Plat Standards Com 1978-; award: Outstanding Young Women of Amer award 1965; individual & church ldrship awards;

civic: Springville Coor Council; VP & pres Springville City Council of Club Presidents; Springville Art Board; sec Com on Children & Youth; PTA Citizenship Chm; 2nd VP Nebo 1st Dist Fed Women's Clubs; pol: Republican; Utah County Party Sec 1968; Dist Sec; rel: LDS, youth ldr, Relief Soc tchr; club: Springville Faits Bien Civic Club; home: 280 E 300 S, Springville; off: 210 County Bldg.

REMINGTON, DENNIS WAYNE   Family Physician, bariatrics; b: 3 Aug 1943; m: Jolayne; p: Donald & Afton; c: Ben 14, Julie 13, Carmen 8; ed: BS MD; mem: Amer Assn of Bariatric Physicians; Amer Med Assn; Utah Med Soc; rel: LDS; club: Riverside Country Club; Sherwood Hills Racquet Club; home: 4141 Dover Ln; off: 1675 N 200 W.

RENCHER, ALVIN C   chm Dept of Statistics BYU; b: 21 Dec 1934; m: LaRue; p: Clarence & Vivian; c: David 17, Michael 12, Ashley 4; ed: BS MS BYU, PhD Virginia Polytechnic Inst; Phi Kappa Phi; grad with honors; former: Evaluation Engr Hercules Inc; mem: Amer Statistical Assn; publ: 20 journal publ; pol: voting dist chm; rel: LDS, h council, bishopric; home: 833 E 2680 N; off: 222 TMCB, BYU.

RHOADS, B ERIC   pres KEYY & KLRZ Radio; pres Mariners Radio Relay Co (KHAA New Orleans); pres Blimpboard Novelty Advertising Co; pres Eric Rhoads & Assoc Marketing & Radio Prog Consultants; b: 30 Aug 1954; m: Gudrun; ed: Harvard Business School; Univ Miami; former: VP New World Communications Co; mem: Natl Assn of Broadcasters; Natl Radio Broadcasters Assn; Radio Adv Bureau; civic: Mayor's Com on Economic Growth, Provo; Boy Scouts; Utah Training Ctr; Easter Seals; March of Dimes; club: Orem Kiwanis Club; home: 1636 N Woodland Dr; off: 307 S 1600 W.

RICHARDS, LORI   instr & coach UTC; b: 16 Jul 1956; m: David G Richards; p: Carl & Bonnie Doerr; ed: BS BYU; masters work; President's Honor Roll; former: instr & coach Hawaii School for Girls; career: Most Outstanding BYU Gerontology Prog; mem: Assn of Athletic Trainers; Eta Sigma Gamma; award: All-Amer volleyball, Long Beach City College; Most Valuable Player Calif State

Volleyball Tournament 1976-8; rel: LDS, Relief Soc pres, tchr, stake board; home: 810 N 250 W; off: PO Box 1609.

RICHEY, MELVA HAMMOND   asst univ archivist BYU; b: 11 Apr 1922; p: Jasper Melvin & Elizabeth Percinda Hale; c: Roger David, Gregory Melvin, Robert Elton; ed: BS Utah State U; MLS BYU; former: home econ tchr; mem: sec Idaho Vocational Home Econ Assn; Idaho Ed Assn; Mormon History Assn; civic: painted *The Lord's Supper* for Aston Ward and *Christ* for Twin Falls Tabernacle; rel: LDS; home: 510 Averett Ave, Springville; off: 5030 HBLL, BYU.

RICHMAN, LARRY LEON   translation supvr LDS Church; pres Richman Communications; pres Richman Publishing; b: 10 Jul 1955; m: Teri Lee Jackman; p: Lynn T & Katheryn Joyce Seely; c: Lanae; ed: BA Spanish, linguistics 1979 MS instructional sci 1981 BYU; PhD work BYU; S&H Foundation scholarship; BYU Translation Cert 1979; Delta Sigma Pi; former: publications proj mgr LDS Church; dir of recording BYU Sound Services, Guatemala; translator & production coord LDS Church; linguistic consultant New World Languages; text writer MTC; test developer Lang & Intercultural Research Ctr; lang specialist for literacy progs David O McKay Inst; mem: Amer Translators Assn; former sec/treas Deseret Language & Linguistics Soc; awards: Eagle Scout; Natl Explorer Presidents Congress, Wash DC; listed in Who's Who in the West, Outstanding Young Men of America; publ: *Culture for Missionaries: Guatemalan Indian; Diccionario Espanol Cakchiquel Ingles; Prominent Men & Women of Provo; Tales of the Cakchiquels;* translations for LDS Church and Guatemalan Ministry of Ed; journal articles on linguistics, Cakchiquel, language learning; rel: LDS, exec sec, clerk, elders pres; home: 553 N 750 E; off: 50 E N Temple, SLC.

RIDDLE, CHAUNCEY CAZIER   prof of Philosophy BYU; b: 18 Dec 1926; m: Bertha Janis Allred; p: Alfred Levi & Frances Grace Cazier; c: Mark, Neil, Robert, Brian, Sara, Paul, Ellen, Seth, Elizabeth, Matthew, Joseph; ed: BA BYU; MA PhD Columbia Univ; former: chm Dept Grad Studies in Rel 1961-9; dean Grad School 1969-76; Asst Academic VP 1976-80; career: Karl G Maeser Teaching

Award 1965; Prof of Yr 1962; Honors Prof of Yr 1967; board of dir 1963-74 pres 1969-74 BYU Credit Union; mem: Utah Acad of Arts, Sci & Letters; Philosophy of Sci Assn; mil: US Army 1945-6; rel: LDS, bishop, h council, stake presidency; home: 1146 Birch Ln; off: 311 KMB.

ROBERTSON, RUSSELL CLARK   sci librarian; b: 30 Dec 1926; m: Yvonne; p: Russell & Christie A Clark; c: Mark, Gaile, Meg, Claire, Amy; ed: BA UCLA; MLS U of Illinois; MEd BYU; Phi Beta Kappa; Phi Eta Sigma; Alpha Mu Gamma; Pi Sigma Alpha; Beta Phi Mu; former: sci librarian Argonne Natl Lab; mem: Mountain Plains Library Assn; Utah Library Assn; publ: articles in library periodicals; civic: dist commissioner Boy Scouts of Amer; pol: precinct com mem; mil: colonel; Army Chaplain 6 yrs; Army Reserve Chaplain 24 yrs; Meritorious Service Medal; Army Commendation Medal; rel: LDS, h council; home: 140 E 100 S, Span Fork; off: 2222 HBLL, BYU.

ROBINS, ROLAND KENITH   prof Chemistry & Biochemistry, dir BYU Cancer Research Ctr; b: 13 Dec 1926; m: Lessa Rasmussen; p: Kenith R & Florence Cropper; c: Corinne Arrington, Kenith Leon, Renee Tannahill, Rhonda Cooper, Rochelle Jarmin, Roy Lynn; ed: BA 1948 MA 1949 BYU; PhD 1952 Oregon State U; former: asst & assoc prof New Mexico Highlands Univ 1953-1957; assoc prof Arizona State U 1960-3; prof U of Utah 1964-9; VP R&D ICN Pharmaceuticals and dir ICN Nucleic Acid Research Inst 1969-77; prof BYU 1977-; career: Utah Award Utah Div Amer Chemical Soc 1981; mem: Amer Chemical Soc; Amer Assn for Cancer Research; publ: over 385 journal articles & patents; editor or editorial board for 4 sci periodicals; mil: US Army Med Corps Cpl 1944-5; rel: LDS, bishop, h council; home: 4006 Sherwood Dr; off: 687 WIDB, BYU.

ROBINSON, DONALD WILFORD   prof of Mathematics; b: 29 Feb 1928; m: Helen Ruth Sorensen; p: Wilford Allen & Thirza Cornick; c: Diane, Allen Conrad, Karen, Janette, Marilyn, Lynae, David William; ed: BS 1948 MA 1952 U of Utah; PhD 1956 Case Inst Tech; NSF Fellow 1962-3; former: res assoc Calif Inst Tech 1962-3; visiting prof US Naval Post Grad School; career: Fulbright-Hayes Lectr U Carabobo, Valencia, Venezuela 1976-7; mem: Amer Math

Soc; Math Assn Amer; Sigma Xi; publ: 35 articles; pol: voting dist chm Republican; rel: LDS, bishop; home: 2380 N 930 E; off: 316 TMCB, BYU.

ROBINSON, HELEN SORENSEN   homemaker, symphony musician, special instr in violin, exec sec; b: 2 Nov 1927; m: Donald Wilford Robinson; p: Conrad Sorensen & Ruth West; c: Diane, Allen Conrad, Karen, Janette, Marilyn, Lynae, David William; ed: BA 1949 U of Utah; Phi Kappa Phi; former: violinist Utah Symphony, Pasadena Symphony, Monterey Symphony, Cleveland Philharmonic; sec Edw L Burton Co, Utah Oil Co; special instr in violin at BYU; career: soloist Utah Valley Symphony; mem: Amer Fed of Musicians; Federated Music Clubs; Amer String Tchrs Assn; award: bowling trophies; civic: concertmaster & board VP Utah Valley Symphony; former Farrer Jr High PTA pres; pol: sec local Republican voting dist; judge of election dist 48; rel: LDS, Relief Soc pres, choir dir, stake primary counselor; club: BYU Women Pres 1979–80; home: 2380 N 930 E.

ROGERS, THOMAS F   prof Russian Lang & Lit; playwright; b: 12 Apr 1933; m: Merriam; p: William A & Lucille Collett; c: Grace, Kyra, Krista, Tommy, Karen, William, Mary; ed: BA U of Utah; MA Yale; PhD Georgetown; Danforth Fellow; former: instr Howard U; asst prof U of Utah; dir BYU Honors Prog; chm BYU Dept of Asian & Slavic Langs; mem: RMMLA; AATSEEL; publ: *Superfluous Men & the Post-Stalin Thaw;* translation: *Turbulence and Random Junctions;* plays: *Huebener, Fire in the Bones, Reunion, The Second Priest;* numerous articles & reviews; civic: Boy Scouts; Amnesty Internatl; rel: LDS, N German Mission presidency; branch pres; home: 939 E Briar Ave; off: 250 FB, BYU.

ROLLINS, LESLIE McKAY   prof of Health Sci BYU; b: 22 Oct 1934; m: Joan; p: J Leslie & Louise; c: Maughn M 20, Bradley M 16, Jacqueline 13, Douglas M 12; ed: BA 1961 MS 1962 BYU; PhD 1971 U of Utah; former: instr health sci Foothill College, Los Altos Hills CA; mem: Utah AAPERD; Amer Alliance for Health, Physical Ed, Recreation & Dance; Eta Sigma Gamma; publ: co–auth 4 books on health sci; civic: barbershop quartet performances in western US; mil: Utah Natl Guard 7 yrs;

Outstanding Trainee of Co; active duty Ft Ord Calif; rel: bishopric, h council, Tabernacle Choir 10 yrs; home: 1860 S Park Ln, Orem; off: 229-H RB, BYU.

ROUNDY, ELMO SMITH   prof & chm of Physical Ed BYU; b: 23 Dec 1928; m: Myrle Pedersen; p: Otho & Verna Fitzgerald; c: Rebecca, Robin Otho, Wade Pedersen, Lisa, Jacquline, Jennifer, Shadrach Joseph; ed: BS MS BYU; PhD UCLA; Phi Kappa Phi; Sigma Xi; Phi Delta Kappa; former: Athletic Dir & Head Football Coach Eastern Arizona JC; principal Snowflake Arizona High School; career: pres Southwest Dist of the Amer Alliance of Health, Physical Ed & Recreation; Arizona High School Coach of the Year 1956; finalist Arizona Coach of the Year 1957; mem: Amer Assn Health, Physical Ed, and Recreation; College of Sports Medicine; Amer Assn of College Physical Educators; award: Outstanding Athlete & Male Student in high school grad class, Palmyra, NY; publ: over 20 professional articles & statistics for res in physical ed; civic: Indian Hills Neighborhood Chm 1972-6; pol: Republican; Utah County Central Com; chm Legislative Dist 37; mil: Provo Natl Guard 145th Field Artillery; master sgt; 6 mo in Korea; rel: LDS, bishop, h council; club: Timpanogos Kiwanis 1970-5; off: 221-f RB, BYU.

ROUNDY, GLEN E   asst dir for Business Affairs BYU Health Ctr; b: 20 Dec 1934; m: Ruth; p: Edmund Eugene & May L; c: Kelly, Brenda, Beth, Kim, Nathan, Jeannette, Michael, Rebecca, Christopher; ed: 2 yrs x-ray school; 2 yrs college; former: X-ray Technologist; grocery clerk; career: 20 Year Award BYU; mem: Amer Soc Radiologic Technologist; BYU Admin Council; publ: *Microfiche An Answer to Medical Records Problems;* mil: Utah Natl Guard staff sgt 3 yrs; rel: LDS, bishop, h council; home: 1137 W 400 N; off: Rm 176 Health Ctr, BYU.

ROUNDY, SHERON KNIGHT   instr Dental Assting UTC; b: 19 Jul 1939; m: Stanley C Roundy; p: Glenn G & Garda G Knight; c: Glenn Q Lowry (Quinn); ed: Certified Dental Asst; former: oral surgery asst to Dr DaCosta Clark; career: Utah Dental Asst Serv Award 1965; mem: Amer Dental Asst Assn 22 yrs; Utah Dental Asst Assn 22 yrs; rel: LDS, MIA pres, jr sunday school 15 yrs, stake coor; home: 313 E 4075 N; off: UTC, Box 1609.

ROUNDY, STANLEY C   court reporter; b: 9 Aug 1928; m: Sheron Knight; p: Clayton & Lyda Parcell; c: Quinn, Clayton R, Paul S, Ruth Ann; ed: UTC; BYU; Lenhardt's College of Court Reporting, San Francisco; career: certified shorthand reporter & registered professional reporter; mil: US Army 2 yrs; rel: LDS, clerk; home: 313 E 4075 N; off: 304 Utah County Bldg.

RUPPER, JOHN H   physician, internal medicine; mem of staff Utah Valley Hospital; internal medicine consul Utah State Hospital; co-developer, sec, mgr of Medical Ctr 1275 N University Ave; b: 19 Feb 1916; m: Bonnie; p: Heber S & Stella McEwan; c: John, Steve, James, Maryann; ed: AB BYU; MD Georgetown Univ School of Medicine; residency, LDS Hospital, Veterans Admin, Dearborne, Mich; former: pres of staff Utah Valley Hospital; pres Utah Heart Assn; pres Utah Society of Internal Medicine; pres Utah State Medical Assn; mem: Utah County Med Soc; Amer Med Assn; Amer Heart Assn; mil: WW II; rel: LDS; club: Rotary Internatl; home: 351 W 1500 N; off: 1275 N University Ave No. 17.

SALAZAR, RICHARD D   asst prof BYU; b: 4 Oct 1936; p: Edifanio C & Esther T; c: Deborah Lynne 5, Meghann Ramona 3; ed: PhD Southern Illinois Univ 1970-2; scholarships for undergrad, masters, doctorate work; former: tchr, coach, Corcoran Calif High School 1959-61, Elsinore Calif High School 1962-3; mem: Amer School Health Assn; Amer Public Health Assn; Phi Kappa Phi; Eta Sigma Gamma; publ: *"Drugs, Youth, and Personality"*; co-auth textbooks: *Preventive Health; Health Management: Promotion & Self-Care;* civic: Red Cross Evaluation Com mem 1981; Pony League baseball coach 1977-present; mil: 6 mo active, 5.5 yrs reserve 1959-65; Provo Reserve Infantry Unit named best unit in 91st Reserve Infantry Div, summer camp, Pakima WN 1965; rel: LDS, temple worker; dist mission pres; home: 821 N Main, Orem; off: 229-C RB, BYU.

SALISBURY, DAVID FRANK   instructional developer; b: 5 Dec 1951; m: Elaine Jenks; p: David & Lois; c: Christianne 2, Julianne 5 mo; ed: PhD instructional sci & tech (comp Aug 1982); 6 half-time fellowships from BYU Grad School; former: Instr Development & Media Serv

Coor, Dixie College; former: tchr BYU Proj Guatemala 3 summers; developed training materials for automated LDS temple recording sys as employee LDS Genealogical Dept; mem: Amer Ed Research Assn; United Families of Amer; publ: *Basic Reading 2;* professional papers; rel: LDS,elders quorum pres, tchr development dir; home: 320 N 800 E; off: 220 KMB, BYU.

SAM, DAVID   Dist Judge 4th Judicial Dist; b: 12 Aug 1933; m: Betty J Brennan; p: Andrew & Flora; c: Betty Jean, David D, Daniel S, Tamara L, Pamela R; Daryl P, Angie E, Sheyla M; ed: BS 1957 BYU; JD 1960 U of Utah; part time prof BYU 5 yrs; former: City Attorney, County Attorney, County Commissioner Duchesne County; mem: Amer Bar Assn; Utah State Bar Assn; award: various public serv awards; civic: Board of Water Resources for State of Utah; Duchesne County Hospital Board; Board of Ed for Continuing Ed Utah State U; pol: Republican county del; mil: US Air Force Captain, Judge Advocate Corps 1961-3; rel: LDS, bishop, stake pres, seminary principal, institute dir; home: 1171 Clairmont Dr, Springville; off: County Courthouse.

SAYER, ROBERT A   owner Sayer Insurance Agency; b: 8 July 1948; m: Miriam; p: Irma Sayer; c: Misty 13, Justin 11, Stacy 7, Jodi 6, Linsey 1; ed: BS BYU; former: sales rep Northwest PMS Feed Co, Caldwell, ID; mem: Independent Agents Assn of Utah; mil: US Navy; rel: LDS; club: BPOE 849; home: 95 E 1600 N, Orem; off: 269 W 400 N.

SEAMONS, MARY LOUISE (MADSEN)   adviser Elementary Ed majors BYU; b: 11 Apr 1930; p: Willis Niel & Louise Frandsen Madsen; c: Debra Anne, Randall "M", Sherri Lou Grigsby, Jerry O; ed: Utah State U; BYU; Scholarship to Utah State U; former: sec O'Leary Jr High, Twin Falls, Idaho; production sec BYU Motion Picture Studio; dept sec BYU Dept of Elementary Ed; mem: Natl Academic Advising Assn; award: Mt Pleasant Centennial Queen; Contestant in Miss Utah Contest; several 1st place awards Saga of the Sanpitch writing contest; Utah Girls' State rep; publ: stories in Saga of the Sanpitch; civic: Jayceettes; PTA Publicity Chm & County Council Mem; rel: LDS, Relief Soc ldr; club: Literary Art Guild; Fed

Music Clubs; Newcomers So-Journey Clubs; home: 1774 S 340 E, Orem; off: 120 MCKB, BYU.

SEKAQUAPTEWA, KENNETH DALE   admin asst Indian Ed Dept BYU; b: 26 Oct 1949; m: Lynne Kalihilihi Laeha; p: Wayne Phillip & Judy Chen; c: Kam Kaohunaniokaleponi 2, Kory Kaheaokalani 1; ed: BA English, secondary ed 1978 BYU; former: assoc producer for weather & sports KSL-TV; career: Outstanding Young Men of Amer 1979; award: Deseret News Marathon 7th place overall 1977; Fiesta Bowl Marathon 40th overall 1975; Lewis Tewanima Memorial Race 1st overall 1975; publ: founding editor & publisher of *Qua'toqti* weekly newspaper for Hopi Indian Tribe 1973-5; editor *Eagle's Eye;* civic: com mem & MC for Miss Indian Scholarship Pageant 1981-2; rel: LDS, bishopric; home 595 W 1850 N; off: 144-A BRMB.

SHUMWAY, LARRY V   assoc prof Humanities BYU; b: 25 Nov 1934; m: Sandra; p: James Carroll & Merle K; c: Nathan 9, Nolan 6, Brendan 4, Kirsten 3, Duncan 1; ed: BA BYU; MA Seton Hall Univ; PhD U of Washington; 2 NDFL Fellowships; 1 Fulbright; former: music tchr Ariz Public Schools, Clayton Jr High SLC; mem: Soc for Ethnomusicology; Soc for Asian Music; publ: "Kibigaku: A Modern Japanese Ritual Music"; "J W 'Babe' Spangler: The Old Virginia Fiddler"; "When is Fiddling Fiddling and When is it Something Else?"; "The Tongan Lakalaka"; rel: LDS, stake music dir, cubmaster; home: 749 E 2550 N; off: 262 JKBA, BYU.

SHURTZ, ROYDEN R   pres & gen mgr Royden Inc; b: 6 Jul 1931; m: Alene Thompson; c: Clark, Marsha Green, Kelly, Tyler, Carolyn, Barbara; mem: former pres Utah County Heating & Cooling Contractors Assn; award: King Scout; Provo Peak Award; civic: VP Provo Chamber of Commerce; former mem Provo City Parks & Rec Board; rel: LDS, stake presidency, bishopric, chm Provo Reg Welfare Dairy Operating Com; club: Rotary Internatl; home: 1916 W Center; off: 177 W 300 S.

SKARDA, R VENCIL   assoc prof Mathematics BYU; b: 22 May 1940; m: Lorraine Clark; p: Ralph V & Pearl D; c: David 10, Brian 8, Kathleen 6, Michael 4, Christopher 2, Johnathan 6 mo; ed: BS 1961 Pomona College; PhD 1966

Cal Tech; former: mathematician at Pacific Missle Range, Sandia Corp & Aerospace Corp; mem: Amer Math Soc; London Math Soc; Mathematical Assn of Amer; civic: Utah Reg Examination Coor for Annual High School Mathematics Examination; rel: LDS; home: 229 E 4075 N; off: 318 TMCB, BYU.

SKINNER, RULON DEAN   assoc prof BYU; b: 26 Jun 1931; m: Margaret Ruth Walters; p: Rulon Moroni & Violet Whipple; c: Kumen Dean, Diane Hazel Holmes, Susan Violet, Maria Ruth, Cheryl Ann; ed: Eastern Arizona Jr College 1950; BA accounting 1954 MA recreation ed 1971 BYU; Phi Kappa Phi; Alpha Phi Omega; Cert Standard Red Cross First Aid instr; former: Professional Training Exec, Natl Staff, Boy Scouts of Amer; Asst Scout Exec & Dist Scout Exec, Utah Natl Parks Council, BSA; career: 1968 Region 12 BSA Career Man of the Yr; Youth Developmental Enterprise Mahelo Awards for service 1977-82; Citations from Amer Camping Assn; listed in 33 biographical publs; mem: Boy Scouts of Amer; Girl Scouts of the USA; Amer Camping Assn; Youth Developmental Enterprises, Amer Red Cross; Natl Rife Assn; Utah Parks & Recreation Assn; award: Provo Peak Award, BSA; 4 Presidential Sports Awards; publ: *That Scouting Spirit; Techniques of Outdoor Adventure With Answers; Community Relationships of Youth Agencies; 100 Youth Agencies & Organizations in the USA; Youth Meetings, Activities, and Conferences; Cub Scouting Workbook; Basic Canoeing Techniques; Twenty-Two Leadership Principles; Keys to Leadership;* over 16 other major publs; civic: community chm Provo United Way 1968; pres elect Big Brothers Big Sisters of Utah County; rel: LDS, stake presidency, stake exec sec, h council, bishopric; club: pres Provo Timpanogos Lions Club 1970-1, zone chm 1971-2; honorary mem Kiwanis Club; home: 1717 W 1460 N; off: 273-D RB, BYU.

SLOVER, ROBERT H   assoc prof Political Sci BYU, Provo, Hawaii, London; ret Col US Army; b: 24 Aug 1913; m: Rosemarie Wood; p: A P Slover; c: Robert H II, Cindy Jo, Timothy W; ed: BA U of Okla; MPA PhD Harvard; Phi Beta Kappa; Phi Eta Sigma; Pi Kappa Alpha; former: US Army Natl Field Supvr WPA, Reg Dir Research & Records WPA; publ: *Bizonal Admin of Western Germany; Case*

Studies on M & Govt; civic: Kiwanis; pol: Democratic candidate for Utah County Commissioner 1979; mil: US Army 2nd Lt to Col 25 yrs active, 5 yrs reserve; 2 Legion of Merit awards; Bronze Star; Korean Ulchi; Annual Award M I Govt Assn; WW II & Korean Ribbons; rel: LDS, Serv Men's Coord Far East, branch pres, bishop, mission pres, reg rep, h council; home: 1717 N Pine N.

SMART, DAVID   pres SOS Computer Sys Inc; b: 5 Mar 1938; m: Pamela; p: Theron; c: Kathy 11, Richard 8, Mellisa 6, Amy 3; ed: BA physics BYU; former: operation mgr DEC System 10, Computer Serv BYU; rel: LDS; home: 889 N 700 E, Orem; off: 1401 W 820 N.

SMITH, BARBARA MCKAY   Asst Dean Continuing Ed UTC; b: 2 Oct 1920; m: Oliver R; p: Thomas E & Fawn Brimhall McKay; c: Barbara Kay Rytting, Olivia Baird, Kenneth M, Ronald M, Rebecca Snyder, Deborah, Dorothy Gillespie, Richard M; former: bookkeeper; mem: Amer Technical Ed Assn Inc; Natl Environmental Training Assn; Utah Adult Ed Assn; civic: Provo City Board of Adjustments 7 yrs; Provo City Planning Commission 5 yrs; pol: Republican, state & county del, precinct chm, former dist chm; home: 970 N 1200 E; off: UTC 1395 N 150 E.

SMITH, BRUCE NEPHI   dean College of Biology & Agriculture BYU; b: 3 Apr 1934; m: Ruth Olean Aamodt; p: N Pratt & Laura P; c: Rebecca, Trudy, Alan, Marilee, Edward, Samual; ed: BS MS PhD; Phi Kappa Phi; former: chm Dept of Botany BYU; asst prof botany U of Texas at Austin; career: SRI Citation Classio 1981; Sigma Xi Paper of the Month; mem: AAUP; AAAS; ASPP; Japanese S Plant Physiol; Geochemical Soc; Sigma Xi; Ecological Soc of Amer; award: Dist Award of Merit BSA; pres Utah Valley Chapter, Sons of Amer Revolution; publ: 1 book; 80 aritcles; civic: Orem City Beautification Com; BSA, SAR; pol: democrat; rel: LDS, bishop, h council; home: 411 W 530 S, Orem; off: 301 WIDB, BYU.

SMITH, CARL V   clinical psychologist; dept head, Specialized Serv for Children & Youth; b: 28 Sep 1947; m: Elizabeth H; p: Vance T, Laura Gunnell, Barbara Loughmiller; c: Shayla 10, David 7, Phillip 6, Jennifer 4; ed: BS 1972 PhD cum laude 1976 BYU; licensed psychologist former: consultant Utah Psychological Serv; intern Timpanogos Community Mental Health Ctr; Timpanogos Community Mental Health Ctr Crisis Team 1979–; clinical psychologist Family Counseling Ctr; therapeutic team coord Reg Adolescent Ctr; dir Carousel Treatment Ctr; mem: board mem Utah Psychological Assn; Mental Health Professional Advisory Council; pres Div of Psychologists in Public Serv; Task Force for Alternatives to Institutionalization for Seriously Delinquent Girls 1979; rel: LDS, bishopric; home: 460 N 880 E, Springville; off: 1169 E 300 N.

SMITH, CRAIG GLENN   accountant; Business Mgr Dept of Special Events; b: 28 Dec 1948; m: Connie Marie Tilton; p: S Glenn & Vivian Poole; ed: BYU 1976 business mgt; mem: NAAMDD; award: Outstanding Young Men of Amer 1981; BSA Second Miler Award; civic: Boy Scouts; rel: LDS, h council; club: Rex Rabbit Club of Amer; home: 312 N 800 E, Springville; off: 2132 MC, BYU.

SMITH, D LOWRY   MD; b: 14 Jun 1918; m: Lily; p: David W & Evalyn Lowry Smith; c: Sherryl, Lester, Kevin, Colin, Steven, Daniel; ed: BYU; MD U of Utah, Ob-gyn, residency LDS Hospital; former: dir Ob-gyn Serv Pleasant Valley Hospital, Calif; dir Ob-gyn Serv Mather AFB; mem: AMA, Utah State Med Soc; Calif Med Soc; Utah County Med Soc; staff BYU Health Serv; mil: US Air Force pilot WWII, Flight Surgeon Utah Natl Guard; USAF Commendation Medal; Air Medals; ret Lt Col; rel: LDS, sunday school pres; home: 927 Quail Valley Dr; off: BYU Health Ctr.

SMITH, ELIZABETH JOYCE   admin asst to asst to pres BYU; b: 19 Feb 1940; c: Elizabeth Marie Baugh 19; former: sec to dept chm Organizational Behavior BYU; mental health worker Millard County; regulatory affairs coord Cutter Labs; rel: LDS, YSI stake ldr, Sunday School tchr, camp dir; home: 685 S Main, Orem; off: C-366 ASB, BYU.

SMITH, GARY RICHARD   BYU prof; b: 20 Oct 1932; m: Rita Palmer; p: Alma Gibson Smith Sr; c: Andrew Gibson 8, Paula Jean 7, Jamie Ann 5, Maren Michelle 3, Stephen Taylor; ed: BA 1954, 59 Idaho State U; EdD 1970 U of

Idaho; Phi Kappa Phi; grad with honors Idaho State U; grad with highest honors U of Idaho; former: tchr Pocatello & Highland High Schools, Utah State U; career: Honorable Order of Kentucky Colonels; Deputy Marshall Dodge City, Kansas; Outstanding Tchr Award Utah Vocational Assn; Open Door Tchr Recognition; DECA Special Recognition Award; mem: Utah Voc Assn; Amer Voc Assn; Natl Bus Ed Assn; Delta Pi Epsilon; Phi Delta Kappa; Utah Bus Ed Assn; Council of Distributive Tchr Educators; Natl Assn of Distributive Ed Tchr; Western Bus Ed Assn; publ: *Display & Promotion; Exploring Marketing Occupations; Communications & Human Relations Activities for Work Adjustment; Profiles of Distinction: College of Business-Century One;* civic: MD campaign chm; pol: Republican dist com 2 terms; mil: US Army Civil Affairs Military Govt Group 1956-8; rel: LDS, stake mission pres, exec sec, bishop; home: 990 E 2680 N; off: 359 JKB, BYU.

SMITH, JAY M JR   Prof of Accounting BYU; b: 14 Jun 1932; m: Jena Vee Cordon; p: Jay & Relia Cooley Smith; c: Michael, Blaine, Jaynie, Relia, Randy, Cynthia, Debra, Frank, David, Kevin, Kristy; ed: BS MS BYU; PhD Stanford; Danforth Scholar 1961-4; former: auditor Arthur Andersen & Co; visiting prof Stanford; prof & dept chm U of Minn 1964-71; prof U of Hawaii; career: CPA 1957 Utah; honorable mention for Natl CPA Exam; Prof of Yr BYU 1982; Distinguished Prof of Yr, School of Mgt 1976; mem: Amer Inst of Cert Public Accountants; Utah State Assn of CPAs; Amer Accounting Assn; publ: co-auth *Intermediate Accounting* 7th ed; journal articles; civic: VP Boy Scouts of Amer Utah Natl Parks Council; mil: US Army 1954-6; rel: LDS, stake pres, bishop, h council, tchr; home: 301 E Maple, Mapleton; off: 337 JKB, BYU.

SMITH, KAY H   prof of Psychology BYU; b: 6 Mar 1935; m: Neva McAllister; p: John L & Olive Smith; c: Carrie, Jennifer, Timothy, Adrianne, Aaron Robert; ed: BA 1957 MA 1958 BYU; PhD 1962 Wayne State U psychology; scholarships; fellowships, assitantships; former: asst prof Detroit Inst of Tech, Mich State U, Field Unit Chief Army Res Inst; mem: former pres Utah Psychological Assn; Soc of Sigma Xi; Amer Psychological Assn; award: All Around Performer of the Year BYU Prog Bureau 1954-5; publ: sci articles & tech reports; civic: mem Adv Board Provo Canyon School; mil: Ensign US Navy; grad with distinction US Naval Preflight School, Pensacola; rel: LDS, mission ldr, h council; home: 3610 N Piute Dr; off: 1094 SWKT, BYU.

SMITH, PHILIP JOHN   asst prof BYU; b: 9 Nov 1951; m: Rosemary Elaine Preete; p: John Gibb & Iris June; c: Chad Philip 6, April Denise 4, Sean Thomas 2; ed: BS 1975 MS 1976 PhD 1979 chemical engineering BYU; Tau Beta Pi; Phi Kappa Phi; Sigma Xi; former: Atlantic Richfield Canada Ltd; Dept of Environment of Canada; career: mem: Amer Inst of Chemical Engineers; Combustion Inst; Amer Inst of Aeronautics & Astronautics; Engineering Inst of Canada; Rocky Mtn Fuel Soc; publ: co-auth book chapters; 8 papers & articles; rel: LDS, bishopric, ward clerk, exec sec; home: 2343 W 300 N; off: 350 CB, BYU.

SMITH, ROBERT JUNIUS   BYU Financial VP; b: 25 Dec 1920; m: Lola Nielson; p: Samuel Francis & Lulu Jane Hatch; c: Junola Bush, Lynn Robert, Lynette Lyman, Shirley Ricks, LaRae Blake, Jeanine Denton, Larry K, Sheldon R; ed: BS accounting & bus admin 1948 BYU; MBA 1949 Northwestern U; DBA 1957 Indiana U; award: Karl G Maeser Outstanding Teaching Award 1967; former: prof of accounting; Assoc Academic VP BYU; career: Elijah Watt Sells Gold Medal, Amer Inst of CPAs for highest grades in May 1949 CPA exam; Natl Assn of Accountants, Outstanding Manuscript Award, SLC Chapter 1957-8, 59-60, 63-4; mem: Amer Accounting Assn; Amer Inst of CPAs; Alpha Kappa Psi; Beta Alpha Psi; Beta Gamma Sigma; Phi Kappa Phi; Utah Assn of CPAs; publ: *Preparing for the CPA Examination* 2 vols; *Thoughts and Verse;* civic: Utah County United Way 11 yrs, pres 1972; controller Utah Parks Council Boy Scouts of Amer; pol: Republican county & state del; mil: US Naval Reserve 1944-6 ETM 2/c; rel: LDS, bishop, h council, stake president, welfare serv reg agent; home: 2465 N 820 E; off: D-387 ASB, BYU.

SMOOT, L DOUGLAS   dean College of Engineering Sci & Tech BYU; prof of Chem Engr; dir BYU Combustion Lab; b: 26 Jul 1934; m: Marian Bird; p: Douglas P & Jennie Hallam; c: Analee, LaCinda, Michelle, Melinda Lee; ed:

BS BES 1957 BYU; MS 1958 PhD chem engr 1960 U of Washington; Registered Professional Engineer; Utah Elks State Scholarship 1952; Outstanding Chem Engr Grad 1957; former: mgr Lockheed Propulsion Co 1963-7; chm Chem Engr Dept BYU 1970-6; natl & internatl consultant to 30 co's; career: Educator of the Yr, SME, Western US 1978; Outstanding Engineer, AIAA, State of Utah 1977; Outstanding Aerospace Educator Award, AIAA, State of Utah 1975; Maeser Research Award 1975; Outstanding Engineering Educator Award, EJC, State of Utah 1975; mem: Amer Inst of Chem Engineers; Amer Inst of Aeronautics & Astronautics; Amer Soc for Engineering Ed; Combution Inst; honor societies; publ: 100 in journal articles & proceedings; *Coal Combustion and Gasification;* civic: tech advisor Provo City Commission 1981; speaker to civic clubs; pol: Republican; mem Governor's council for Sci & Tech 1979-; rep USA in natl & internatl sci & tech coms; rel: LDS, stake presidency, bishop; club: Kiwanis; home: 1881 N 1500 E; off: 270 CB, BYU.

SNOW, KARL NELSON JR   Prof of Public Admin BYU; b: 1 Jul 1930; m: Donna Jean Dain; p: Karl N & Wanda McGregor; c: Karl N III, Melissa, Daniel D, Jeanmarie, Howard H, Elisabeth; ed: BS BYU; MA U of Minn; Doctorate of Pub Admin USC; scholarships USC & U of Minn; former: Utah State Leg Analyst 1966-9; Dir Inst of Govt BYU 1969-79; mem: board of editors *Public Administration Review* and *State and Local Government Review;* award: Utah State Off Personnel Mgt & Governor of State of Utah Award for Excellence in Mgt Reform 1980; Outstanding Elected Official 1981, Utah Public Employees Assn; civic: chm Citizens Com on Provo City Govt 1980; chm Utah State House Fellowship Commission 1973-9; chm Utah State Constitutional Revision Commission 1977-; pol: elected to Utah State Senate 1972; Republican Majority Leader; rel: LDS, bishopric, h council, tchr; home: 1847 N Oak Ln; off: 210 JKB, BYU.

SNYDER, BRENT   Chief Building Official; b: 9 May 1943; m: Sharon; p: Mary; c: Patrick 18, Kevin 17, Michael 11, Jaime 2; ed: Western Nevada CC; Utah Tech; Colorado Northwestern CC; 4.0 at WNCC; former: Chief Bldg Official Provo 1979-81; Plans Examiner 1978-9; career: 4 Resolutions of Commendation; Provo City Commission; 1

of 23 bldg officials in world to receive Cert of Achievement, Internatl Conf of Bldg Officials; mem: com mem Natl Ed Com for ICBO; IAMPO, IAEI, Colorado ICBO, Utah UAMPO; civic: scout ldr; rel: LDS, elders quorum pres, stake scoutmaster, bishopric; home: 699 W 1440 S; 2470 S Redwood Rd, W Valley City.

SNYDER, CRAIG MORGAN   attorney; partner Howard, Lewis & Petersen; b: 19 Jul 1947; m: Nancy Kay Throckmorton; p: William M & Martha J; c: Travis 11, Brady 7, Matthew 3; ed: BA history BA political sci U of Utah 1970; JD U of Utah 1972; licensed to appear before 10th Circuit Court of Appeals; former: staff attorney Exxon, Houston, Texas 1972-3; career: pres Central Utah Bar Assn 1978; mem: Utah State Bar Assn; State Bar of Texas; civic: Cub Scout Pack Ldr; home: 1144 E 435 N, Orem; off: 120 E 300 N.

SORENSEN, MARILYN HALVORSEN   Registered Family Nurse Practioner BYU Health Ctr; b: 16 Sep 1955; m: Asael T Sorensen Jr; p: Gail S & Alta J Halvorsen; c: Asael H; ed: BS; MS 1982; academic scholarships, honors prog, grad high honors, BYU; former: RN Utah Valley Hospital; mem: UNA; award: Ballroom Dance Team; pol: county del; rel: LDS, stake board; home: 579 N 400 E; off: BYU Health Ctr.

SOTER, NICHOLAS GREGORY   pres Soter Associates Inc Advertising Agency; partner Council Press; b: 26 Apr 1947; m: Kathleen Lyman; p: Sam N & Bernice Bennett; c: Nichole 12, Erin 10, Samuel Scott 7, Kara 5, Stephen Andrew 3; ed: BS communications BYU 1971; former: VP & account exec McLean Associates Advertising Agency; career: world Finalist CLIO Advertising Awards 1982; NY Art Director's The One Show Advertising Fed, SL Art Directors & Communications Assn of Utah Valley; mem: former pres Communications Assn of Utah Valley; publ: magazine articles; civic: Provo Chamber of Commerce; United Way; pol: Republican voting dist chm; rel: LDS, bishop, branch pres, h council, varsity scout coach; home: 1728 S 290 E, Orem; off: 209 N 400 W.

SOWELL, MADISON U   prof BYU; b: 8 Mar 1952; m: Debra Sue Hickenlooper; p: M U & Ora H S Blair; c:

MariLouise 2; ed: AM, PhD Harvard, BA BYU; grad summa cum laude BYU 1975; Joan Jacoby Award for Italian Lit & Travel Study Prize for Excellence in Teaching; former: asst prof Italian & Comp Lit BYU 1979–; career: research fellowships; mem: Phi Kappa Phi; Dante Soc of Amer; Medieval Acad of Amer; Amer Assn Of Tchrs of Italian; Renaissance Soc of Amer; Soc for Italian Studies; Modern Language Assn; Amer Assn of Univ Prof of Italian; Philological Assn of the Pacific Coast; Amer Boccaccio Assn; publ: articles; pol: Republican canvasser; rel: LDS, organist, sunday school tchr, elders presidency, stake clerk; home: 810 E 2730 N; off: 230 MSRB, BYU.

SPENCER, HERBERT BECK   physician (urologist); b: 6 May 1929; m: Mavis; p: Herbert G & LaZella Beck; c: David, Anne, John, Susan, Julie; ed: BS MD U of Utah; Phi Kappa Phi; Alpha Omega Alpha; former: consultant in urology US Air Force Surgeon Gen in Europe; pres med staff Utah Valley Hospital; mem: fellow Amer College of Surgeons; diplomate Amer Board of Urology; publ: med articles; mil: US Air Force major; rel: LDS, bishop, stake pres, mission pres, reg rep; home: 2060 N Oak Ln; off: 930 N 500 W.

SPENCER, RUSSELL LARRY   exec dir Central Utah Enterprises Rehabilitation Facility; b: 2 Jan 1940; m: Kathryn Hunsaker; p: Richard L & Nina F; c: Ellen 15, Robert 12, Christine 4, Douglas 2; ed: BA 1967 BYU Spanish/German; MA 1970 BYU Spanish/Ed Admin & Curriculum; grad study fellowships BYU; La Sociedad Nacional Hispanica Sigma Delta Pi; former: Spanish tchr BYU; mem: pres Utah Assn of Rehabilitation Facilities; Senator Hatch's Adv Com for the Handicapped; pres Board of Dir Alpine House; Utah and Natl Rehabilitation Assn; pol: del Utah County Republican Convention; mil: US Army 1963–5; US Air Force Reserves 1967–9; rel: LDS, bishopric, h council; home: 1136 Birch Ln; off: 1170 S 350 E.

SPINDLER, GREGORY H   prof BYU; b: 12 Nov 1948; m: Laurel L; p: Herman; ed: PhD U of Illinois; U of Illinois Grad Fellow; Phi Kappa Phi; Amer Philological Assn; Rocky Mtn Modern Languages Assn; publ: journal articles pending; work on *Oresteia* commentary; rel: Assembly of God; home: 893 N 400 W, PG; off: A-206 JKBA, BYU.

SPOTTEN, RON   catering, wedding services; b: 20 Aug 1943; m: Beth C; p: Thomas C & Latell; ed: BYU; former: insurance salesman; career: Salesman of the Yr awards; mil: US Air Force 4 yrs; rel: LDS, sunday school dist supt, 70s pres; home: 699 E 500 S; off: 189 W 300 S.

STANFORD, MELVIN JOSEPH   prof Business Mgt BYU; b: 13 Jul 1932; m: Linda Barney; p: Joseph Sedley & Ida Pearl Ivie; c: Connie Tendick, Cheryl Gordon, Joseph, Theodore, Emily, Charlotte, Charles, Sarah; ed: BS business 1957 Utah State U; MBA 1963 Harvard; PhD 1968 Illinois; Phi Kappa Phi; First Security Found Scholar; Donald Kirk David Fellow; former: visiting prof of mgt, Boston U, Europe; accounting staff analyst Arabian Amer Oil Co, Dhahran, Saudi Arabia; career: Scroll of Appreciation, Heilbronn Community, W Germany; Cert of Merit, US Small Business Admin; mem: Acad of Mgt; Amer Inst for Decision Sci; Alpha Kappa Psi; Beta Gamma Sigma; Internatl Council for Small Business & Entrepreneurship; Utah Assn of CPAs; Sons of the Amer Revolution; Sons of the Utah Pioneers; award: Meritorious Serv Award, Sons of the Amer Revolution; publ: 6 books; over 100 journal articles & mgt cases; civic: treas Provo High School Acad Boosters; Mayor's Com for Business Enhancement; mil: US Air Force, Korea; Lt Col US Army Reserve; commander of unit recd Superior Unit Cert; Natl Defense Serv Medal; rel: LDS, stake Sunday School presidency, ward music chm, h council, bishopric, presiding elder, Tabernacle Choir; home: 1163 E 820 N; off: 203 JKB, BYU.

STEED, HARMAN C   VP & mgr 1st Interstate Bank Provo Office; b: 4 Oct 1924; m: Margaret Smith; p: Milton E & Ida H; c: Douglas A, Debra S Parks; ed: BS BYU; former: mgr 1st State Bank, Salina, Kanab Branch; mem: Robert Morris Assoc Commercial Lending Frat; dir Utah State Bankers Assn; former pres Utah County Bankers Assn; civic: former dir Chamber of Commerce; dir Utah Housing Authority; comptroller Metropolitan Water Dist of Provo; former pres Utah County United Way; pol: former mayor Kanab, Utah; former Kane County

Republican Chm; mil: US Infantry 2.5 yrs; 2 yrs European Theater of Operation; Purple Heart; Unit Citation; rel: LDS, bishop; club: Rotary Internatl Club; Riverside Country Club; home: 469 E 4380 N; off: 300 W Center.

STEELE, ROBERT FOSTER   tchr cabinetmaking UTC, gen contractor; b: 17 Mar 1936; m: Marilyn Deem; p: Robert B & Ruby F; c: Bert 18, Brent 15, Brian 13, Blaine 11, Merrilynn 8, Mallene 6; ed: BS MS BYU; former: pres UTC Faculty assn; career: Tchr of the Year UTC 1980-1; sect pres Gen Const Dept, June Workshop; production mgr Utah Small Business of the Year, UTEFAB Ltd; mem: Utah Public Employees Assn; Utah Industrial Arts Assn; Utah Vocational Assn; Amer Vocational Assn; award: Scouting Second Miler; publ: masters thesis; civic: Lions Club pres 1980-1; dist Scout Commissioner; pol: commissioner Lindon City Planning Board; rel: LDS, bishop, h council; home: 558 N 200 E, Lindon; off: UTC, 1395 N 150 E.

STEVENS, DALE J   prof of Geography; b: 27 Jun 1936; m: Mary L; p: Lawrence C; c: Clarke 19, Alan 15, Jill 13, Sue Ann 12, Kaylane 3, Cherie 2; ed: Assoc Arts Weber State; BA BYU; MA Indiana Univ; PhD UCLA; Res & tchg Assistantship; res awards; former: instr Univ of Wyoming; career: res grants in geomorphology & climatology; mem: Assn of Amer Geographers; Pacific Coast Geographers; publ: 14 journal articles; author, co-auth 2 books; civic: PTA, juror in dist & city courts; pol: county del; rel: LDS, h council; home: 471 W 600 S, Orem; off: 622 SWKT, BYU.

STEVENSON, CLAUDIUS E   photographer, portrait, commercial & industrial; b: 26 Apr 1915; m: Marie Douglass; p: Dr Lester A, MD & Bertha Starley; c: Douglass E; ed: LLB 1939 U of Utah; Beta Theta Pi; Delta Theta Phi; former: head of Photographic Dept during construction of Geneva Steel Plant; career: 6 Awards of Merit, Professional Photographers of Amer; listed in Who's Who in Amer Politics, Who's Who in the West, Community Ldrs & Noteworthy Americans, Dictionary of Internatl Biography; mem: Intermtn Professional Photographers Assn; Professional Photographers of Amer; Creative Photographers of Amer; Professional Photographers of Utah; Royal Photo Soc Gt Brit; publ:

photos publ in Life, Time, Fortune, Popular Sci, Ladies
Home Journal; civic: Govt Study Commission of Utah
County 1973; pol: treas 1965-71, chm 1971-5, Utah
County Republican Party; del Natl Republican Conv 1972;
state & county convs; mil: US Marine Corps 1943-6; North
Amer Theatre; Good Conduct; Victory Medal; rel: LDS, 70
quorum pres; club: Provo Rotary Club 1947-60; home: 340
W 400 N, Payson; off: 87 N University Ave.

STIGGINS, CHARLES F   Strength & Conditioning Coach
BYU Athletic Dept; b: 3 Sep 1953; m: Rebecca Allen; p:
Frank & Juanita; ed: assoc degree Ricks College; BS MS
BYU; doctorate work BYU; career: Region 5 Strength &
Conditioning Coach of the Year 1981; one of four finalists
Natl Strength & Conditioning Coach of the Year 1981;
mem: Board of Dir Natl Strength & Conditioning Assn;
publ: conditioning articles in Natl Conditioning Journal;
rel: LDS; off: 233 SFH, BYU.

STIMPSON, MIRIAM   asst prof, assoc chm Dept of
Design; b: 6 May; m: David; p: Cecil Ray Furr & Lucile
Hawkins; c: Todd 15, Greg 13, Ryan 9, Lynley 2 mo; ed:
BS BYU; MA BYU 1972; former: flight stewardess; private
design consul; mem: Amer Soc of Interior Design; publ:
Contemporary Architecture & Furnishings home study
course; *Perceptual Motor Skills Relation of Personality
Char and Color Preferences;* rel: LDS, tchr, Relief
Society counselor; home: 1661 N 1500 E; off: 233 BRMB,
BYU.

STODDARD, DARRELL J   dir of marketing BYU Media
Serv; b: 29 Aug 1934; m: LaRae; p: Earl S & Helen
Froerer; c: James, Mark, Paul, Laura, Lisa, Amy; ed:
Weber State; SE Okla State; BYU; former: reg mgr Ed
Marketing & Research; co-founder Aro Publishing Co &
Reading Research; mem: Assn for Media Educators in
Religion; Univ Film Assn; rel: LDS, stake mission pres,
elders presidency, tchr; home: 266 E 3200 N; off: MPS,
BYU.

STRONG, WILLIAM J   prof of Physics BYU; b: 1 Jan
1934; m: Charlene F; p: William A & June E; c: William,
Stephen, Kathleen, John, David, Richard; ed: BS 1958 MS
1959 BYU; PhD 1964 MIT; Whitney Fellow MIT 1959-60;

former: lecturer in physics Northeastern U & Holy Cross College; career: Sr Fullbright Fellow 1980; mem: fellow Acoustical Soc of Amer; Sigma Xi, IEEE; publ: *Music, Speech & High Fidelity;* mil: US Air Force 1964-6; rel: LDS, bishop, scoutmaster, elders quorum pres, ward clerk; home: 2250 N 800 e; off: Physics Dept, BYU.

STUBBS, DARREL W   prof of Music BYU; b: 7 Dec 1925; m: Eva Stokes; p: John W & Ella R; c: Brian, Eric, Rita, Alan, Carrie; ed: Eastman School of Music; Indiana U; USC; Performers Cert, Eastman; studied oboe with Louis W Booth, Robert Sprenkle, Robert Bloom; former: faculty Indiana U, U of Hawaii, U of S Calif; career: Amer Woodwind Quintet; Los Angeles Woodwinds; Monday Evening Concerts; BYU & U of Utah faculty quintets; soloist Berkshire String Quartet; soloist Indianapolis & Penninsula Festival Orchestras; mem: Orchestras in Rochester NY, Indianapolis, Los Angeles, Honolulu, and Utah Symphony (principal oboist 13 yrs); mil: US Army WWII Sgt, Bandsman; Good Conduct; Marksmanship; rel: LDS, bishop, h council, elders pres, reg music ldr; home: 592 E 2200 N; off: E-575 HFAC, BYU.

STUM,　ROBERT　WILSON　film　producer, cinematographer; b: 22 Jan 1920; m: Gladys; p: Samuel A & Olive O; c: Susan, Karl, Julie, Richard, Sherri; ed: BYU; Art Center School; Hollywood Evening School; Los Angeles Polytechnic School; former: mgr Biddulph-Stum Studios, Provo; award: Professional Photographers of Amer Natl Award 1981; BYU Media Serv Outstanding Serv Award 1978; BYU Meritorious Serv Award in Photo Communications; BYU Exemplary Serv Award 1970; BYU Purposive Creativity Award 1970; mem: Professional Photographers　of　Amer;　Intermtn　Professional Photographers Assn; Associated Latter-Day Media Artists board mem; Photographic Soc of Amer; publ: still photos in *Life; Look; Radio-TV Mirror; Pageant; Jord Jimes; Improvement Era; Coronet; Church News;* dir of photography, set designer, or director for over 115 films; civic: chm Provo 4th of July Queen Contest 2 yrs; pol: Republican dist chm; mil: US Army Signal Corps with Patton's 3rd Army 1942-5; Staff Sgt; rel: LDS, bishopric, h priest asst, youth ldr; club: Timpanogos Kiwanis Club; home: 320 E 2100 N; off: MPS, BYU.

STUTZ, HOWARD C   prof Botany & Genetics; b: 24 Aug 1918; m: Mildred Robison; p: Joseph Reuben & Clara M Coombs; c: Kent, Craig, Thomas, Joseph, Ellen, John, Susan; ed: BS 1940 MS 1950 BYU; PhD 1956 U of Calif Berkeley; former: high school principal, dept head Snow College; career: Guggenheim Fellowship 1960-1; Fulbright Scholarship 1966-7; Maeser Teaching Excellence Award 1970; Sigma Xi Res Award 1972; College Res Award 1976; Cooley Natl Plant Taxonomy Award 1977; mem: Phi Kappa Phi; Sigma Xi; Botanical Soc of Amer; Soc for Study of Evolution; award: Jr Chamber of Commerce Outstanding Young Man Award 1950; publ: 50 sci articles on genetics and evolution; civic: pres Jr Chamber of Commerce 1950; mil: USAF Combat Engineers WW II Europe; rel: LDS, bishop, h council; home: 531 W 3700 N; off: 451 WIDB, BYU.

SUDWEEKS, RICHARD R   evaluation specialist, David O McKay Inst of Ed BYU; b: 9 Jun 1940; m: Josephine Shurtliff; p: Raymond & Jessie May Hansen; c: Ray Richard 16, Sterling 13, Celestia 11, Crystallyn 8, Emily 6; ed: PhD ed measurement & res U of Illinois at Urbana-Champaign; former: evaluation specialist Syracuse Univ 1979-80; dir of res & evaluation LDS Church Ed Sys 1975-78; mem: Amer Ed Res Assn Evaluation Network; publ: co-author "A Comprehensive Approach to Course Evaluation", *Journal of Instr Development;* pol: voting dist chm, del to state conv; rel: LDS, writer for Sunday School Gen Board, h council, bishopric; home: 5977 W 10620 N, Highland; off: 111 KMB, BYU.

SUNDQUIST, EUGENE   owner Gene's Oak Hills Serv; b: 11 Mar 1923; m: Jeanne A; p: Edna & Emil; c: Bonnie, Michael, Jeffrey; ed: vocational school; former: County Assessor; State Personnel Dir; civic: Jr Chamber of Commerce; coor State Flood Com; pol: 1st paid organizer State Republican Party; county chm; campaign dir Gov J Brackon Lee; mil: US Navy WW II; Admiral's Citation; rel: LDS; club: Elks; Moose; Kiwanis; home: 1745 S Sandhill Rd, Orem; off: 1220 N 900 E.

SWINDLE, JOHN C   Utah State Mgr Amer Family Life; b: 6 Oct 1929; m: Sharon B; p: Emil & Hazel; c: Jon,

Shane, Stacey, Stuart, Stephanie, Seth, Jeremy, Alison, Sara; ed: BA U of Utah; Phi Beta Kappa, Phi Delta Phi; former: mgr Canada Life; mgr Prudential Insurance Co; mem: Chartered Life Underwriter, LUTC, grad mem, NALU, Central Utah Assn Life Und; civic: Provo Freedom Festival, former VP, Chamber of Commerce; rel: LDS, bishop, h council; home: 1506 E 1650 N; off: 379 N University.

SWINYARD, WILLIAM RIGBY   assoc prof of Business Mgt; b: 23 Jun 1940; m: Fae; p: William O & Gwendolyn Rigby; c: William E 12, Julia Fae 11, Lara Joy 5, Tyler R 2; ed: BS English 1965 BYU; MBA 1967 U of Michigan; PhD business 1976 Stanford U; former: Brand Res Mgr Carnation Co 1967-8; Corp Marketing Planner MSL Industries 1968-9; Product Mgr Ponder & Best Inc (now Vivitar Corp) 1969-71; Saga Enterprises Inc 1974-5; instr Southern Utah State College 1971-2, U of Santa Clara 1975; asst prof Arizona State U 1976-8; career: Outstanding Business Prof 1977 Arizona State U; 1st place Amer Marketing Assn Dissertation Competition 1976; mem: Amer Marketing Assn; Assn for Consumer Research; publ: editor Marketing Communications issue of Journal of Business Research; 24 articles; 7 papers; rel: LDS, h council; home: 1056 E 850 N, Orem; off: 236-Q JKB, BYU.

SYBROWSKY, PAUL K   marketing mgr CTI; b: 22 Aug 1944; m: Lynne; p: Paul H & Betty; c: Joel 12, Kristen 9, Rebecca 7, Joshua 5, Jacob 2, Joseph 6 mo; ed: BS sociology, psychology 1968 BYU; former: gen mgr Europe ADP Dealer Serv; mil: US Air Force; rel: LDS, bishop; home: 4230 Scenic Dr; off: 1455 S State, Suite 3, Orem.

SZALKOWSKI, BRUNO   laboratory glassblower; b: 20 Jun 1936; m: Helga Ursula; p: Bruno & Lotte; c: Tody 13, Monique 18, Nicole 20; ed: tech college, aprenticeship, masterglassblower Germany; former: foreman Glassblowing Plant, Milwauke, Wis; career: BYU 1875-1975 Centenial Creative Craftsmanship Award $1000; mem: Amer Sci Glassblowing Soc; Natl Rifle Assn; club: Elks; home: RFD 2 Box 160, Springville; off: BYU.

TANNER, GEORGE WOOLF   librarian; b: 5 Apr 1919; m:

Laura; p: John Sidney & Orrilla Woolf; c: Craig, Stephen, Jean, Wayne, Kara; ed: MFA master of arts U of Iowa; MLS U of Denver; former: UCLA 1 yr; USU 4 yrs; BYU 2 yrs; Church College of New Zeland 5 yrs; Weber State 6 yrs; UTC 12 yrs; mem: former pres Utah Library Assn; Amer Library Assn; Amer Ed Theatre Assn; Mtn Plains Library Assn; civic: BSA; Freedom Festival; Pioneer Days, Ogden; rel: LDS, sunday school pres; h priest grp ldr; home: 655 E 400 N, Orem; off: UTC Box 1609.

TANNER, RICHARD S   Gen Mgr & Gen Partner, Extra Space Devel Co; b: 28 Aug 1952; p: William C, Jr & Athelia S; ed: BS BYU, MBA U of Utah; Honors Prog Designation, Honors with Distinction; former: VP & Dir Oberon Oil; Sec/Treas & Dir Black Gnat Devel; mem: Self Service Storage Assn, region 3 VP; licensed real estate agent; publ: co-editor *One Hundred Years Young*, BYU 1976; civic: Utah Youth Soccer Assn, dist 21 comm; pol: sustaining mem Republican Natl Com; rel: LDS; club: Blue Key Natl Honor Fraternity; Sunstone Foundation; home: 755 N 100 E; off: 1675 N 200 W No. 9C.

TAYLOR, JOHN L   commercial estimator Jones Paint & Glass; b: 29 Sep 1947; m: Dee; p: John L & Susan; c: Clint 9, Farrah 5; career: professional horse trainer; civic: March of Dimes co-chm Ride-a-long 4 yrs; mil: Utah Natl Guard 12 yrs; rel: LDS; club: board of dir Utah Appaloosa Horse Club; former pres Provo Riding Club; home: Rt 1 Box 323A; off: 1250 W 100 N.

TAYLOR, RICK   wholesale, retail, Beauty & Theatrical Supply; b: 13 Oct 1946; m: Paula; p: Lynn T & Margene Lowe; c: Richard 19, Tammy 18, Adam 13, Isaac 1; ed: BYU 2 yrs; former: sales mgr & gen mgr Frend Beauty Supply; rel: LDS, elders quorum pres, priests & tchrs advisor; home: 3027 Cherokee Ln; off: 46-B University Mall.

TAYLOR, ROBERT C   chm Dept of Travel Study BYU; b: 17 Apr 1927; m: Katherine; p: Frank C & Bessie T; c: Michael, Mark, Michele; ed: MA U of Utah; former: asst to pres Howard Hughes Productions; mem: VP, Western States Council on Ed Travel; pol: former dist chm Republican; mil: US Coast Guard WW II; rel: LDS, bishop, h council; home: 1723 Driftwood Dr; off: 310 HCEB, BYU.

TERRY, ELMER L   lawyer; b: 15 Sep 1912; m: Edna G; p:
Willis E & Pearl Ekins; c: Robert L, attorney, Carolyn
Faux, Bryan G, MD, Janet Head; ed: BS, Bachelor of
Laws, JD; Phi Beta Kappa, Phi Kappa Phi, Order of the
Coif Legal Fraternity; mem: Central Utah Bar Assn; Utah
State Bar Assn; civic: former pres Provo Lions Club; pol:
Deputy Utah County Attorney 28 yrs; sec Utah County
Democratic Central Com 20 yrs; rel: LDS, bishop, stake
presidency 17 yrs; home: 1219 Elm Ave; off: 192 S 100 E.

THACKERAY, RENEE   asst prof BYU; b: 27 Jan 1931; p:
Horace E & Margaret B Thackeray; ed: MS Oregon State
U; post grad work UC Berkeley, Utah State U; 2
scholarships; research assistantship; former: faculty Chico
State U; instr, salesman Singer Sewing Co; career: Phi
Kappa Phi; Gamma Phi Omicron; mem: Amer Home Econ
Assn; Assn College Prof of Cl Tx; Internatl Fabric Care
Inst; Amer Assn Textile Chemist & Colorists; publ:
*Exploring Textiles: A Basic Workbook; Textiles:
Performance Tests & Evaluations; Apparel Evaluation
Syllabus;* civic: Cancer Drive; neighborhood activities; 2
summers in Guatemala on home & family preparedness;
rel: LDS, Relief Soc & sunday school stake boards,
homemaking ldr; club: University Women; home: 364 E
Stadium Cr; off: 2251 SFLC, BYU.

THOMAS, DARWIN LaMAR   prof of Sociology BYU; b: 3
Dec 1933; m: Beverly Morrison; p: David Bynon & Grace
Rebecca Hartvigsen; c: Kim, Suanne, Becky, Kristi, sara,
david; ed: BA 1962 MA 1964 BYU; PhD 1968 U of Minn;
Outstanding Sr Achievement Award BYU; grad with
honors BYU; NIMH Fellowship U of Minn; former: asst
prof Sociology Wash State U 1968-72; career: Virginia F
Cutler Award BYU; Sigma Sci Research Award BYU;
research awards Natl Sci Found & Natl Inst of Mental
Health; mem: Amer Sociological Assn; Natl Conf on
Family Relations; Utah Council on Family Relations; publ:
*Family Socialization & the Adolescent; Population
Resources & the Future; Social Psychology;* over 30
journal articles on family & social psychology; pol: chm
Young Republicans BYU; mil: US Army 1956-8; rel: LDS,
elders pres, 70s pres, bishop, h council; home: Rt 1 Box
59, Spanish Fork; off: 233-A SFLC, BYU.

THOMAS, DIAN   demonstrator on NBC's Today Show, author, lecturer; b: 19 May 1945; p: Julian & Norene Thomas; ed: BA 1968 MA 1973 BYU; Corning Glassware scholarship; former: tchr Orem Jr High 1968-71; part-time faculty BYU 1971-5; self-employed 1975-; career: Forecast Magazine service award 1975; Utah Home Economics Assn Outstanding Home Economist 1981; mem: Amer Home Econ Assn; Utah Home Econ Assn; Amer Fed of TV Assn; Internatl Microwave Power Assn; award: Outstanding Young Woman of Amer 1976-8; Outstanding Young Woman of Utah 1976; Granite High School Hall of Fame 1977; publ: *Roughing It Easy; Roughing It Easy 99; Backyard Roughing It Easy; Today's Tips for Easy Living;* civic: volunteer lecturer; pol: Republican party campaign; rel: LDS, Relief Soc pres, MIA pres, youth tchr; off: PO Box 7530 University Station.

THOMASON, ANNETTE JOHNSON   prog coord Accounting Data Proc UTC; b: 1 Oct 1937; p: Marion & Verl Johnson; c: Allen Floyde, Mark Richard; ed: LDS Business Col; BS magna cum laude 1969 MS 1971 bus ed BYU; EdD 1979 bus ed Oklahoma State U; Cert Professional Sec 1971; Phi Kappa Phi; Beta Gamma Sigma; Phi Delta Kappa; fellowships & scholarships; research awards; former: asst prof Weber State Col; specialist Utah State Off of Ed; tchr Amer Fork High School; mem: pres elect Utah Business Ed Assn; Utah State Office of Ed; Amer Vocational Assn; Utah Vocational Assn; Natl Business Ed Assn; Natl Ed Assn; Western Business Ed Assn; Utah Vocational Assn; Delta Pi Epsilon; Internatl Word Processing Assn; publ co-auth: *State Business & Office Occupational Curriculum Guide; Century 21 Shorthand: Skill Building Tapes; Mountainlands Curriculum Materials for Typewriting 9, 99, & 999; Century 21 Shorthand: Theory & Practice Instr Tapes; Dictation Materials for the Most Frequently Used Words in Business Correspondence;* civic: workshops & presentations; rel: LDS, Relief Soc social relations; home: 299 E 260 S, Orem; off: BU 288 UTC, Box 1609.

THOMPSON, JANIE (JANE)   artistic dir Lamanite Generation, BYU Entertainment Div 1971-; p: J Henry & Lora Harmon; ed: BA music BYU; grad with honors;

former: professional vocalist with Ike Carpenter's Band, Los Angeles; entertainer in Europe; music tchr; dir BYU Program Bureau 1952-70; organized "Young Ambassadors" singing group; traveled over half million miles with performing groups; 2,463 shows in first yr at BYU; career: "Janie Thompson Day" declared by Provo Mayor & city commissioners 14 Nov 1968; Six Outstanding Women Award BYU 1971; The Lamanite Vision Award, Amer Indian Serv BYU; US Defense Dept Outstanding Serv Award, presented by Senator Moss 1971; numerous other awards by US State Dept & Dept of Defense; mem: Musician's Union SF Local; AGVA; award: Cert of Recognition from BYU Athletic Dept Lighting the Y Ambassador's Award; songs: How Near to the Angels, Families to Match the Mountains, Thanksgiving Hymn Medley; civic: dir first 4 panorama shows for Provo Freedom Festival; talent & programming for many civic affairs; rel: LDS, gen YWMIA board 16 yrs; home: 781 N 1000 E; off: 20 KMH.

THOMPSON, PAUL H   prof of Organizational Behavior BYU; b: 28 Nov 1938; m: Carolyn L; p: Harold M & Elda Skeen; c: Lori 18, Kristyn 16, Shannyn 11, Robbyn 8, Daylyn 6, Nathan 3; ed: BS economics 1964 U of Utah; MBA 1966 Dr Business Admin 1969 Harvard Grad School of Business Admin; Baker Scholar; grad U of Utah magna cum laude; honors prog; former: asst dean BYU School of Mgt 1978-81; dept chm Organizational Behavior BYU 1974-8; asst prof Harvard Grad School of Business 1969-73; consul for Citibank, Gen Electric, Fiber Tech, Esso Resources Ltd; mem: dir of career interest group in Acad of Mgt; publ: co-auth *Organization & People: Readings, Cases, and Exercises in Organizational Behavior;* chapter in book; 18 articles; civic: 4-H Ldr; PTA; pol: Democratic del to county & state conv; rel: LDS, stake presidency, branch pres, Gen Church Com Evaluation Correlation; home: 1300 Maple Ln; off: 1070 SWKT, BYU.

THOMPSON, RANDY C   bank mgr; b: 18 Dec 1949; m: Sandra; p: Cliff & Elaine; c: 2 girls, 2 boys; ed: BA Spanish & Communications BYU; grad work economics Utah State U; high honor; President's List; former: educator, coach, commercial loan officer; career: President's Club;

coached Reg I Champ High School Debate Squad 1975;
mem: AIB; BAI; Utah County Bankers; award: all-reg
basketball player high school; civic: dir Chamber of
Commerce; VP United Way; campaign cabinet Mayorial
Coms; pol: Republican county del; rel: LDS, elders pres,
stake mission presidency, YMMIA & Sunday School
presidency, clerk; club: Rotary; off: First Sec Bank, 1389
N University.

THORSTENSON, CLARK T   prof of Recreation Mgt &
Youth Ldrship BYU; b: 15 Apr 1936; m: Colleen; p:
Goodman & Florence Angus; c: Kevin 17, Lisa 15,
Elizabeth 11, Daniel 9, Jill 6; ed: BS 1962 MREd 1965
BYU; PhD 1969 U of Utah; professional development
training at hospitals; Phi Kappa Phi; former: research
coor BYU Outdoor Survival School; chm BYU Outdoor
Survival Com; career: Registered Master of Therapeutic
Recreation Specialist, Natl Therapeutic Recreation Soc;
VIP Del & Speaker, 1st Presidential Conf on Fitness &
Aging, Washington DC; Utah Recreation & Parks Assn
Service to the Assn Award; NRPA/CPRS Distinguished
Fellow Award & Outstanding Contributions Cert; mem:
Utah Assn of Recreational Therapists; Utah Health Care
Assn; 1st Western Symposium on Therapeutic Recreation;
NRPA/CPRS Treasuere dist advisory council;
NRPA/CPRS Natl & Dist Advisory Councils; Rocky Mtn
Ctr for Gerontology; BYU Ctr for Environmental Studies;
board of dir Utah Recreation & Parks Assn; publ:
Activities: Therapeutic & Recreational; co-auth *Planning
for Social Recreation* and *Issues in Outdoor Recreation;*
20 articles; editor Utah Assn of Health, Physical Ed &
Recreation Journal; editorial board UAHPER Journal;
civic: chm Utah Recreation Therapy Advisory Com; Utah
Governor's Com on Health & Fitness; Utah Governor's
Com on Employment for the Handicapped; dir Nordic
Adventure Cruise to Scandanavia, Poland & Russia; BYU
Community School Advisory Council; SPRE Com for
Community Schools; Family Ctr for Research Inst; rel:
LDS, bishop, h council, church athletic com, church
special interest com, gen activities com; home: 2797
Apache Ln; off: 273-G RB, BYU.

THYGERSON, ALTON L   prof of Health Sci; b: 23 Apr
1940; m: Ardith Moss; p: Luie S & Callie N; c: Scott 14,

Michael 10, Steven 8, Whitney 6, Matthew 5, Justin 2; ed: EdD 1969; former: instr Chabot College, Calif; tchr Blackford High School, Calif; visiting lecturer to U of Wyoming, Slippery Rock College, Penn, U of Utah; career: Fellow of Amer Acad of Safety Ed; Health Ed Writer's Award; KSL Safety Award; Who's Who in the West & 8 other biographical publs; mem: Natl Safety Council; Amer Alliance for Health, Physical Ed, Recreation; publ: "The Safe Life", weekly *Deseret News* column; monthly feature in *Emergency: The Journal of Emergency Services; The First Aid Book; Disaster Survival Handbook; Study Guide for First Aid Practices; Accidents & Disasters: Causes & Countermeasures; Safety: Concepts & Instruction; Health Perspectives; Health Management; First Aid: Contemporary Practices & Principles;* civic: Scouting; volunteer Amer Red Cross instr; consultant to State Depts of Ed in Utah, Wyoming, Nebraska; consultant to Utah Energy Office, Utah Alcohol Safety Action Proj, US Army Dugway Proving Grounds; rel: LDS, stake exec sec, area emergency prepare spec, bishopric; home: 3300 Mohican Ln; off: 229-J RB, BYU.

TIMMINS, WILLIAM M   prof of Personnel Admin & Labor/Mgt Rel, mgt counsultant; b: 13 Mar 1936; m: Theda Laws; p: W Mont & Mary Brighton; c: Mont 19, Clark 17, Laurel 14, Sally 11, Rebekah 8; ed: BS 1960 U of Utah; MA 1962 Harvard U; PhD 1972 U of Utah; post doct U of Calif at LA; fellowship, Redd Ctr for Western Research 1981; former: asst dir Utah State Personnel Office; asst State Planning Coor; asst VP & asst dean, U of Utah; dir Interstate Projs, Utah State Board of Ed; acting personnel dir SLC Corp; VP Consalt Inc; career: listed in Who's Who in the West & Who's Who in Politics; Teaching Excellence 1974,6,80; mem: Internatl Personnel Mgt Assn; Amer Soc for Public Admin; award: Citation for Excellence in Voluntarism 1973,4, Natl Ctr for Voluntary Action; Outstanding State Volunteer 1977, Utah State Office of Voluntarism; Exemplary Community Serv 1978, SL Community Serv Council; publ: asst editor, *Public Admin Review;* books, articles, manuals; civic: Silver Beaver, Boy Scouts of Amer 1974; pres-elect Natl Assn of Civil Serv Commissioners; pres Utah Assn of Civil Serv Commissioners & Merit System Councils; chm SL County Merit System Council; VP Rocky Mtn Public

Employer Labor Rel Assn; chm adv board, SL County Youth Serv Ctr; board of dir SL Community Serv Council; chm of board School Volunteers, Inc; Citizen's Adv Com, Wasatch Front Reg Council; various task forces, study coms, labor rel assns, advisory coms; pol: treas SL County Republican Party; rel: LDS, bishop, h council, stake mission pres; club: President's Club at Utah State U & BYU; home: 5419 Wayman Ln, Holliday; off: 210 JKB, BYU.

TOOKE, WILLIAM H owner Tooke's Tours & Travel and Tooke's Real Estate & Land Development; b: 29 Aug 1926; m: Shirley Davis; p: Stratton William & Lily W; c: William D, Julie Christensen, Suzanne Lewis, Michael D, Heather; ed: BS business BYU; former: First Security Bank 10 yrs; owner Royal Vista Home Supply; owner Tooke's Carpeting; owner Tooke's Furniture; career: travel school & seminar awards; mem: Amer Soc of Travel Agents; award: sporting awards; civic: Red Cross; March of Dimes; United Fund; pol: Republican; mil: US Navy, South Pacific; rel: LDS; club: former board mem Riverside Country Club; BPOE No. 849; home: 334 S 530 E, Orem; off: 480 N 200 W.

TUCKER, KARL BYU Mens Golf Coach, Ski School Dir; b: 18 Nov 1926; m: Joanne Eliason; p: George Traverse & Della Redd Spilsbury; c: Jackie, Shellie, Larry, Philip; ed: BS 1952 MS 1964 BYU; former: tchr in Portland & SLC 1953-61; career: Dale Rex Award 1976; Coach of Yr Dist 7 NCAA 1973,5,6,8,80; NCAA Ntl Coach of Yr 1981; mem: Golf Coaches Assn NCAA; chm Selection Com Dist 7 PSIA 25 yrs; award: Outstanding Contribution to SL Jr Golf Assn & Utah Golf Assn; publ: contributing writer Jr World of Golf; Skiing Revisions 1968, 72, 76; College Football Rules Interpreter 1965-80; civic: fund raiser speaker; mil: US Army 1946; rel: LDS, stake athletic dir, elders pres; club: Sherwood Hills Racquet Club; Riverside Country Club; home: 730 E 360 S; off: 54 SFH, BYU.

TUCKETT, GLEN Athletic Dir BYU; b: 11 Dec 1927; m: Josephine Whittaker; p: William Cameron & Bessie Farrell; c: Alison, Shannon, Kendall, Erin; ed: BS Utah; MS EdD BYU; former: professional baseball; high school coach; college coach; career: AACBC Hall of Fame;

Coach of the Year; mem: NCAA; CFA; AACBC; award: Exemplary Manhood Award; publ: articles; mil: US Army 18 mo; rel: LDS, bishop, h council, stake presidency; home: 3815 N 700 E; off: 106 SFH, BYU.

TURNER, LANCE   interior designer, pres Lance Turner & Associates; b: 4 Jan 1927; m: Marilyn; p: Lance H & Mary Ferguson; c: Heidi, Joshua, Chip, Matthew; former: art dir Foote, Cone & Belding, world's 3rd largest advertising agcy; career: Dillon Lauritzen Memorial Award, LA Art Dir's Club; USDA Commendation as co-developer of Smokey Bear; Industrial Showplace of Amer for Valtek Bldg, Springville; award: World Class Birdcarver; mil: Veteran WW II; rel: LDS, bishopric, youth ldr; home: 276 E 4000 N; off: 3707 N Canyon Rd.

VANCE, CLAIR W   restraunt owner; b: 16 Feb 1920; m: Venna B; p: Willard & Ellis J; c: Stephanie L, Cathy L, Vickie, Julie, Kelly J; ed: BS BYU; masters work; former: school tchr; publ: articles in Provo Herald; civic: Chamber of Commerce; mil: WWII Veteran B-25 pilot Pacific Campaign; Letters of Recognition; rel: LDS; club: Provo Jaycees; Exchange Club; Athletic Club; Elks Club; home: 985 S 500 E, Orem; off: 154 N University Ave.

VANFLEET, HOWARD B   Prof & Chm, BYU Dept of Physics & Astronomy; b: 5 Jun 1931; m: Helen (Haacke); p: Willard Parker & Celia May (Bay); c: Pamela (deceased) 32, Vennette Seymour 25, L Howard 23, James P 22, May Lyn 18, David C 16, Richard R 14; ed: BS 1955 BYU; PhD 1961 U of Utah; teaching & res fellowships 1956–60, U of Utah; former: 1973–4 Visiting Prof, Amer Univ in Cairo, Egypt; career: Karl G Maeser Res & Creative Arts Award 1973 BYU; fed funding, 7 grants, 1962–74; mem: Sigma Pi Sigma, Physics Hon Soc, Sigma Xi Sigma, Res Soc, Amer Physical Soc, Amer Assn of Physics Tchrs; publ: 43 publ in natl & intl refereed journals; mil: US Army 1952–4; rel: LDS; home: 1722 N 1500 E; off: Dept of Physics & Astronomy, BYU.

VIGO-ACOSTA, CARMEN   instr of Spanish; b: 31 Jul 1932; m: Frank N Acosta; p: Julio Vigo Carcia & Carmen Salgado Rodriguez; c: Frank C, Ruben C, Jon C Acosta; ed: BS MA BYU; Sigma Delta Pi pres 1967–8; former:

Peace Corps Language Tchr; mem: Utah Foreign Language Assn; Rocky Mtn Modern Language Assn; Amer Assn of Tchrs of Spanish & Portuguese; Amer Translators Assn; publ: co-auth *Learn Spanish Through The Book of Mormon; Culture for Missionaries - Spain;* rel: LDS, RS cultural ref tchr; home: 859 N 440 W; off: 113 FOB, BYU.

VIGOREN, RONALD W   CPA Fox & Company; b: 18 May 1943; m: Liz; p: Max & Lorraine; c: Scott 11, Julie 9, Ronna 7, Kristopher 6, Lorriann 2; ed: BS 1965 BYU; acad scholarship BYU; Beta Alpha Psi; mem: Amer Inst of CPAs; Utah Assn of CPAs; civic: Chamber of Commerce; Accreditation Com; Rotary Internatl; mil: US Army; rel: LDS; home: 4088 Foothill Dr; off: 1675 N 200 W.

VODOPICH, VIVIAN CLARK LOVELESS   owner & operator Vivian's Beauty Salon; b: 3 Dec 1924; m: Anton; (1st husband Dean E Loveless); p: Oliver C Clark & Maude Ferre; c: Dena Marie Kimber, Patricia Christensen, Georgia V Brown; step: Dolly Mayne, Linda Ransdall, Toni hurst; former: Thomas Dept Store; Sutton Cafe; Hedquist Drug; Elliotts Cafe; JC Penneys; mem: former pres Eagles, Natl Beautician; award: Sweetheart of the Eagles; Mr & Mrs Eagle Award 1982; publ: recipies for natl magazines; civic: ALTURSA Service Club; rel: LDS, Primary sec & couns, MIA pres, Relief Soc work dir; club: Handicraft of Provo; Hands & Feet; Doc Amiga; REAC of Provo Eagles; REAC of Pleasant Grove Eagles; home: 1360 W 900 N; off: 358 N 500 W.

WALDEN, DAVID M   rep Life Story Enterprises; b: 6 Nov 1947; p: Blake & Charlotte; ed: BS zoology 1969 Iowa State; MA behavioral sci 1979 U of Guam; Secondary Tchng Cert 1981 BYU; U of Guam Honor Soc; former: secondary school tchr, Guam; MTC culture tchr; mem: Utah Folklore Soc; Soc for Sociological Study of Mormon Life; Cultural Survival Inc; Amer Chess Federation; award: 1st place BYU Student Research Poster Contest 1980; publ: articles in progress; pol: Republican county del, election judge, campaigner; BYU Coll Republican Club; mil: US Navy 1969-73; hospital corpsman & lab asst; 2nd Class PO; San Diego Hospital Corps A School honor student; rel: LDS, stake missionary, exec sec, tchr; club: former pres Guam Shell Club; BYU Chess Club; off: 100 E 580 N, No 4.

WALKER, O LEE   technical dir & asst prof BYU Theatre Dept; b: 1 Jul 1937; m: Eula Rae Johnson; p: Asael O; c: Asena Smith, Daniel L, Breta Finlinson, John A, Merri Malin, Emily Rae, Spencer M; ed: BS 1968 MIE 1975 BYU; U of Utah; Industrial Arts Club Outstanding Scholarship Award; former: school tchr Jordan School Dist; technical dir & construction supvr for over 130 main stage productions at BYU; mem: life mem Amer Industrial Assn; US Inst for Theatre Technology; former v-chm 2 yrs, Rocky Mtn Section USITT; publ: *Design & Construction of a Low Budget Vacuum Former;* mil: Utah Natl Guard 6 yrs; Sgt 1st Class & Mess Sgt; rel: LDS, elders quorum pres, Sunday School pres, scoutmaster; home: 3000 N 600 E; off: B-249 HFAC, BYU.

WALKER, STANLEY H   Utah County Treasurer, BYU personal finance tchr, bank dir, broker; b: 3 Jul 1924; m: Lorna Cowley; p: Harold S & Lucile M Harvey; c: Patricia, Jeanne, Harold, Holly; ed: BS BYU; advanced business Wharton School of Business; former: sales mgr Mtn Bell 15 yrs; stock broker Merrill Lynch & Hogle; career: "Top 10" JA Hogle Award; mem: dir of boards of Assn Treasurers, Geneva State Bank, Bank of Pl Grove, Utah Local Govt Trust; award: Outstanding Public City Official; Cert of Merit Assn of County Treasurers; publ: co-auth *Pleasant Grove School History;* civic: BSA 3 yrs; Mayor Lindon City 4 yrs; pol: county & state del, dist chm, republican; mil: Sgt Major Coast Artillery & 12th Airborne Asia-Pacific 27 mo; Sharpshooter; Glider Wings; rel: LDS, stake mission, stake financian advisor; club: Jr Chamber; Lions; Rotary; home: 445 N 645 E; off: County Bldg.

WALKER, STEVEN C   assoc prof English BYU; b: 15 Oct 1941; m: Ardith; p: Jess & Elaine; c: Scott 12, Rebecca 10, Emily 7; ed: BS MA BYU; AM PhD Harvard U; Graduate Prize Fellow & Traveling Fellow at Harvard U; former: Teaching Fellow, Harvard U; career: English Dept Prof of Year 1979-80; BYU Prof of Year 1980-1; mem: Victorian Studies Assn; Internatl Conf on the Fantastic; award: prize-winning poem in Natl League of Amer Pen Women 1981 Contest; publ: *Ronald Reagan: Mr President; A Book of Mormons;* 23 articles, essays, poems; mil: US Army Reserve sgt E-6 1961-8; Expert Rifleman; rel: LDS, bishopric, dir of writers Relief Soc lessons; home: 385 S 1280 E; off: A-239 JKBA, BYU.

WALLACE, LON   prof   of   bldg   construction   &
architectural drafting BYU; b: 15 Apr 1930; m: Lynnette
Cariz; p: Arthur Noble & mary Ellen Hobbs; c: Kent Booth
20, Valerie 18; ed: Fine Arts & Architecture; Denver U;
BYU; U of Utah; former: prog supvr Bldg Const; asst dept
chm Ind Ed Dept; mem: Amer Inst of Architects; Natl
Assn of Home Builders; Associated General Contractors
of Amer; award: Outstanding Board of Dir JC Party Chm;
JC Provo Peak Award BSA; civic: former pres, 1st VP,
dir, Provo Jaycees; mil: US Air Force, Korean War;
Comindation Medal; Bronze Star; rel: LDS, scoutmaster,
cub scout ldr; club: Provo Jayces; Provo Elks 25 yrs;
home: 2880 N 175 E; off: 230 SNLB, BYU.

WALTON, WILBUR T   assoc prof & Coor of Special Ed
BYU; b: 2 Oct 1929; m: Wilma Toone; c: Eric, Thomas,
Bruce, Carolee, William, Kristine, Laurie, James; ed: BA
1957 BYU; MS 1965 PhD 1969 U of Utah; former: dir Day
Hospital, Primary Children's Hospital Psych Ctr; career:
Corp for Public Broadcasting's 1978 Best Ed Film Award
for "Worth of a Child"; Best of the West Award in ed instr
for Balance of Life Series 9 films on Special Ed; mem: Pi
Mu Epsilon Natl Honorary Math Fraternity; Natl Ed Assn;
Natl Council for Exceptional Children; Natl Council for
Tchr Ed for Child with Behavioral Disorders; publ:
*Education & Treatment of Emotionally Handicapped
Children; The Emotionally Handicapped Individual in an
Educational Setting; Behavioral Modification Techniques
for Teachers of Exceptional Children;* co-auth *Emotional
Disturbance;* co-auth *Train Up a Child - Discipline in the
Home;* ed & coop writer Balance of Life Series Workbook
The Exceptional Child in the Classroom; 2 syllabi; 10
articles & papers; civic: developed & dir Family Living
Seminar for Orem Social Serv; State Competencies Com
for Ed of the Emotionally Handicapped; exec com Higher
Ed Training Progs for tchrs of the emotionally
handicapped; Salt Lake County Library sys circuit
presenter; LDS YM YW com special needs; State Advisory
Com on Handicapped Advisory Com State Board of Ed;
exec com Utah Comprehensive Sys for Personnel
Development Council for Special Ed; mil: US Navy
1948-52; rel: LDS, bishop; home: 2880 N 840 E; off: 322
MCKB, BYU.

WARD, LANE DENNIS   assoc dir Res & Development
MTC; b: 22 Apr 1948; m: Julie Glazier; p: Orville M &
Mildred T; c: Glazier 9, Johnathan 7, Joseph 5, Christian
3; ed: BA cross-cultural training & comms; Master ed
admin; Doctorate training & development; post-dr
business admin; Phi Delta Kappa; former: educator; mgr,
asst dir of training & development; career: Master Tchr
Award; Sup Development Awards; lecturer at natl mgt &
training conventions; mem: TRAINING Human Resources
Development; Amer Soc for Training & Development;
Amer Soc for Personnel Admin; rel: LDS, h council,
bishop; home: 1304 N 800 W, Orem; A-121 MTC, BYU.

WARNER, DELBERT R   merchant, pres Utah Office
Supply; b: 6 Apr 1921; m: Jacqueline; p: Leo A & Eva; c:
Susanne, Cathy, Lee; ed: 2 yrs BAC, Cedar City; civic:
former pres Provo Chamber of Commerce; mil: US Army
Air Force; Distinguished Flying Award; Purple Heart;
POW 13 mo; rel: LDS, bishop, h council, stake Sunday
School, stake missionary; club: Timpanogos Lions; home:
1066 E 250 S, Orem; off: 595 S University Ave.

WARNER, DORIS S   dept chm Home Econ, Timpview
High School; b: 9 Jan 1929; m: Ted J; p: Emmett R &
Mable R Stroud; c: Kathryn A Christiansen; Cecelia,
Carolyn; ed: BS, East Carolina U; MEd BYU; EdD BYU
1981; Delta Kappa Gamma Internatl Scholarship; former:
high school tchr; career: Home Econ Tchr of the Year for
Utah 1976; mem: NEA, UEA, PEA, Amer Vocational
Tchr's Assn; Utah Vocational Ed Assn; pres 1981-2 Utah
Vocational Tchr's Assn; publ: several articles in
professional journals; civic: pres Delta Kappa Gamma;
sponsor of 4-H Clubs; pol: county del Democratic Party;
rel: LDS, YWMIA Presidency; club: Pro Libris; home: 1375
Apple Ave; off: Timpview High School.

WARNER, TED J   Asst Dean for Grad Studies & Res
BYU; prof of History; b: 2 Mar 1929; m: Doris Stroud; p:
George W & Cecelia J; c: Kathryn A Christiansen,
Cecelia, Carolyn; ed: AS Weber State; BA MA BYU; PhD
U of New Mexico; Phi Kappa Phi; former: history instr
Carbon College; Special Collections Librarian U of New
Mexico; career: Karl G Maeser Distinguished Teaching
Award 1979; mem: Amer Historical Assn; Organization of

Amer Historians; Utah Historical Soc; New Mexico Historical Soc; Mormon History Assn; Gran Quivera Historical Assn; publ: *The Dominguez-Escalante Journal 1776;* journal articles; pol: precinct chm, del county conventions, Democratic party; mil: S/Sgt 82nd Airborne Div, Korean War 1951-4; Sr Parachutist Badge; Div Commander's Award; rel: LDS, branch pres, h council, bishopric; home: 1375 Apple Ave; off: 972 SWKT, BYU.

WASHBURN, AlDEAN dentist; b: 27 Sep 1926; m: Clara Broderick; p: Alvin Lavell & Wasel A Black; c: Berk, Ann, Allen, Linda, Anderson, Hugh, Ruth, Sam, Sarah, Joseph, Cathy, Dan; ed: BS 1951 BYU; DDS 1958 U of S Calif; Omicron Kappa Upsilon; Phi Kappa Phi; former: high school basketball coach; math instr at USC & BYU; mem: Amer Dental Assn; Utah Dental Assn; Provo Dist Dental Soc; civic: Trona Unified School Dist board 8 yrs; Indian Wells Valley School Dist board 5 yrs; mil: US Navy Air Corp WWII; rel: LDS, stake pres, patriarch; home: 1350 Apple Ave; off: 1275 N University Ave No. 16.

WATABE, MASAKAZU asst prof BYU; b: 11 May 1947; m: Rosaline I; p: Masao & Hisako; c: Michelle Kimiyo 7, Paulette Sayo 6, Foster Masahito 3; ed: BA MA BYU; PhD U of S Calif; magna cum laude; former: escort interpreter US State Dept; mem: Linguistic Soc of Amer; Tchrs Assn of Japanese; Phi Kappa Phi; award: Outstanding Young Men Of Amer 1981; publ: Japanese textbooks; papers on language learning & US-Japan relations; rel: LDS, bishop; home: 814 N 470 E, Orem; off: 243 FB, BYU.

WATKINS, ARTHUR RICH prof Germanic Languages BYU; b: 31 July 1916; m: Ruth Hansen; p: Arthur V & Andrea Rich; c: Annette, Arthur Lynn, Laurel, Bryan, Marie, Denise, Paul, Ronald; ed: BA MA BYU; PhD Standord; U of Besancon, France; U of Oslo, Norway; Georgetown U; George Washington U; former: official guest Fed Republic of Germany for 3-week study-tour 1958; chm Dept of Modern & Classical Languages BYU; chm Dept of Germanic & Slavic Languages BYU; chm Dept of Germanic Languages BYU; publ: *Interessantes Deutsch; German through Conversational Patterns,* incl **workbook & teacher's manual,** *Reviewing German; Scenes from German Drama; Norwegian Through Conversational*

Patterns; mil: US Army Signal Intelligence Corps crypt analyst 1943-5; rel: LDS, h council, pres Austrian Mission 1936-9, Gen Sunday School Board 1969-72, pres Italy Padova Mission 1978-80, MTC branch pres; home: 351 E 720 S, Orem; off: 463 MSRB, BYU.

WAYCASY, MILT   owner Casey's Nite Club; m: Carol; c: Jimmy, Sherry, Debbie; ed: high school; former: gen mgr KFTN Radio Station; Sports Dir KFTN-K96; part owner & gen mgr Miracle Bowl Bowling Lanes; head of corp who built Miracle Bowl; awards: outstanding achievements in bowling, softball, table tennis, golf; publ: *All American Sports Stories;* mil: Navy 3 yrs; club: Riverside Country Club; home: 63 E 600 N; off: 345 S 100 W.

WEAVER, MAX DICKSON   prof of Art & Design BYU; b: 14 Mar 1917; m: Ruth Kimball; p: David Christopher & Sophia Dickson; c: Max Kimball, Kurt Stoddard, Katherine Genee Walker, Scott Dickson, EdWynn Stoddard, Ruth Kay Merrell; ed: BA MA Utah State U; grad work U of S Calif, Long Beach State, BYU, U of Utah; former: school tchr; head of Art Dept S Utah State College; career: awards in pottery, prints, painting, jewelry exhibited widely; work publ in Sage magazine; mem: former pres Utah Designer Craftsmen; del first Natl Congress of Craftsmen, NY; Sigma Alpha Epsilon Fraternity; civic: former chm Orem City Art Board; Orem City Library & Arts Board; lectures to schools, clubs, civic orgs; pol: Democratic Party del to state, county conventions; mil: US Army Engineer Corps WW II; rel: LDS, Provo Temple ordinance wrkr, stake missionary, stake 7 pres of 70; home: 216 E 1864 S, Orem.

WEBER, DARRELL JACK   prof of botany BYU; b: 16 Nov 1933; m: Carolyn Foremaster; p: John & Norma; c: Brad 18, Becky 15, Brian 13, todd 10, Kelly 7, Jason 6, Trent 3; ed: BS 1958 biochem U of Idaho; MS 1959 PhD 1963 U of Calif; Karl G Maeser Award 1974; Fellow of Utah Acad of Sci 1972; former: post doc biochem U of Wisconsin 1963-5; ast prof U of Houston 1965-9; career: 30 res grants of $800,000 over 18 yrs; NIH Fellowship Michigan State; mem: Alpha Zeta; Amer Soc of Microbiologists; Sigma Xi; AIBS, Amer Mycological Soc; Phytochemical Soc; Amer Botanical Soc; Amer Phytopathological Soc; publ: 75 sci articles, 3 books;

civic: Boy Scout Com; mil: 2 yrs ROTC; rel: LDS, h
council, bishopric, mission presidency; home: 560 E Robin,
Orem; 285 WIDB, BYU.

WEIDNER, LEO ALBERT   business consul in motivation,
sales, marketing, fund raising; part owner Weidner
Communications; b: 12 Jun 1934; m: Shirley Bench; p: Leo
F & Francis C; c: Leo E, Erin G, Amber L, Tiffany B,
Trevor C; stepchildren: Michael J, Robert D, Kent R,
Steven L; ed: BA finance & banking, economics 1959
BYU; former: area mgr Lever Bros; VP of Ins Co;
Co-founder Weidner Communications; civic: Boy Scout
Adv Chm 9 yrs; pol: finance dir Beckham for Congress
Campaign; mil: US Navy Submarine Serv, Korean War; rel:
LDS; bishop, h council; club: Val Hyric BYU; home: 3695
N Littlerock Terrace.

WEIGHT, DAVID G   assoc prof Clinical Psychology BYU;
consult Utah Valley Hospital; b: 16 Nov 1936; m: Shauna
Swensen; p: Gordon & Lucile Collins; c: Eric 19, Craig 17,
Jeffrey 13, Kevin 9, Cynthia 6; ed: BA MA BYU; PhD U of
Wash; US Public Health Serv Traineeship; internship
Seattle & Amer Lake VA Hospitals; former: lab tech Utah
Valley Hospital; tching fellow Congenital Defects Ctr U
of Wash; consult clinical psychologist Jordan School Dist;
mem: Amer Psychological Assn; Utah Psychological Assn;
APA Div Clinical & Experimental Hypnosis; publ: journal
articles; chapters; civic: Provo City Govt Transition
Team; former VP Provo Board of Ed; former pres Utah
County Mental Health Assn; school board; mil: Air Natl
Guard 6 yrs; Outstanding Airman 151st USAF Dispensary;
rel: LDS, h council, bishop; home: 3695 N 820 E; off: 293
CCB, BYU.

WELCH, BRUCE L   Principle Research Plant Physiologist
BYU; b: 15 Jan 1943; m: Susan A Welch; p: Clyde E &
Ardella B; c: Shamayne 17, Michael 16, Darin 14, Melissia
13, Andrea 11, Jon 5, Jeffery 1; ed: BS 1966 Utah State U;
MS 1969 PhD 1974 U of Idaho; scholastic honor rolls;
research fellow; former: Vocational Agriculture instr;
biological technician; career: adjunct assoc prof of Range
Mgt BYU; mem: Soc for Range Mgt; Sigma Xi; award:
Outstanding Ldrship in Scouting; publ: 40 sci articles on
plant diseases, wildlife; assoc editor Journal of Range

Mgt; civic: Scouting; rel: LDS, branch pres, elders quorum pres; home: 1061 W 860 N; off: BYU Shrub Sci Lab, 735 N 500 E.

WELCH, JOHN W   Assoc Prof of Law; b: 15 Oct 1946; m: Jeannie; p: John S & Unita Woodland; c: John Sutton 10, Christina 8, Allison 5, James Gregory 2; ed: BA 1970 MA 1970 BYU; Oxford Univ; JD 1975 Duke Univ; Woodrow Wilson Fellow; Valedictorian 1970 BYU; former: O'Melveny & Myers Attorneys, Los Angeles; mem: Calif & Utah Bar Assns; dir Found for Ancient Research & Mormon Studies; Jewish Law Soc; SBL; IAC; publ: *Chiasmus in Antiquity;* articles editor Duke Law Journal; articles; rel: LDS, h council; home: 3970 N Quail Run; off: 522 JRCB, BYU.

WELLESLEY, GEORGE M   electrician, electrical contractor; b: 27 Jun 1925; m: Edna Lou; p: George M; c: Craig, Chad, Kris; ed: grad Benson Polytechnical School, Portland OR; 2 yr BYU; career: Master Electrical Utah & Wyoming; mil: 1st Class Electrician US Navy 1943-6; 9 ribbons, 3 stars; rel: LDS; club: pres Edgemount Lions; former mem Elks Lodge 849, 32 yrs; home: 3020 N 600 E.

WELSH, STANLEY LARSON   prof of Botany & Range Sci BYU; Dir of Herbarium; b: 7 Sep 1928; m: Stella L Tree; p: David H & Amanda; c: Julie, Kent, Ruth, Blaine, Kathy, Jean, Martin, Eric; ed: BS 1951 MS 1957 botany BYU; PhD systematic botany 1960 Iowa State U; Sigma Xi; Researcher of the Month BYU Chapter Sigma Xi 1975; former: consultant, proj dir & investigator on various studies for Natl Park Serv, Natl Geographic, Bureau of Land Mgt, US Forest Serv, US Fish & Wildlife Serv, various companies; mem: Utah Native Plant Soc, Internatl Assn for Plant Taxonomy; publ: 63 publ; mil: US Army 1946-7; rel: LDS; home: 129 N 1000 E, Orem; off: 375 MLBM, BYU.

WHEELER, DORETTA C   librarian BYU; b: 13 Oct 1927; p: Henry Calvin & Doris Kathleen Wheeler; ed: BA 1954 BYU; former: staff Davis County Library 4 yrs; career: 10 and 15 yr certs BYU; mem: Timpanogos group, Natl Audubon Soc; Natl Wildlife Assn; BYU Library Assn; rel: LDS, librarian; club: Sierra Club; home: 449 W 700 N; off: 6380 HBLL, BYU.

WHEELER, GLORIA EILEEN   asst prof Inst of Business Mgt BYU; b: 6 Jun 1943; p: William Edwin & Lida Jane Mulliner; ed: BS 1965 Montana State U; AM 1966 MS 1968 PhD 1972 U of Michigan; Phi Kappa Phi; Pi Mu Epsilon; undergrad scholarships; former: sr assoc Rensis Likert Associates Inc; special assoc Office of Exec Personnel, US Dept of Health & Human Serv; career: Federal Faculty Fellow for Natl Assn of Schools of Public Affairs & Admin 1980; mem: Amer Inst for Decision Sci; Amer Psychological Assn, Div 14 Industrial & Organizational Psychology; publ: journal articles; civic: former Girl Scout ldr; charity fund drives; rel: LDS, YW pres, camp dir; home: 570 W 300 N; off: 395 JKB, BYU.

WHITAKER, WILLIAM   artist; b: 5 Mar 1943; m: Jenny Marie; p: W Ferrin & Martha B; c: Matthew 12, Caitlin 8; ed: BA 1967 U of Utah; Otis Art Inst; former: assoc prof BYU to 1980; career: Gold & Silver medals Natl Acad of Western Art; Gold & Silver medals Springville Museum of Art; awards Utah Inst of Fine Art; listed in Who's Who in Amer Art & Who's Who in the West; mem: Natl Acad of Western Art; Western Heritage Art Boards; Artists of Amer; publ: in *Arizona Highways, Artists of the Rockies, Southwest Art*, rel: LDS, h council, bishop; club: Mtn Oyster Club; home: 2846 Marrcrest Cr West.

WHITEHEAD, ARMAND   assoc prof of Zoology BYU; b: 19 May 1936; m: Rose Afton Jensen; p: Earnest & Verda; c: Steven, Roseann, Richard, Irene, Mary; ed: BS zoology 1965 cum laude BYU; PhD entomology 1969 U C Berkeley; Natl Inst of Health Grad Fellow; former: visiting asst prof U of Illinois; mem: Sigma Xi; publ: 8 papers; pol: Republican dist del; mil: US Air Force 8 yrs; Airman of the Yr, Keesler AFB, Miss 1961; rel: LDS bishop, elders pres, h council; club: exec committeeman BYU Apple Computer Users Group; home: 120 E 350 N, Orem; off: 621 WIDB, BYU.

WHITENIGHT, KATHY ANN   asst to dean BYU College of Nursing; b: 21 May; p: Herman David & Margie Ann Whitenight; ed: AS psychology Ricks College; BS psychology BYU; Phi Theta Kappa; Dean's List; former: dir Behavioral Services; career: qualified Mental Retardation Specialist; mem: licensed social worker in

Idaho; publ: *Independent Living Programs for Mentally Retarded;* civic: volunteer Utah State Hospital Children's Ward; pol: appointed mem Mayor's Com to Hire the Handicapped; rel: LDS, youth tchr; home: 31 E 925 N, Orem; off: 591 SWKT, BYU.

WIGGINS, MARVIN E   chm Gen Reference Dept, Assoc Librarian BYU Library; b: 25 Mr 1941; m: Annette Christensen; p: Eugene Howard & Delores Hokanson; c: Nathan 14, Michael 11, Evan 9, Allan 6, Isaac 5, Ana 3, Andrea 2, Beth 2; ed: AS Weber State College; BA BYU; MLS Rutgers, New Jersey; former: chm College & Univ Sect, Utah Library Assn 1974-5; chm Utah Public Serv Com Utah College Library Council 1972-6; mem: Utah Library Assn; publ: co-author *Using the Library: The Card Catalog;* chapter in *Sign Systems for Libraries;* articles on library use instr; biographical index in progress; civic: Provo City Rock Canyon Neighborhood chm 1971-9; pol: Republican dist 48 chm 1980-2; rel: LDS, Sr Pres Stake 70's Quorum; home: 742 E 2730 N; off: 3224 HBLL, BYU.

WILKES, DORAN F   prof Design & Computer Graphics BYU; b: 26 Feb 1929; m: Nola A; p: O Frane; c: Koray, Kevan, Kellen, Kody, Karlin; ed: BS 1951 MS 1955 Utah State U; Doctorate 1966 U of Missouri; former: instr Utah State U; instr U of Mo; tchr Utah & Wyoming public schools; career: research assistantship Utah State U & U of Mo; mem: Amer Soc Engineering Ed; Natl Computer Graphics Assn; publ: articles; 2 workbooks; pol: county & state del; mil: Lt Col US Air Force 2 yrs; 20 yrs reserve; instl engineering; rel: LDS, clerk, elders pres, bishop, h council; home: 646 S 400 W, Orem; off: 472 CB, BYU.

WILKIN, KATHRYN   branch mgr Utah State Tax Commission Motor Vehicle Div; b: 31 Jan 1938; p: Gale & Donna Bachman; c: Pam Bair, Vicki McLellan, Kelly Ackerman; ed: high school; Comtomator Course; adult ed; former: title clerk, Chuck Peterson Motors, Household Finance, Utah Finance Co; mem: Ladies Auxilary; club: Eagles Lodge, Pleasant Grove; off: State Tax Commission, 129 S University Ave.

WILLIAMS, DIANE HART   home econ tchr Provo High; Provo High Preschool; b: 3 Feb 1956; m: Zane Stephenson

Williams; p: Philip James & Olive Winterton Hart; ed: BS
1977 BYU; MS 1980 Utah State U; Phi Kappa Phi; grad
magna cum laude; Pres Scholarships; FBLA Scholarship;
Home Econ Club 4 yr Scholarship; former: home econ tchr
Weber High 2 yrs; instr Utah State U 1 yr; mem: Amer
Home Econ Assn; Natl Ed Assn; Utah Ed Assn; Provo Ed
Assn; Utah State Univ Family Life Council; civic: candy
striper; rel: LDS, Relief Soc presidency, YA presidency,
tchr; club: Future Business Ldrs of Amer; Home Econ
Club; home: 619 E 2780 N; off: 1125 & 887 N Univeristy
Ave.

WILSON, ARNOLD   prof of Civil Engineering; b: 1 Feb
1933; m: Joyce Hutchings; p: Robert L & Luella; c:
Dennis, Sharon, Diana, Kerry, Craig, Christine, Kendall,
Mark, Annette, Michael; ed: BES 1957 MS 1962 civil
engineering BYU; PhD 1973 Oklahoma State U;
Outstanding Prof BYU 1967, 80; Prof of the Year BYU
1980; career: Registered Professional Engr in Utah, Idaho,
Kansas, Alberta Canada; listed in Who's Who in
Engineering & Who's Who in the West; mem: Fellow Amer
Concrete Inst; Internatl Assn for Shell & Spacial
Structures; Sigma Xi; award: BSA Silver Beaver; publ:
*Concrete; Concrete Thin Shell Structures; Steel Space
Frame; Housing;* civic: chm Mapleton City Planning
Commission 1968-72; City Engr 1972-; rel: LDS, bishop, h
council, scoutmaster; home: 415 E Maple, Mapleton; off:
368 CB, BYU.

WILSON, WARREN BINGHAM   artist; BYU prof; b: 4 Nov
1920; m: Donna Van Wagenen; p: Alma Lavoy & Pearl
Bingham; c: Vaughn Warren, Michael Alma, Annette,
Pauline, Douglas George, Craig Aaron, Robert Kevin; ed:
BS ed 1943 Utah State U; MFA sculpture 1949 State U of
Iowa; BYU research grants 1963, 65, 67, 78; faculty
fellowship Charles Redd Ctr for Western Studies 1974;
former: asst prof Utah State U 1949-54; visiting lecturer
U of Cal at Davis 1967; visiting instr Salt Lake Art Ctr
1951; visiting instr Pioneer Craft House SLC 1969-70;
visiting artist Utah Artist in the Schools Prog 1972-4;
career: numerous awards & prizes for sculpture, painting,
pottery, printmaking, mosaics; Craftsmen of the
Southwest Directory 1965; mem: pres Logan Artists Group
1950-1; pres 1957 VP 1958 Provo Fine Arts Board; pres

Utah Designer Craftsmen 1963-5; Utah Rep Southwest Reg Assembly of Craftsmen 1961-5; Utah Rep 1st World Congress of Craftsmen, NY 1964; Utah Chm Art Tchrs in Higher Ed NAEA 1969-73; Natl Council on Ed for the Ceramic Arts; award: BSA Silver Beaver Award 1973; publ: 3 magazine articles; civic: Scoutmaster 40 yrs; Scout Commissioner 7 yrs; Natl BSA Jamboree Staff 1973; chm Utah County Art Exhibits 4 yrs; pol: Republican; mil: Air Force Cadet 1942-4; Air Force Flying Instr 1944; Pilot US Air Force 1944-5; US Air Force Reserve 1950-8; rel: LDS, bishopric, h council, youth ldr; home: 1000 Briar Ave; off: B-481 HFAC, BYU.

WIMMER, LARRY TURLEY   chm & prof of Economics; b: 8 Dec 1935; m: Louise Johnson; p: James Ivan & Corinne; c: Brian, Greg, Kendall, Eric, Brett; ed: BA 1960 BYU; PhD 1967 U of Chicago; Maeser Distinguished Tchr BYU 1978; career: Fulbright Fellow 1972-3; mem: Amer Econ Assn; Econ Hist Assn; Mormon Hist Assn, Mont Pelerin Soc; publ: co-author *The Kirtland Economy Revisited;* journal articles; rel: LDS; home: 810 E 3950 N; off: 700 SWKT, BYU.

WINEGAR, JAMES STODDARD   VP marketing; b: 21 Sep 1936; m: Brenda Parcell; p: Glen S & Lulo; c: Stephen, Angela, Kristen, Eric, Warren, Becca; ed: marketing U of Utah; former: Area Trade Mgr; Reg Mgr; Dist Mgr; career: Mgr of the Yr 3 yrs; Presidents Award; mem: SAMPE; civic: pres Downs Syndrome Parents Group; Parent To Parent, Utah Valley Hospital; pres of Recep Group; home: 4037 Foothill Dr; off: 765 S 100 E.

WINTERTON, DOYLE W   pres Winterton's Audio, retail sales; b: 5 Feb 1933; m: Donna Bunnell; p: Stafford Winterton & Maud Winterton Giles; c: Vickie, Mark, Gary, Linda, Scott, Neal, Amy; ed: BES BYU; former: US Bureau of Reclamation, civil & field engr; BYU Fine Arts Ctr design engr; Utah State Dept of Highways; mem: Audio Engineering Soc; civic: Boy Scouts of Amer Com; mil: US Army 1953-5; rel: LDS, MIA pres, exec sec; home: 4321 N 100 E; off: 83 N University.

WINWARD, EDWARD J   assoc prof, counseling psychologist; b: 27 Oct 1931; m: Margaret B; p: Bert &

Elizabeth; c: Kirk, Karrie, Clay, Jill, Kristi, Rand, Rick, Troy; ed: BS MS Utah State U; PhD U of Missouri; Psy Chi; Phi Kappa Phi; former: chm BYU Testing Serv; counselor U of Missouri; mem: AMCAP; UPGA; APGA, UACES; mil: US Army 1953-5; rel: LDS, bishopric, h council; home: 556 E 1200 N, Orem; off: 158 Health Ctr, BYU.

WOOD, STEPHEN LANE   prof Zoology & Entomology BYU; Curator of Insects, BYU Life Sci Museum; editor, Great Basin Naturalist; b: 2 Jul 1924; m: Elizabeth Griffin Wood; p: John Karl & Phebe Ricks; c: Katherine Wood Brown, John Griffin Wood, Marian Wood Pickerd; ed: BS 1946 MS 1948 Utah State U; PhD 1953 U of Kansas; Phi Beta Kappa; Phi Kappa Phi; former: sci tchr Beaver County High School; emtomologist Canada Dept Agriculture; career: College Creative Achievement Award; Sigma Xi annual lecture; visiting prof of res at U of Costa Rica; visiting prof of res Laboratorio Nacional de Productos Forestales, Merida, Venezuela; Natl Sci Found res awards 1959-78; mem: Entomological Soc of Amer; Amer Registry of Professional Entomologists; Coleopterists soc; Utah Lepidoptera Soc; Soc Indian Foresters; publ: over 90 sci journal articles in 7 countries; civic: Timpanogos Kiwanis Club; mil: US Army; rel: LDS, h council, clerk; home: 1286 Apple Ave; off: 332 Life Sci Museum, BYU.

WOODBURY, LAEL J   Dean, College of Fine Arts & Communications, BYU; b: 3 Jul 1927; m: Margaret Swenson; p: Raymond & Wanda; c: Carolyn, Shannon, Jordon, Lexon; ed: BS Utah State U 1952, MA BYU 1953, PhD U of Illinois 1954; Karl G Maeser Res & Creative Arts Award; Sidney B Sperry Symposium Award; former: assoc prof, U of Iowa, Bowling Green State U, Colorado State U; career: BYU Alumni Distinguished Service Award; Univ Fellow, U of Illinois; award: co-chm Utah Alliance for Arts Ed; board of adv Eagle Marketing Corp; mem Utah Arts Festival Adv Board; publ: *Mosiac Theatre; Mormon Arts,* vol 1, co-author; over 30 magazine articles & book reviews; civic: dir, Las Vegas, Nev, Centennial Pageant; co-author & co-dir of Nephi, Utah & Provo, Utah Centennial Pageants; mil: EM/c, US Navy; rel: LDS, stake pres, sealing officiator, Provo Temple; home: 1303 Locust Ln.

WOODBURY, RICHARD COULAM prof Electrical Engineering; b: 19 Apr 1931; m: Patricia Anne Johnson; p: Harvey C & Lucille Coulam; c: Pamela, David Eric, Marie, Ann, Karen, Sandra; ed: BSEE U of Utah 1956; MSEE Stanford 1958; PhD EE Stanford 1965; grad high honors U of Utah; Phi Kappa Phi; Tav Beta Pi; Eta Kappa Nu; former: integrated circuit designer AMS 1974-5, Hewlett Packard 1956-9; mem: chm, reg VI, NE area, Inst of Elec & Electronic Engrs; Amer Soc for Eng Ed; publ: 5 journal articles on circuit design, magnetic materials, radiation damage to silicon; patent for analog magnetic memory; rel: LDS, bishop; home: 2891 N 175 E; 459 CB, BYU.

WOODWARD, RALPH Prof of Music BYU; b: 21 Nov 1918; m: Margaret; p: Alonzo & Alta; c: Ralph Barclay, Bruce Gregory, Polly Jean; ed: BM 1940 U of Idaho; MM 1948 Cincinnati Conservatory of Music; DMA 1964 U of Illinois; Cert for Teaching Excellence 1965-6; Karl Maeser Award for Teaching Excellence 1973; former: asst prof Drake Univ, Des Moines, Iowa; award: choirs won Internatl Choral competition in Wales; Linz, Austria festival; Spittal, Austria, Internatl competition; featured in natl & internatl tours; mem: Phi Kappa Phi; MENC; ACDA; NATS; Phi Mu Alpha; award: Utah Valley Council of the Arts medal for contributions to area arts; publ: articles on voice & choral conducting; 2 books in progress; civic: conductor & founder Ralph Woodward Chorale; mil: US Army Special Serv Officer 8th Army Japan WW II; rel: LDS, ward choir dir, sunday school gen board, gen music com, h council; club: Rotary Internatl; home: 2860 N 220 E; off: E-439 HFAC, BYU.

WOOTTON, NOAL T attorney; b: 8 Sep 1941; p: O DeVere & Nora; c: Lisa 18, Christopher Noall 14, Leslie 11; ed: JD U of Utah, NW Univ Prosecutor's Course, Natl Dist Attorney's Assn course; former: Deputy Couty Attorney, Asst Dist Attorney; Utah County Attorney, BYU instr; career: Outstanding Contribution to Law Enforcement, Provo BPO; mem: Utah Bar Assn, Assn of Amer Trial Lawyers, Amer Judiciate Soc; pol: Utah Rep Party; rel: LDS; club: Provo Lodge 849 BPOE, Alpine Country Club; off: 8 N Center, Amer Fork.

WRIGHT, STEVEN RICH   dir language training MTC; b:
22 Aug 1950; m: Hariella Haws; p: Warren G & Donna
Bowen; c: Rich 8, Anamarie 6, Brent 4, Carl 2; ed: BA
Spanish MA linguistics BYU; Phi Kappa Phi; grad magna
cum laude; former: ESL dir Fillmore Refugee Proj;
career: Outstanding Young Amer Award; mem: Intermtn
TESOL, Internatl TESOL; ACTFL; SEITAR; publ: articles
in language journals; pol: Republican dist rep; rel: LDS,
branch pres MTC; home: 781 E 50 S; off: A-113 MTC.

WUDEL, JAMES "JIMBA" MARTIN   owner & operator
Jimba's Restaurant; b: 4 Jul 1939; m: Pamela Norris; p:
Reinhold Henry & Katheryn; c: Christopher James 11,
Jaclyn Kay 3; ed: BYU, Los Angeles Art Ctr College of
Design, Woodbury College; career: Good Dining Award
1976; mem: Provo Chamber of Commerce; Internatl Food
Serv Exec Assn, Utah Valley Chapter; Utah County Com
for a Better Environment; mil: US Marines; Western US
Rifle Team; rel: LDS, venture ldr; home: 278 W Center.

WUDEL, JOHN ANTHONY   pres Wudel Inc, pres Jimba's
Inc, co-owner & creator of Jimba's Restaurant; b: 14 May
1941; m: Nancy Twitty; p: Dr & Mrs R H Wudel; c: Tricia
10, Robyn 9, David 5, John 3; ed: BS zoology & chemistry
BYU 1964; Masters of Theology work BYU; former: area
dir Seminaries & Institutes LDS Church Ed System;
career: Teacher of Yr 1969 Juab High School; mem: Utah
Retail Grocers Assn; Utah Restaurant Assn; US Chamber
of Commerce; award: featured on Natl TV PM Magazine;
publ: patent filled for Jimba's Fabulous Fructose Ice
Cream & Soft Serve; civic: sponsor of Girl Scout Troop;
pol: Republican county del 5 yrs; rel: LDS, h council,
bishop; home: 734 Sunny Ln, Orem; off: 278 W Center.

YAMADA, EUGENE S   gen mgr Kamon Restaurant of
Japan; b: 20 Aug 1943; m: Tatsue; p: Shichiya & Yaeko; c:
Starla 12, Skyli 6; ed: BS BYU; former: chm of board
Internatl Star Commerce Corp; home: 731 Northland Dr,
SLC; off: 40 N 400 W.

YOUNG, WAYNE   Head Men's Gymnastic Coach BYU; b:
1 Jun 1952; m: Carol Broadhead; p: Clair & Chrystal
Mathis; c: Jessica Leigh 6, Guard Wayne 4, Britney Anne
3, Heather Carol 1; ed: BS BYU; masters Penn State;

NCAA Post Grad Award; former: head coach Odessa College; career: 1974 WAC AA, Vaulting Champ, 1974 3rd AA NCAA, 1974 1st World Game team USA, 1975 1st WAC Still Rings, Long horse, Parallel Bars, All Around, 1st NCAA All Around; 4th Still Rings, Parallel Bars, High Bar, 1976 1st USA Olympics Team Captain; 1979 Jr College Coach of the Year; 1981 Mid-West Coach of the Year; mem: Athlete Rep on USGF Board of Dir, NCAA Rules Com (Gymnastics), NCGCA, USGF Utah State Chm USGF Age Group; award: Outstanding Research Award 1976; publ: *Mechanical Analysis of Arm Movement in Longhorse Vaulting;* rel: LDS; club: Cougar Club; home: 1128 E 435 N, Orem.

ZAKRZEWSKI, LIDIA   writer; Polish teacher at BYU; c: Wojciech, Antoni; Szczepan, Edmund; Maciej, Marceli; Jacek, Mikolaj; ed: BA MA PhD in Slavic Lit; studied medicine at Medical School of Poznan Univ in Warsaw; Warsaw Conservatory and Guildhal School of Music, London; 4-yr scholarship to study piano in England; former: volunteer tchr at New England Conservatory; resident dir Keene State College, New Hamp; career: 1st prize short story from Polish literary magazine Wiadomosci, London; publ: 144 short stories & poems publ by Wuadomosci, London, Bog i Ojczyzna, Buenos Aires, White Eagle, New York, et al; civic: concerts in Poland, England, and USA; mil: mem of Polish Underground; messenger during Warsaw uprising; WAAF, London; Cross of Valor, Warsaw; Air Force War Medal, England; rel: LDS, music dir, stake missionary; home: 1000 E Center No. 10; off: 244 FB, BYU.

ZIRBES, JOHN A "JACK"   Provo City Engineer; b: 1 Aug 1932; m: Dolores; p: Ray & Marie; c: Sharon Bowles, Debbie, Jeff, Nancy, Tom; ed: BS civil engineering U Wisconsin; former: Onalaska Wisc City Engineer; Design Engineer, Los Angeles; career: nominated for top 10 public works officials in US 1979; mem: APWA; ASCE; NSPE; publ: papers at public works confs; pol: Republican; mil: US Army 2 yrs; rel: LDS, h council, bishopric; club: Rotary; home: 1380 E 330 S; off: PO Box 1849.